*The Churching of America, 1776–1990*

# The Churching of America, 1776–1990

## Winners and Losers in Our Religious Economy

**ROGER FINKE**
and
**RODNEY STARK**

RUTGERS UNIVERSITY PRESS     New Brunswick, New Jersey

Library of Congress Cataloging-in-Publication Data

Finke, Roger, 1954-
    The churching of America, 1776–†990: winners and losers in our
religious economy / Roger Finke and Rodney Stark.
        p.   cm.
    Includes bibliographical references and index.
    ISBN 0–8135–1837–7
    1. United States—Church history. 2. Sociology, Christian—United
States.   I. Stark, Rodney.   II. Title.
    BR515.F56 1992
    277.3'08-dc20                                        91–45908
                                                             CIP

British Cataloging-in-Publication information available

# Contents

# List of Illustrations

# List of Figures

# List of Tables

# *Preface*

It is appropriate to thank a number of people and institutions who helped us complete this study. First of all we wish to express our debts to our friend and sometime collaborator Laurence Iannaccone of Santa Clara University, whose work greatly informed Chapter 7. We also must acknowledge that it was Jeffrey K. Hadden of the University of Virginia who first made us aware of the many decades of efforts by the National Council of Churches to monopolize radio and television time for religious programs. Jeff also made useful suggestions about revising the initial draft of the manuscript. Many colleagues have provided advice, encouragement, and counsel as we have completed this study, but we are especially grateful to those who have offered comments on early drafts of various portions of the manuscript: Andrew Greeley, David Hackett, James McCann, Richard Shiels, Steve Warner, and an anonymous reviewer.

Locating the necessary documents and books for the completion of this project required the assistance of many. We are indebted to librarians at numerous institutions: the Archives of the Archdiocese of Chicago, the Billy Graham Center Library and Archives, the University of Chicago, Concordia College, the Christian Theological Seminary, Franklin College, the Garrett Evangelical Theological Seminary, Loyola University of Chicago, the Newberry Library, the University of Notre Dame, the University of St. Mary of the Lake, Purdue University, Seattle Pacific University, the Southern Baptist Theological Seminary, and the University of Washington. Benjamin and Linda de Wit of Chalcedon Books in East Lansing, Michigan, located copies of many original sources for us, including James R. Rogers's *The Cane Ridge Meeting-house*, which unexpectedly turned out to consist mainly of Barton W. Stone's *Autobiography.*

Illustrations for this book were taken from ten different collections and benefited from the advice of archivists from many others. We offer a special note of thanks to Cathy Koves and Wendy McDowell, curators at the Billy Graham Center Museum, for their tireless search for the perfect pictures.

Statistical analysis was done with the Microcase Analysis System, which was also used to create the maps of the United States.

The senior author wishes to thank the Louisville Institute for the Study of Protestantism and American Culture for providing a summer stipend to support the completion of the manuscript.

Finally, and foremost, we thank our families.

*The Churching of America, 1776–1990*

# Chapter 1

# *A New Approach to American Religious History*

We did not intend to make major revisions in the history of American religion. But unless reason and arithmetic have failed us, we have done precisely that. It seems appropriate, therefore, to begin this study with an explanation of how it took shape and why we were so often forced to challenge the received wisdom about American religious history.

The most striking trend in the history of religion in America is growth—or what we call the churching of America. The backbone of this book consists of our attempt to explore and explain how and why America shifted from a nation in which most people took no part in organized religion to a nation in which nearly two thirds of American adults do. Along the way we shall discover that the churching of America was not simply a rise in participation. Many observers have discounted the rise in church membership on the grounds that it was accompanied by a decline in acceptance of traditional religious doctrines. But this simply isn't so. Not all denominations shared in this immense rise in membership rates, and to the degree that denominations rejected traditional doctrines and ceased to make serious demands on their followers, they ceased to prosper. The churching of America was accomplished by aggressive churches committed to vivid otherworldliness.

We began tracing this trend in church membership with quite modest aims. We intended merely to provide more adequate quantitative evidence for the study of American religion and to resolve more fully such limited questions as: How religious was colonial America? Have church membership rates risen constantly over the past two centuries or have there been cycles of ups and downs? But as our work progressed we were drawn to some rather blunt questions about the characteristics of winners and losers in a free market religious environment that exposed religious organizations to relentless competition. To be more specific, we were led to ask questions such as: Why had the leading denominations of 1776 gone into such rapid eclipse by the turn of the century? Why were the Methodists and the Baptists able to win such huge and rapid victories, making them the dominant religious organizations during the first half of the nineteenth century? And then what happened to the Methodists? Why did their nearly miraculous rise soon turn into a long downward slide?

As we assembled and constructed evidence appropriate to answering such questions, we began to discover that many general historians of American religion seemed to be ill at ease with arithmetic and to "borrow" numerical claims from one another quite uncritically.[1] We often found that the same wrong number had been repeated by one writer after another across the decades. Some of these errors have caused major falsifications of the past. Every important general historian of American religion, for example, has passed along patently absurd statistics about Catholic membership during the latter half of the nineteenth century. Having greatly exaggerated Catholic membership, each was forced to present a very misleading historical account, as we shall see in Chapter 4.

In similar fashion, general historians of American religion (as well as many specialists) have been content to trust the claims of proponents of the federated church movement that there was a severe crisis facing the churches in rural America. Everyone reports that during the first three decades of the twentieth century, thousands of rural churches closed for lack of members because of the rapid decline in the rural population caused by urbanization. And everyone agrees that this state of affairs is well described as "the lamentable overchurching of many rural communities" (Sanderson, 1942, p. 318). But, as will be discussed in Chapter 6, far from shrinking, the rural population continued to *grow substantially* throughout the period. Although some denominations were closing rural congregations, others were opening new ones at such a rate that the total number of rural churches grew. The real concerns of the proponents of federated churches had to do with rural America's taste for "unsuitable" denominations.

As we became increasingly familiar with the literature we began to notice that it wasn't only numbers that the major writers seemed to borrow. Across the decades the general histories included virtually identical selections of quotations. As we consulted the original sources of these quotations we noted how frequently the same minor error was repeated or the same odd omission occurred. For example, every general history of American religion or of religion in the colonial period reports details of George Whitefield's revival preaching in Boston during September 1740. Everyone includes crowd estimates and colorful quotations taken from Whitefield's *Journals*. These crowd estimates agree across historians, but deviate in small ways from the ones actually reported by Whitefield. And most authors chose precisely the same quotations from among the many quite similar ones provided in the original source. But it is striking that these authors could have read Whitefield and yet have failed to report his great anguish over the fact that five people were killed one afternoon (September 22, 1740) when panic seized a crowd awaiting his arrival at the Reverend Checkley's Meeting House:

> The meeting-house being filled, though there was no real danger, on a sudden all the people were in an uproar, and so unaccountably surprised, that some threw themselves out of the gallery, and others trampled on one another; so that five were actually killed, and others dangerously wounded. I happened to come in the midst of the uproar, and saw two or three lying on the ground in pitiable condition. God was pleased to give me the presence of mind; so that I gave notice I would immediately preach upon the common. The weather was wet, but many thousands followed in the field. . . . (Whitefield, [1756] 1969, p. 462)

Is it credible that authors who reported that Whitefield preached on the Boston Common that afternoon would have failed to mention why he had led the crowd out into wet weather, had they actually read the passage reported above? Every author of a general history of American religion mentioned Whitefield's preaching on the Common that day, but only Martin E. Marty (1984) noted the deaths that led to the shift in plans.

We found the prevalence of these patterns quite surprising. Having noticed these things for ourselves, however, we were better prepared when we encountered the findings of Douglas H. Sweet (1976). He reported that the characterization of the religious situation in the immediate aftermath of the American Revolution as the "lowest ebb-tide" in our history was used nearly word for word by all the leading authors from Robert Baird in 1844 to Sydney Ahlstrom in 1972. Having noted the common language, Sweet traced it to a common source—Lyman Beecher's autobiography. Sweet shows that Beecher's gloomy description of the period was at best reflective of the hard times on which Congregationalism had fallen. In fact, as we shall see in Chapter 3, the Baptists and Methodists were booming in this era and the ebb-tide characterization was as mythical as was the overchurching of rural America.

We shall meet variations of this myth many times as the book goes along. Frequently, a lack of religious activity is asserted when all that is lacking is a *preferred brand* of religious activity. In Chapter 3 we shall see that the American Home Missionary Society claimed to be a nondenominational movement devoted to bringing religion to unchurched areas. Most general historians accept this claim. However, many of the areas pronounced as unchurched by the society abounded in Baptist and Methodist churches and were lacking only in Congregationalists, Presbyterians, and Episcopalians.

We do not mean to suggest that scholars should not rely on one another or that a quotation in a secondary source should not be repeated without consulting the original. We have done both in this book and have tried to make it clear to readers when we have done so. However, because of the many errors we discovered early in our research, we have tried to rely on primary sources whenever it was feasible to do so. As we continued to read histories of American religion we also soon discovered that many of the chronic errors in the familiar historical story reflect far more than sloppy scholarship. The field of general American religious history suffers from glaring, systematic biases.

## Ideas or Actions?

Much of what we have found unattractive and biased in accounts of the history of American religion is rooted in the definition of the subject matter. *What* is American religion? For most historians, religion means theology, and therefore the history of American religion is the history of religious ideas. There is nothing wrong with writing histories of ideas, of course. But when historians trace the history of American religious ideas they nearly always adopt (at least implicitly) a model of intellectual progress. Their history is organized on the basis of showing how new religious ideas arose and were progressively refined. Moreover, the standards against which refinement is usually judged are entirely secular—parsimony, clarity, logical unity, graceful expression, and the like. One never encounters standards of theological progress or refinement based on how effectively a doctrine could stir the faithful or satisfy the heart. As a result, the history of American religious ideas always turns into an historical account of the march toward liberalism. That is, religious ideas always become more refined (i.e., better) when they are shorn of mystery, miracle, and mysticism—when an active supernatural realm is replaced by abstractions concerning virtue.

Even so, if historians were very careful to limit themselves to a history of religious ideas, we would find little in their work to criticize. But many historians of religion slip over the line and soon are linking individuals and organizations to these ideas. And it is here that the very strong preference for a more refined theology causes profound misreporting. An example may prove helpful. In Chapter 5 we shall encounter the Holiness Movement. As presented by historians, those involved in the Holiness Movement were unsophisticated souls, sadly out of joint with modern times. They were losers: not only were these misguided conservatives expelled from the mainline bodies, they were thereby consigned to historical insignificance as well.

Such an interpretation is possible only if one values theological refinement more than religious commitment and participation. For it is only in terms of a progressive history of theology that the Holiness Movement can be assigned to the losing side. Any fair history based on the subsequent fate of religious organizations would have to acknowledge that the Holiness Movement gave birth to denominations that have been growing rapidly, while the denominations that drove out the Holiness Movement have been rapidly losing out ever since.

In this book the history of American religion is the history of human actions and human organizations, not the history of ideas (refined or otherwise). But this is not to say that we regard theology as unimportant. To the contrary, we shall argue repeatedly that religious organizations can thrive only to the extent that they have a theology that can comfort souls and motivate sacrifice. In a sense, then, we are urging an underlying model of religious history that is the exact opposite of that based on progress through theological refinement. We shall present compelling evidence that theological refinement is the kind of progress that results in organizational bankruptcy.

Having made clear our intentions, in the remainder of this chapter we introduce the two primary ingredients on which the study rests, one empirical, the other theoretical. The empirical ingredient has to do with data on religious membership, broken down by denomination and region, in various eras. The theoretical ingredient involves a basic model of religious economies—a device that allows us to examine the dynamic interplay of religious bodies as they seek to attract and hold a committed membership.

## Data on American Religion

In 1962 the distinguished American demographer William Petersen published an essay on religious statistics in the United States in which he flatly stated that the "census in this country has no data on religion." In addition, Petersen lamented, few denominations possessed more than fragments of historical data on their membership, and it of dubious reliability. Worse yet, the religious data from national opinion polls are "not an adequate substitute for official statistics" (1962, p. 166).

Although Petersen's essay was published in a journal for specialists in the social scientific study of religion, many of them sophisticated quantitative data analysts, no one raised the slightest challenge to his claims, for they were not controversial. Unlike national census forms in many nations of Europe and Latin America, the United States Census has never asked citizens to report their personal religious affiliation. Hence, it seemed self-evident that quantitative studies of American religious history are precluded.

Fortunately, Petersen was wrong. At the time he wrote, an amazing array of "official statistics" on religion could be found in any well-stocked university library. Indeed the United States Census began to collect detailed statistical information from all American religious bodies—from the largest to the most obscure—every ten years from 1850 through 1890 (with a gap for 1880) and then from 1906 through 1936. Many eastern states also conducted their own census at mid-decade, and many of these include religious statistics. Furthermore, after federal and state governments ceased gathering religious statistics in the 1940s, private organizations soon filled the gap—although these data offer little more than membership counts. Finally, it proved relatively easy to re-create detailed denominational statistics for the nation in 1776, broken down by colonies.

It seems worthwhile to recount briefly how we have discovered, evaluated, and reconstructed the data on which we shall examine the churching of America. Because luck and coincidence played such a major part in this process, and because we played different roles at various points along the way, we have chosen to write first-person accounts of key episodes.

## Stark: The Religious Census, 1890–1936

One day I was sitting in my office at the University of Washington when Kevin Welch, one of my graduate students, brought me a two-volume set of books, published by the Bureau of the Census, titled *Religious Bodies, 1926.*

"What do you know about these?" he asked.

"I've never heard of them," I confessed. "Where did you get them?"

"In the census section of the library. There are sets for other years too: 1890, 1906, 1916, and 1936."

As I leafed through the volumes I was stunned at their range and depth. They provided the most extraordinary historical, doctrinal, and statistical information on 256 separate religious bodies, including very tiny ones as well as those outside the Judeo-Christian tradition. As I grew excited about the possibilities the volumes presented, I also grew increasingly embarrassed. I had been publishing studies in the sociology of religion for more than fifteen years and I had never known such books existed. How could I have been so uninformed? Then I recalled Petersen's paper, which I had read during my second year in graduate school. How could he not have known? How could generations of scholars have remained ignorant of what was clearly a massive census undertaking? Indeed, how could demographers, and especially their graduate students, fail to notice a whole shelf of books of religious statistics located alongside the regular census volumes? In fact they didn't overlook them—the books weren't missed, they were dismissed. I have since talked with many demographers who noticed these volumes while in graduate school, but in each case they were informed by faculty members that these statistics were nothing but junk that the Bureau should never have bothered with. Why? Because they were not based on tabulations of individual responses to a question on the regular census form. Instead, they were based on reports prepared by individual pastors or boards of elders. And, it was claimed, such people were not to be trusted. The figures would necessarily be hopelessly inflated.

Perhaps these demographers knew little about American religion and had never bothered to examine the data with care. Hopelessly inflated statistics are precisely what are obtained when *individuals* are asked their religious affiliation. Ever since the start of public opinion polling in the late 1930s, surveys have always found that virtually *everyone* has a religion. I know of no national survey in which as many as 10 percent answered "none" when asked their religious affiliation. But the nations churches cannot possibly seat 90 percent of the population. More careful investigation reveals that for many, their claim to a religious affiliation amounts to nothing more than a vague recollection of what their parents or grandparents have passed along as the family preference. Consider that substantial numbers of students at major universities commit the most unlikely spelling errors when filling out a questionnaire item on their denomination. Can students who think they go to the Pisscaple Church have ever seen the word Episcopal? Or what of Presditurians? If one wishes to know which churches have how many members (that is, people sufficiently active to have their names on the membership rolls), one needs to visit churches and count the rolls. Or one can ask how many names are on the rolls. But it takes very careful and elaborate research techniques to calculate membership by summing the responses given by individuals.

Rather than being hopelessly inaccurate, then, there are strong prima facie grounds for thinking that these old census statistics are relatively accurate. But there are other strong indications of their accuracy as well. The first of these is that the numbers claimed by the churches are modest. The national rate of religious adherence based on the 1890 data is only 45 percent. Second, the data are extremely stable over space and time. Had there been substantial local misrepresentation, then the data ought to jump around between nearby communities, and they do not. By the same token, there should have been a great deal of inconsistency from one decade to the next, and there is not. Finally, the Bureau of the Census was very concerned with accuracy and provided extensive, sophisticated, and persuasive evaluations of its procedures.[2]

These volumes offer a glittering array of scholarly possibilities. For example, each set of volumes contains a carefully researched section reporting on the history, doctrine, and organizational features of every

A page from the 1926 census of religious bodies showing a portion of the detailed membership statistics for Buffalo, New York. (From Bureau of the Census, 1930, vol. 1.)

| CITY AND DENOMINATION | Total number of churches [1] | MEMBERSHIP BY AGE [2] | | | | SUNDAY SCHOOLS [3] | | |
|---|---|---|---|---|---|---|---|---|
| | | Total number [4] | 13 years and over | Under 13 years | Per cent under 13 [5] | Churches reporting | Officers and teachers | Scholars |
| **Brookline, Mass.**—Continued. | | | | | | | | |
| Jewish Congregations | 4 | 7,500 | ------ | ------ | ------ | 2 | 22 | 530 |
| Methodist bodies: | | | | | | | | |
| Methodist Episcopal Church | 1 | 810 | 789 | 21 | 2.6 | 1 | 24 | 375 |
| Presbyterian bodies: | | | | | | | | |
| Presbyterian Church in the United States of America | 1 | 448 | 448 | ------ | ------ | 1 | 25 | 344 |
| Protestant Episcopal Church | 3 | 2,745 | 2,217 | 528 | 19.2 | 3 | 90 | 612 |
| Roman Catholic Church | 3 | 9,975 | 7,975 | 2,000 | 20.1 | 3 | 57 | 1,739 |
| Unitarians | 2 | 522 | 522 | ------ | ------ | 2 | 23 | 177 |
| Universalist Church | 1 | 295 | 268 | 27 | 9.2 | 1 | 16 | 45 |
| **Buffalo, N. Y.** | 341 | 351,907 | 236,275 | 75,677 | 24.3 | 261 | 5,201 | 66,037 |
| Adventist bodies: | | | | | | | | |
| Seventh-day Adventist Denomination | 3 | 267 | 254 | 13 | 4.9 | 1 | 29 | 158 |
| American Rescue Workers | 3 | 53 | 36 | 17 | ------ | 3 | 4 | 37 |
| Bahá'is | 1 | 15 | 15 | ------ | ------ | ------ | ------ | ------ |
| Baptist bodies: | | | | | | | | |
| Baptists— | | | | | | | | |
| Northern Baptist Convention | 25 | 6,265 | 5,904 | 194 | 3.2 | 25 | 534 | 5,322 |
| Negro Baptists | 5 | 2,383 | 2,285 | 98 | 4.1 | 5 | 71 | 856 |
| Brethren, Plymouth: | | | | | | | | |
| Plymouth Brethren I | 1 | 52 | 52 | ------ | ------ | 1 | 9 | 100 |
| Plymouth Brethren II | 2 | 213 | 213 | ------ | ------ | 2 | 34 | 225 |
| Catholic Apostolic Church | 1 | 136 | 125 | 11 | 8.1 | 1 | 5 | 55 |
| Christadelphians | 2 | 77 | 77 | ------ | ------ | 2 | 8 | 36 |
| Christian and Missionary Alliance | 1 | 73 | 73 | ------ | ------ | 1 | 14 | 100 |
| Church of Armenia in America | 1 | 126 | 92 | 34 | 27.0 | ------ | ------ | ------ |
| Church of Christ, Scientist | 3 | 939 | 939 | ------ | ------ | 2 | 111 | 594 |
| Church of God (Headquarters, Anderson, Ind.) | 1 | 40 | 39 | 1 | ------ | 1 | 6 | 50 |
| Church of God and Saints of Christ | 1 | 8 | 7 | 1 | ------ | ------ | ------ | ------ |
| Church of God in Christ | 2 | 115 | 72 | 3 | ------ | 2 | 10 | 75 |
| Churches of God, Holiness | 1 | 105 | 80 | 25 | 23.8 | 1 | 9 | 70 |
| Churches of the New Jerusalem: | | | | | | | | |
| General Convention of the New Jerusalem in the United States of America | 1 | 59 | 39 | 20 | ------ | 1 | 4 | 59 |
| Congregational Churches | 5 | 1,385 | 1,186 | 12 | 1.0 | 5 | 77 | 833 |
| Disciples of Christ | 8 | 2,534 | 1,674 | 70 | 4.0 | 8 | 196 | 1,987 |
| Eastern Orthodox Churches: | | | | | | | | |
| Greek Orthodox Church (Hellenic) | 1 | 1,632 | 655 | 977 | 59.9 | ------ | ------ | ------ |
| Roumanian Orthodox Church | 1 | 300 | 269 | 31 | 10.3 | 1 | 1 | 20 |
| Russian Orthodox Church | 1 | 2,550 | 1,800 | 750 | 29.4 | ------ | ------ | ------ |
| Evangelical Church | 6 | 1,069 | 1,042 | 27 | 2.5 | 6 | 103 | 914 |
| Evangelical Synod of North America | 20 | 10,634 | 10,634 | ------ | ------ | 20 | 554 | 5,073 |
| Friends: | | | | | | | | |
| Religious Society of Friends (Hicksite) | 1 | 30 | ------ | ------ | ------ | ------ | ------ | ------ |
| Jewish Congregations | 14 | 20,000 | ------ | ------ | ------ | 1 | 16 | 300 |
| Latter-day Saints: | | | | | | | | |
| Church of Jesus Christ of Latter-day Saints | 1 | 58 | 40 | 18 | ------ | 1 | 4 | 25 |
| Reorganized Church of Jesus Christ of Latter Day Saints | 1 | 107 | 100 | 7 | 6.5 | 1 | 13 | 45 |
| Liberal Catholic Church | 1 | 27 | 24 | 3 | ------ | ------ | ------ | ------ |
| Lutherans: | | | | | | | | |
| United Lutheran Church in America | 15 | 14,347 | 10,437 | 3,910 | 27.3 | 15 | 390 | 4,410 |
| Evangelical Lutheran Augustana Synod of North America | 1 | 406 | 258 | 148 | 36.5 | 1 | 12 | 101 |
| Evangelical Lutheran Synodical Conference of America— | | | | | | | | |
| Evangelical Lutheran Synod of Missouri, Ohio, and Other States | 12 | 6,562 | 4,588 | 1,974 | 30.1 | 12 | 178 | 1,867 |
| Lutheran Synod of Buffalo | 4 | 1,525 | 942 | 263 | 21.8 | 4 | 70 | 669 |
| Methodist bodies: | | | | | | | | |
| Methodist Episcopal Church | 27 | 10,667 | 9,494 | 548 | 5.5 | 27 | 801 | 9,451 |
| Free Methodist Church of North America | 2 | 140 | 140 | ------ | ------ | 2 | 21 | 288 |
| African Methodist Episcopal Church | 1 | 300 | 225 | 75 | 25.0 | 1 | 15 | 125 |
| African Methodist Episcopal Zion Church | 2 | 780 | 711 | 69 | 8.8 | 2 | 64 | 430 |
| Colored Methodist Episcopal Church | 1 | 80 | 75 | 5 | ------ | 1 | 8 | 60 |

See footnotes on p. 360.

religious body in the nation, along with detailed statistics on such things as total membership (also separated by age and by sex), Sunday school enrollment, number of congregations, value of church property, amount of debt, total expenditures, minister's salaries, contributions to foreign missions, and so on—presented separately for every state. In addition, statistical summary volumes organize membership data by counties and for all cities having more than 25,000 inhabitants.

To provide a glimpse of these materials, we reproduce two sample pages from the 1926 volumes. The first is part of a one-and-a-half page table for the city of Buffalo, New York. Here we can see the inclusiveness of the Bureau's definition of a religious body. In 1926 the Baha'is had one church and 15 members, all of them age thirteen and over. The Christadelphians had two churches and 77 members. The Swedenborgians, already split into two denominations, appear under the heading of "Churches of the New Jerusalem."

The second page is one of seven tables from the section devoted to the Methodist Episcopal Church. Summary statistics are given for several of the measures collected by the Bureau and are broken down by urban and rural territory. Notice how very disproportionately female the Methodists had become, having but 66.8 males for every 100 female members.

Initially, I believed that the Census Bureau began this massive work in 1890, but I soon discovered that they had actually begun in 1850, piggybacking the project on the regular census conducted that year. In addition to their other duties, local census supervisors (often U.S. deputy marshals) were asked to assemble a list of every organized religious body meeting within the community and then to visit each with a questionnaire. This was repeated in 1860 and 1870. For reasons that remain obscure, the census of religious bodies for 1880 was never published and now is thought to be lost. But publication was resumed in 1890. The project was then shifted to the sixth year of the decade in order to relieve the workload on the Bureau of the Census—so the next one was conducted in 1906, and again in 1916, 1926, and 1936. The 1936 census

A page from the 1926 census of religious bodies showing a portion of the detailed membership statistics for the Methodist Episcopal Church. (From Bureau of the Census, 1930, vol. 2.)

# METHODIST EPISCOPAL CHURCH

## STATISTICS

**Summary for the United States, with urban-rural classification.**—A general summary of the statistics for the Methodist Episcopal Church for the year 1926 is presented in Table 1, which shows also the distribution of these figures between urban and rural territory.

In the Methodist Episcopal Church persons are received into full membership upon public profession of faith (usually after six months' probation) and a pledge to conform to the discipline and rules of the church. Baptism is required and those baptized in infancy must publicly renew their vows.

TABLE 1.—SUMMARY OF STATISTICS FOR CHURCHES IN URBAN AND RURAL TERRITORY, 1926: METHODIST EPISCOPAL CHURCH

| ITEM | Total | In urban territory [1] | In rural territory [1] | PER CENT OF TOTAL Urban | PER CENT OF TOTAL Rural |
|---|---|---|---|---|---|
| **Churches** (local organizations) | 26, 130 | 5, 489 | 20, 641 | 21. 0 | 79. 0 |
| **Members** | 4, 080, 777 | 2, 212, 180 | 1, 868, 597 | 54. 2 | 45. 8 |
| Average per church | 156 | 403 | 91 | | |
| Membership by sex: | | | | | |
| Male | 1, 518, 791 | 818, 438 | 700, 353 | 53. 9 | 46. 1 |
| Female | 2, 274, 615 | 1, 228, 612 | 1, 046, 003 | 54. 0 | 46. 0 |
| Sex not reported | 287, 371 | 165, 130 | 122, 241 | 57. 5 | 42. 5 |
| Males per 100 females | 66. 8 | 66. 6 | 67. 0 | | |
| Membership by age: | | | | | |
| Under 13 years | 313, 840 | 164, 350 | 149, 490 | 52. 4 | 47. 6 |
| 13 years and over | 3, 250, 505 | 1, 782, 927 | 1, 467, 578 | 54. 9 | 45. 1 |
| Age not reported | 516, 432 | 264, 903 | 251, 529 | 51. 3 | 48. 7 |
| Per cent under 13 years [2] | 8. 8 | 9. 1 | 9. 2 | | |
| **Church edifices:** | | | | | |
| Number | 25, 570 | 5, 516 | 20, 054 | 21. 6 | 78. 4 |
| Value—Churches reporting | 25, 290 | 5, 358 | 19, 932 | 21. 2 | 78. 8 |
| Amount reported | $406, 165, 659 | $274, 162, 895 | $132, 002, 764 | 67 5 | 32. 5 |
| Average per church | $16, 060 | $51, 169 | $6, 623 | | |
| Debt—Churches reporting | 5, 064 | 2, 286 | 2, 778 | 45. 1 | 54. 9 |
| Amount reported | $42, 749, 854 | $35, 971, 915 | $6, 777, 939 | 84. 1 | 15. 9 |
| Churches reporting "no debt" on church edifice | 15, 346 | 2, 433 | 12, 913 | 15. 9 | 84. 1 |
| **Parsonages:** | | | | | |
| Value—Churches reporting | 13, 665 | 4, 362 | 9, 303 | 31. 9 | 68. 1 |
| Amount reported | $60, 724, 434 | $32, 057, 564 | $28, 666, 870 | 52. 8 | 47. 2 |
| Debt—Churches reporting | 2, 041 | 976 | 1, 065 | 47. 8 | 52. 2 |
| Amount reported | $4, 547, 967 | $3, 159, 937 | $1, 388, 030 | 69. 5 | 30. 5 |
| Churches reporting "no debt" on parsonage | 8, 805 | 2, 568 | 6, 237 | 29. 2 | 70. 8 |
| **Expenditures during year:** | | | | | |
| Churches reporting | 25, 790 | 5, 466 | 20, 324 | 21. 2 | 78. 8 |
| Amount reported | $89, 422, 307 | $57, 411, 370 | $32, 010, 937 | 64. 2 | 35. 8 |
| Current expenses and improvements | $68, 949, 285 | $43, 038, 086 | $25, 911, 199 | 62. 4 | 37. 6 |
| Benevolences, missions, etc. | $20, 462, 262 | $14, 372, 684 | $6, 089, 578 | 70. 2 | 29. 8 |
| Not classified | $10, 760 | $600 | $10, 160 | 5. 6 | 94. 4 |
| Average expenditure per church | $3, 467 | $10, 503 | $1, 575 | | |
| **Sunday schools:** | | | | | |
| Churches reporting | 24, 730 | 5, 404 | 19, 326 | 21. 9 | 78. 1 |
| Officers and teachers | 382, 043 | 156, 744 | 225, 299 | 41. 0 | 59. 0 |
| Scholars | 3, 796, 561 | 1, 910, 259 | 1, 886, 302 | 50. 3 | 49. 7 |

[1] Urban territory includes all cities and other incorporated places which had 2,500 inhabitants or more in 1920, the date of the last Federal census; rural territory comprises the remainder of the country.
[2] Based on membership with age classification reported.

was distorted by the decision of some bodies not to report.[3] The 1946 religious census was suspended after a number of groups challenged its propriety. The Jewish community voiced special concern in the immediate aftermath of the Holocaust that all efforts to count or otherwise emphasize the Jewish presence could only inflame anti-Semitism.

Although the statistics go back to 1850, there was one very serious problem with the first three reports. Despite recording a wealth of valuable statistics, the census failed to ask the single most important question: "How many members do you have?"

## Finke: Turning Pews into People, 1850–1870

Soon after I enrolled in graduate school at the University of Washington, I became Rodney Stark's research assistant. We used church membership rates based on the 1926 census in several papers in which we found that cities and states having higher rates of church membership had lower rates of crime, delinquency, suicide, alcoholism, and venereal disease. But my interests gradually shifted from criminology to questions that eventually led to this book. And that made the lack of membership statistics in the mid-nineteenth-century reports very frustrating. For every church in the nation, we know details such as the value of the church buildings and land, the number of organizations sponsored by each, and the seating capacity of the church. But we have no information on how many of those pew seats were ever filled.

In 1890 the census takers still asked about total seating capacity, but finally they also asked about total membership. It struck me that it might be possible to take advantage of this fact to construct a statistical procedure that would, in effect, turn counts of pews into counts of people. The details of such predictive models have been reported elsewhere (Finke and Stark, 1986). The logic involved was to try to construct a model, based on the value of church property, the number of organizations, and the seating capacity, that would accurately predict membership—using the actual membership in 1890 as the standard. When this attempt turned out to be successful (Finke and Stark, 1986), I applied the model to the 1850, 1860, and 1870 data to provide the missing membership statistics. As a check on these results, I compared them with official statistics available from some denominations for the pertinent years. Once again the match-up was very close, giving us confidence that our estimates of membership are an adequate substitute for the actual statistics. These estimates enabled me to chart denominational membership and total church membership by individual states and regions for 1850, 1860, and 1870.

I then worked on shifting patterns of denominational success and the rising church membership rate. My analysis began in 1850, and when the census data are combined with membership data for 1952 and 1980, the study spanned 130 years. It seemed impossible to go any further back.

## Stark: Reconstructing Colonial Religious Statistics

Soon after we began to outline this book, luck struck again. My colleague James C. McCann showed me an old book: *Atlas of the Historical Geography of the United States,* by Charles O. Paullin, published jointly in 1932 by the Carnegie Institution of Washington, D.C., and the American Geographical Society. Seeking historical data on the locations of Indian reservations, McCann had discovered that this atlas included a set of maps purporting to show the location of *every* religious congregation in the thirteen colonies, plus Maine and Georgia, in 1776. There was a separate map for each denomination. The careful discussion of methods included in the text convinced me that the data were of the highest quality—many years of well-funded, original research by historians specializing in the period had produced the results. Nothing of their original work remained in the Carnegie Institution's archives, so I began to count dots in order to recover the actual numbers of congregations for each denomination in each colony.

Unfortunately, for some denominations, their density was so great in parts of some colonies that solidly black areas resulted and not even computer enhancement techniques were of any use in deciphering them. The map that gave the greatest difficulty was the one for the Congregationalists (see Figure 1.1). Clearly there are areas in Connecticut, Massachusetts, and New Hampshire that cannot be counted. When a denomination produced only one uncountable area, since I knew the total number of congregations for each denomination, the problem was solved by subtracting the counted dots from the total. But it seemed unlikely that I could ever unscramble the Congregationalists in New England into their proper states. Then, by accident, I stumbled on a set

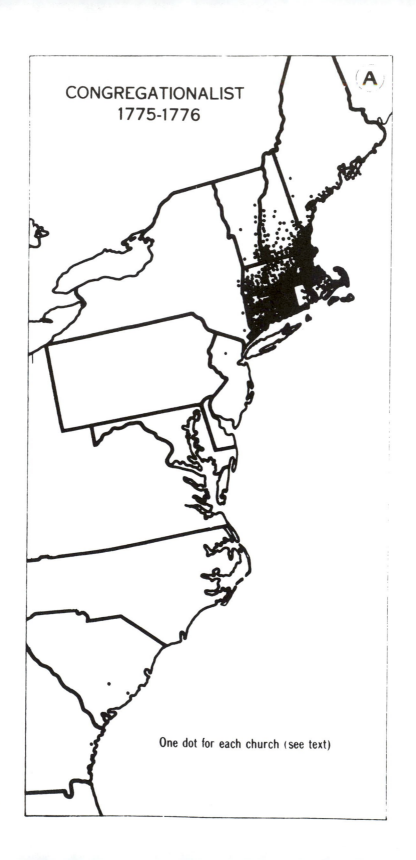

CONGREGATIONALIST
1775-1776

(A)

One dot for each church (see text)

of volumes compiled by Frederick Lewis Weis with the support of the Society of the Descendants of Colonial Clergy. One of these, *The Colonial Clergy and the Colonial Churches of New England* (1936), was the needed Rosetta Stone. It listed all men who had ever held pulpits in New England during colonial times. And in the last section of the book, the names were listed by congregation, showing the period of tenure of each man to hold that pulpit (there were, in effect, no female clergy in this era). This gave me an independent list of all the Congregationalist churches by location. By eliminating those not shown to have been occupied in 1776, it was possible to create the missing Congregationalist statistics for Connecticut, Massachusetts, and New Hampshire. This volume, and others by Weis (1938, 1950, 1955) containing similar data for the other colonies, filled in the blanks everywhere the dots were too thick to count. By comparing Weis's lists with dot counts it was also possible to cross-check the sources. The level of agreement was consistently very high. In this way it proved possible to reconstruct a detailed portrait of the denominational make-up of America on the eve of the Revolution. Finally, as will be explained in Chapter 2, we established a basis for estimating the number of members a denomination had from the number of its churches.

## 1776–1980: The Churching of America

At this point it seems appropriate to present the primary fruits of our adventures with religious statistics. Figure 1.2 plots the overall trend in the rate of religious adherence[4] for two centuries. This pattern can truly be called the churching of America. On the eve of the Revolution only about 17 percent of Americans were churched. By the start of the Civil War this proportion had rise dramatically, to 37 percent. The immense dislocations of the war caused a serious decline in adherence in the South, which is reflected in the overall decline to 35 percent in the 1870 census. The rate then began to rise once more, and by 1906 slightly more than half of the U.S. population was churched. Adherence rates reached 56 percent by 1926. Since then the rate has been rather stable although inching upwards. By 1980 church adherence was about 62 percent.

Figure 1.1. Jernegan's Map of Congregationalist Congregations in 1776, Showing the Uncountable Areas. (From Paullin, 1932, Plate 82.)

FIGURE 1.2 Rates of Religious Adherence, 1776–1980

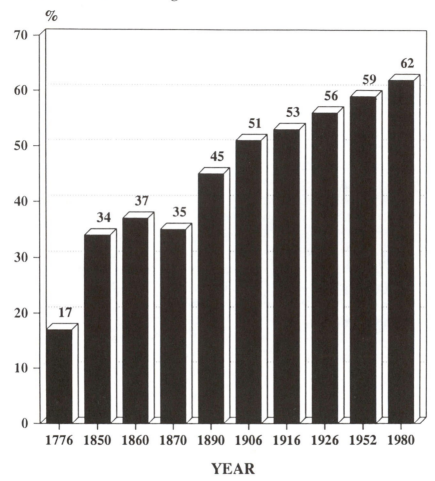

(On calculation of rates, see Stark and Finke, 1988, for 1776; Finke and Stark, 1986, for 1850–1926; Zelinsky, 1961, for 1952; and Stark, 1987, for 1980.)

This is the phenomenon we shall try to explain in this book. Why did the rate rise so greatly? Which denominations contributed most to the great increase in religious adherence, and which failed to benefit? These issues lead directly to our key analytical device: religious economies.

# On Religious Economies

Some readers may shudder at the use of "market" terminology in discussions of religion. But we see nothing inappropriate in acknowledging that where religious affiliation is a matter of choice, religious organizations must compete for members and that the "invisible hand" of the marketplace is as unforgiving of ineffective religious firms as it is of their commercial counterparts.

We are not the first to use an explicit market model to explore the interplay among religious organizations. Indeed, as we shall see in Chapter 2, Adam Smith did so very persuasively back in 1776. Moreover, it was typical for European visitors to use economic language to explain the religious situation in America to their friends back home. For example, Francis Grund, an Austrian who eventually became an American citizen, wrote in 1837: "In America, every clergyman may be said to do business on his own account, and under his own firm. He alone is responsible for any deficiency in the discharge of his office, as he alone is entitled to all the credit due to his exertions. He always acts as principal, and is therefore more anxious, and will make greater efforts to obtain popularity, than one who serves for wages. The actual stock in any of these firms is, of course, less than the immense capital of the Church of England; but the aggregate amount of business transacted by them jointly may nevertheless be greater in the United States" (in Powell, 1937, p. 77).

We will use economic concepts such as markets, firms, market penetration, and segmented markets to analyze the success and failure of religious bodies. Religious economies are like commercial economies in that they consist of a market made up of a set of current and potential customers and a set of firms seeking to serve that market. The fate of these firms will depend upon (1) aspects of their organizational structures, (2) their sales representatives, (3) their product, and (4) their marketing techniques. Translated into more churchly language, the relative success of religious bodies (especially when confronted with an unregulated economy) will depend upon their polity, their clergy, their religious doctrines, and their evangelization techniques.

The use of economic tools in no way suggests that the content of religion is unimportant, that it is all a matter of clever marketing and energetic selling. To the contrary, we will argue that the primary market weakness that has caused the failure of many denominations, and the impending failure of many more, is precisely a matter of doctrinal content, or the lack of it. That is, we will repeatedly suggest that as denominations have modernized their doctrines and embraced temporal values, they have gone into decline.

The primary value of analyzing American religious history through a market-oriented lens is that in this way some well-established deductions from the principles of supply and demand can illuminate what might otherwise seem a very disorderly landscape (as it indeed often appears to be in standard histories of the subject). Consider the following examples.

First, as in the analysis of market economies, a major consideration in analyzing religious economies is their degree of regulation. Some are virtually unregulated; some are restricted to state-imposed monopolies. In keeping with supply and demand principles, to the degree that a religious economy is unregulated, pluralism will thrive. That is, the "natural" state of religious economies is one in which a variety of religious groups successfully caters to the special needs and interests of specific market segments. This variety arises because of the inherent inability of a single product to satisfy very divergent tastes. Or, to note the specific features of religious firms and products, pluralism arises because of the inability of a single religious organization to be at once worldly and otherworldly, strict and permissive, exclusive and inclusive, while the market will always contain distinct consumer segments with strong preferences on each of these aspects of faith. This occurs because of "normal" variations in the human condition such as social class, age, gender, health, life experiences, and socialization.

In fact, because of this underlying differentiation of consumer preferences, religious economies can never be successfully monopolized, even when a religious organization is backed by the state. At the height of its temporal power, the medieval church was surrounded by heresy and dissent. Of course, when repressive efforts are very great, religions in competition with the state-sponsored monopoly will be forced to operate underground. But whenever and wherever repression falters, lush pluralism will break through.

Sociologists have long been fascinated with religious pluralism and its consequences for the religious landscape. Unfortunately, their grasp of both economics and history has been imperfect. The received wisdom is that pluralism weakens faith—that where multiple religious groups compete, each discredits the other and this encourages the view that religion per se is open to question, dispute, and doubt. Peter Berger

(1967, 1979) is the most eloquent and effective contemporary representative of this position. His work is suffused with a very European belief
that religious disintegration set in when pluralism shattered the "sacred
canopy" of "one true faith" that inspired the universal piety we often
associate with the medieval village.

Historical evidence says otherwise. There is ample evidence that in
societies with putative monopoly faiths, religious indifference, not
piety, is rife. Our contrary perceptions are nostalgic error. As we shall
see in the next chapter, in the Puritan Commonwealth of Massachusetts
religious adherence probably never exceeded 22 percent. It is becoming
increasingly well known that religious participation was very low in
medieval Europe (Stark and Iannaccone, forthcoming). And today, close
inspection of the religious situation in societies where "everyone" is a
Roman Catholic reveals levels of religious participation that are aston-
ishingly low compared with those in America—the exceptions being
places such as Ireland and Quebec where the church has also served as
the primary vehicle for political resistance to external domination (Stark
and McCann, 1989).

In addition to being based on bad history, faith in the power of monopoly religions is rooted in bad economics. We have already noted that
the inability of the monopoly church, despite its sacred canopy, to mobilize massive commitment is inherent in the segmentation of any religious economy. A single faith cannot shape its appeal to suit precisely
the needs of one market segment without sacrificing its appeal to another. But a second, equally compelling, principle of economics also applies: Monopoly firms always tend to be lazy.

In contrasting the American and European religious situations, Francis Grund (1837) noted that establishment makes the clergy "indolent
and lazy," because "a person provided for cannot, by the rules of common sense, be supposed to work as hard as one who has to exert himself for a living. . . . Not only have Americans a greater number of
clergymen than, in proportion to the population, can be found either
on the Continent or in England; but they have not one idler amongst
them; all of them being obliged to exert themselves for the spiritual welfare of their respective congregations. The Americans, therefore, enjoy
a threefold advantage: they have more preachers; they have more active
preachers, and they have cheaper preachers than can be found in any
part of Europe" (in Powell, 1967, pp. 77, 80).

A similar argument was developed by the prominent and colorful
English traveler William Cobbett (1818):

Taxes and Priests; for these always lay on heavily together. . . . I will, on
these subjects, address myself more immediately to my old neighbours of
Botley, and endeavour to make them understand what America is as to
taxes and priests. . . .

I have talked to several farmers here about the tithes in England; and,
they *laugh* . . . they seem, at last, not to believe what I say, when I tell
them that the English farmer gives, and is compelled [by law] to give, the
Parson a tenth part of his whole crop. . . . They cannot believe this. They
treat it as a sort of *romance*. . . .

But, my Botley neighours, you will exclaim, "No *tithes!* Why, then,
there can be no *Churches* and no *Parsons!* The people must know nothing
of God or Devil; and must all go to hell!" By no means, my friends. Here
are plenty of Churches. No less than three Episcopal (or English)
Churches; three Presbyterian Churches; three Lutheran Churches; one or
two Quaker Meeting-houses; and two Methodist places; all within *six miles*
of the spot where I am sitting. And, these, mind, not poor shabby
Churches; but each of them larger and better built and far handsomer than
Botley Church, with the church-yards all kept in the neatest order, with a
head-stone to almost every grave. As to the Quaker Meeting-house, it
would take Botley Church into its belly, if you were first to knock off the
steeple.

Oh no! Tithes are not necessary to promote *religion*. When our Parsons
. . . talk about *religion,* or *the church,* being in danger; they mean that the
*tithes* are in danger. They mean that they are in danger of being compelled
to work for their bread.

But, the fact is, that it is the circumstance of the church being established by law that makes it of little use as to real religion. . . . Because . . .
establishment forces upon the people, parsons whom they cannot respect. . . .

The most likely way to insure [a clergyman is both sincere and indus-
trious] is to manage things so that he may be in the first place, selected by
the people, and, in the second place, have no rewards in view other than
those which are to be given in consequence of his perseverance in a line
of good conduct.

And thus it is with clergy in America, who are duly and amply rewarded for their diligence, and very justly respected for the piety, talent,
and zeal which they discover; but, who have no tenure of their places
other than that of the will of the congregation. (in Powell, 1967, pp. 43–
44, 47)

Where many faiths function within a religious economy, a high degree of specialization as well as competition occurs. From this it follows
that many independent religious bodies will, together, be able to attract

a much larger proportion of a population than can be the case when only one or very few firms have free access.

This last point obviously helps to explain why American religious participation has been rising for two centuries. However, we shall postpone more extended discussion of this and other details of our model until the need arises in the chapters that follow.

## Disclaimer

We must emphasize that this book *is not* a general historical account of religion in America. Our aim is to place the history of American religion within a dynamic, interpretive model and to correct some major misconceptions. To do this does not require that we cover every significant topic or include every significant figure—indeed, such inclusiveness would have produced an exhausting work in which the model would have been buried in detail. Our decisions about what to include have been based on what is most pertinent to our analysis. Thus we give extensive coverage to George Whitefield and to Charles Grandison Finney in order to dispel claims about Great Awakenings, but we make no mention of two equally important figures, Dwight L. Moody and Billy Graham. Moreover, many religious groups of considerable historical and cultural significance are also essentially ignored, including Jews, Christian Scientists, Jehovah's Witnesses, Mormons, Pentecostals, Unitarians, and the many Eastern Orthodox bodies. We also have paid no attention to nineteenth-century millenarian movements, to Mennonites, or to the Amish. Lutherans are mentioned only in passing, primarily in a section on Muhlenberg's confrontations with clerical impostors. We had planned a few pages on black Baptists in Chapter 5, but we discovered that unless we were willing to undertake a substantial amount of new research, we should say nothing.

We justify these omissions on the grounds that our primary aim is not to *describe* the history of American religion, but to *explain* it. To the best of our knowledge we have omitted nothing that would modify any of our conclusions.

# Chapter 2

# The Colonial Era Revisited

Nostalgia is the enemy of history. No educated person any longer believes that the ancients were correct about a fall from a Golden Age. Yet we frequently accept equally inaccurate tales about more recent "good old days"—tales that corrupt our understanding of the past and mislead us about the present.

Americans are burdened with more nostalgic illusions about the colonial era than about any other period in their history. Our conceptions of the time are dominated by a few powerful illustrations of Pilgrim scenes that most people over forty stared at year after year on classroom walls: the baptism of Pocahontas, the Pilgrims walking through the woods to church, and the first Thanksgiving. Had these classroom walls also been graced with colonial scenes of drunken revelry and barroom brawling, of women in risqué ball-gowns, of gamblers and rakes, a better balance might have been struck. For the fact is that there never were all that many Puritans, even in New England, and non-Puritan behavior abounded. From 1761 through 1800 a third (33.7%) of all first births in New England occurred after less than nine months of marriage (D. S. Smith, 1985), despite harsh laws against fornication. Granted, some of these early births were simply premature and do not necessarily show that premarital intercourse had occurred, but offsetting this is the likelihood that not all women who engaged in premarital intercourse would have become pregnant. In any case, single women in New England during the colonial period were more likely to be sexually active than to belong to a church—in 1776 only about one out of five New Englanders had a religious affiliation. The lack of affiliation does not necessarily

For generations of American schoolchildren this picture *was* the colonial era, supposedly an age of piety and faith: devout Puritans walk through the snow to church, many of the men bearing arms as protection against Indians. The schools chose not to hang portrayals of colonial revelers alongside those of the churchgoers. But Boston's taverns were probably fuller on Saturday night than were its churches on Sunday morning. (Courtesy of the Billy Graham Center Museum, Wheaton, Ill.)

mean that most were irreligious (although some clearly were), but it does mean that their faith lacked public expression and organized influence.

In several colonies, especially Massachusetts, small religious minorities dominated public life to the extent that they gave the illusion of nearly universal membership. Indeed, because the Congregationalists were the established church in New England and drew support from all taxpayers, they sometimes placed their membership close to the total population figure. The Congregationalist minister Ezra Stiles, for example, set the number of Congregationalists in New England in 1760 at 445,000, or just about 4,000 persons short of the total population of the time (Sweet, 1939, p. 3).[1] Such optimistic counting, combined with the superficial aura of respectability sustained by legalized Puritanism, often badly misled visitors about the religious situation. The Church of England's Society for the Propagation of the Gospel in Foreign Parts reported that New England was the "only well-churched area in the American colonies" (in Ahlstrom, 1975, vol. 1, p. 215). Not only was there no well-churched area in America, however, but New England's religious adherence rate was not significantly higher than that of the Middle Colonies, and New Jersey and Pennsylvania had slightly higher rates than Massachusetts. What were the denominational profiles of the colonies on the eve of the Revolution? Why, in particular, were so few of the colonists church members?

## Religious Adherence

The original research for the maps in the *Atlas of the Historical Geography of the United States* (Paullin, 1932) was supervised by M. W. Jernegan, professor of history at the University of Chicago and one of the major figures in colonial history in the 1920s and 1930s. Jernegan's totals, unlike his data for individual colonies, appeared in the *Atlas* and thus survived. Consider Jernegan's denominational totals for 1776 (see Table 2.1). As might be expected, the Congregationalists had the most churches and the Presbyterians were a solid second. But many will be surprised that the Baptists were already in third place, exceeding the Episcopalians by two congregations. Interestingly, although there were only five synagogues in the nation by 1776, Rhode Island, New York City, and Georgia had one each and two were in South Carolina. However, although counting dots on the *Atlas* maps and consulting Weis's (1936, 1939) data on clergy allow us to break these denominational totals down by colony, even this information doesn't answer the question of how many people belonged to these congregations.

Historians of American religion are well aware that the colonies did not exude universal piety. There has been general agreement that in the colonial period no more than 10 to 20 percent of the population actually belonged to a church (W. W. Sweet, 1947; Ahlstrom, 1975; Hudson, 1981). But we mistrust statistics not based on something resembling an actual count, and these are not. We are sure that this range defines the ballpark, but we would like to be much more precise. To do so, we must discover a basis for estimating the average size of these congregations, for then membership rates require nothing but simple multiplication.

The 1890 census reported that the average Protestant congregation in the nation had 91.5 members. Surely they would have been smaller than this in 1776, because population density was much less then. In fact, lack of population density was commonly cited by religious leaders of the time as a primary barrier to sustaining churches. But if churches

TABLE 2.1
## Number of Congregations per Denomination, 1776

| Denomination | Number of congregations |
|---|---|
| Congregational | 668 |
| Presbyterian* | 588 |
| Baptist† | 497 |
| Episcopal | 495 |
| Quakers | 310 |
| German Reformed | 159 |
| Lutheran§ | 150 |
| Dutch Reformed | 120 |
| Methodist | 65 |
| Catholic | 56 |
| Moravian | 31 |
| Separatist and Independent | 27 |
| Dunker | 24 |
| Mennonite | 16 |
| Huguenot | 7 |
| Sandemanian | 6 |
| Jewish | 5 |
| TOTAL | 3,228 |

SOURCE: Paullin (1932).
*Includes all divisions such as New Light, Old Light, Associate Reformed, etc.
†Includes all divisions such as Separate, Six Principle, Seventh Day, Rogerene, etc.
§Includes all synods.

were smaller in 1776, how much smaller were they? This question caused us to search for any fragmentary statistics that might have survived.

The Methodists have quite complete and apparently accurate statistics for this period. The 1776 *Minutes of the Annual Conference of the Methodist Episcopal Church* report a total membership of 4,921. If we divide this number by the 65 Methodist congregations reported by Jernegan, we arrive at an average of 75.7 members. This is closely matched by Baptist data. Rufus Babcock (1841) reported that the average Baptist congregation in 1784 had 74.5 members. In 1790, John Asplund reported the results of an eighteen-month, seven-thousand-mile journey (most of it on foot) to visit all the Baptist congregations, which he numbered at 867 with a total of 65,233 members, or an average of 75.2. Finally, Herman C. Weber (1927) reported that in 1826 the average Presbyterian congregation had 70 members.

Let us cautiously assume that the average congregation in 1776 had 75 members.[2] If we multiply this by the 3,228 known congregations, we arrive at a total of 242,100 members. Factoring in children, in order to be comparable with later data, and dividing by the total population produces a national religious adherence rate of 17 percent for 1776. This percentage falls nicely within the ballpark limits. But it has the advantage of having been based on an actual enumeration of churches and on an average congregational size supported by church records.

Now let us consider the adherence rate for each colony, given in Table 2.2. The rates have been rounded to the nearest whole number, because the use of even one decimal place would give a very unwarranted impression of precision. There is substantial variation, from as low as 7 percent in Georgia and 9 percent in Vermont and North Carolina, up to 26 percent in New Jersey, 24 in Pennsylvania, and 22 in Massachusetts. The rates for New England (20%) and for the Middle Colonies (19%) are essentially the same, but the rate for the Southern Colonies (12%) is substantially lower. This difference is partly an artifact of slavery.

In 1776 slaves made up 42 percent of the population of the Southern Colonies, and they are included in the population denominators on which the adherence rates are based. But, in those days very few slaves had the option of belonging to a church (Raboteau, 1978; Butler, 1990). Jernegan himself wrote in 1916: "Though so many forces . . . were favorable to the conversion of slaves, progress was nevertheless exceedingly slow, and the results attained at the opening of the Revolution were comparatively meager" (p. 516). Not until later did the denominations invest much in ministries to the slaves, and slave owners continued to resist these efforts until well into the nineteenth century, fearing that religion would cause discontent.

For this reason the adherence rates in Table 2.2 have also been calculated using only the total white population in the denominators. With

TABLE 2.2
Religious Adherence Rates by Colony, 1776   (in percent)

| Colony | Adherence rate | White adherence rate |
|---|---|---|
| NEW ENGLAND | 20 | 20 |
| Maine | 19 | 20 |
| New Hampshire | 20 | 20 |
| Vermont | 9 | 9 |
| Massachusetts | 22 | 22 |
| Rhode Island | 20 | 20 |
| Connecticut | 20 | 20 |
| MIDDLE COLONIES | 19 | 20 |
| New York | 15 | 17 |
| New Jersey | 26 | 26 |
| Pennsylvania | 24 | 24 |
| Delaware | 20 | 22 |
| Maryland | 12 | 17 |
| SOUTHERN COLONIES | 12 | 20 |
| Virginia | 12 | 22 |
| North Carolina | 9 | 14 |
| South Carolina | 14 | 31 |
| Georgia | 7 | 20 |
| NATIONAL | 17 | 20 |

SOURCE: The data in Table 2.2, 2.4, 2.5, and A.1 are based on a series of estimation procedures described in the text. The number of congregations is estimated from Paullin (1932) and Wers (1936, 1938, 1950, 1955); the number of members per congregation is estimated from existing denominational totals.

this taken into account, all regional differences disappear. New England, the Middle Colonies, and the Southern Colonies all have the same rate as the nation overall, 20 percent. In our judgment, the rates based on whites only are probably a bit too high—it is certain that some blacks were churched in this period. The true rates for the Southern Colonies, therefore, probably lay somewhere between the two rates shown.

If we now know approximately how many church members there were in each colony, to what denominations did they belong? The data on numbers of churches allow us to present regional profiles of denominational make-up (see Table 2.3). To the degree that it was churched at all, New England was a bastion of Congregationalism. The Baptists were second, followed by a scattering of Episcopalian, Presbyterian, and Quaker congregations.

Compared with the other regions, New England was very lacking in diversity. Not only was there no dominant denomination in the other regions, but there was strong representation by "non-British" denominations—German and Dutch Reformed, Lutheran, and Moravian—especially in the Middle Colonies. This too emphasizes that New England was well named, for it was equally lacking in terms of ethnic diversity—its limited set of British denominations reflected its almost exclusively British ethnicity. The 1790 census classified 82 percent of the population of Massachusetts as English, as compared with 52 percent in New York and 35 percent in Pennsylvania. Adding in Scots and Protestant Irish accounted for 90 percent of the residents of Massachusetts, but only two thirds of New Yorkers and just over half of Pennsylvanians. Even the Southern Colonies had considerable religious and ethnic diversity in this period. Interestingly, the immense success of Baptists in the South had already begun.

Appendix Table A.1 presents similar breakdowns for each colony. There are no real surprises here, but the data suggest that many historical generalizations are rather exaggerated.

As expected, Rhode Island is the most Baptist of colonies, but it wasn't very Baptist. Given that only about half of its churches were Baptist and that only 20 percent of Rhode Islanders were churched, only about one person in ten would have been a Baptist.

Next, examine the profile of the "Quaker State." Quakers made up only the third largest denomination in Pennsylvania, far behind the Presbyterians, and behind the German Reformed. Moreover, Quakers

TABLE 2.3
## Denominational Percentages by Region, 1776, Based on Number of Congregations

| | |
|---|---:|
| **NEW ENGLAND (N = 1,039)** | |
| Congregationalist | 63.0 |
| Baptist | 15.3 |
| Episcopal | 8.4 |
| Presbyterian | 5.5 |
| Quaker | 3.8 |
| Other* | 3.6 |
| **MIDDLE COLONIES (N = 1,285)** | |
| Presbyterian | 24.6 |
| Quaker | 14.1 |
| Episcopal | 12.9 |
| German Reformed | 9.8 |
| Dutch Reformed | 8.9 |
| Lutheran | 8.6 |
| Baptist | 7.6 |
| Roman Catholic | 4.2 |
| Methodist | 3.8 |
| Moravian | 1.8 |
| Congregationalist | 0.3 |
| Other* | 3.1 |
| **SOUTHERN COLONIES (N = 845)** | |
| Baptist | 28.0 |
| Episcopal | 27.8 |
| Presbyterian | 24.9 |
| Quaker | 9.0 |
| Lutheran | 3.8 |
| German Reformed | 2.8 |
| Methodist | 1.4 |
| Moravian | 0.6 |

TABLE 2.3 (*Continued*)

| | |
|---|---|
| SOUTHERN COLONIES (*N* = 845) | |
| Congregationalist | 0.1 |
| Roman Catholic | 0.1 |
| Other* | 1.2 |

SOURCE: See Table 2.2.
NOTE: Only 3,169 of Jernegan's 3,228 congregations could be located by colony.
*"Other" includes Separatist and Independent, Dunker, Mennonite, Huguenot, Sandemanian, and Jewish.

represented less than 5 percent of Pennsylvanians. Indeed, Quakers were more common in Delaware and North Carolina.

Founded by Lord Baltimore as a haven for Roman Catholics, Maryland was the most Catholic colony in 1776. But that wasn't very Catholic—about three people in a hundred.

In any event, what is most noticeable about religion in the colonial era is how poorly the denominations were doing. To put it another way, these firms had failed to make any serious dent in the market. Whatever their religious needs, preferences, or concerns, the vast majority of Americans had not been reached by an organized faith. What factors produced such a lack of religious mobilization? And was anything brewing? Were new firms about to inject new methods and energy into the religious economy?

To begin to answer these questions, it is important to realize that most colonial settlements, even in the eighteenth century, were part of an untamed frontier. Everyone knows that in the "Wild West" of the nineteenth century, towns such as Dodge City, Tombstone, and Deadwood were not filled with God-fearing, Sunday-go-to-meeting folks, but were wide open, lawless capitals of vice and violence. Why should it have been any different when the frontier boom towns were New York or Charleston?[3] It wasn't. On any given Sunday morning there were at least as many people recovering from late Saturday nights in the taverns of these seaport towns as were in church.

Appearing on the front page of *Harper's Weekly* in the early 1880s, these pictures served to authenticate nostalgic memories of colonial religion. The picture to the left was entitled "Early Settlers on Their Way to Church," and for the picture to the right the caption read "The Call to Church—Early Colonial Times in New England." (Courtesy of the Billy Graham Center Museum, Wheaton, Ill.)

## The Sociology of Frontiers

By definition, a frontier is an area of new settlement and rapid population growth. As a result, frontiers are populated with newcomers and strangers. Quite aside from whether those attracted to frontiers tend to be deficient in moral character, wherever large numbers of people lack social ties, or what are often called interpersonal attachments, the result is social disorganization.

The real basis of the moral order is human relationships. Most of us conform to laws and social norms most of the time because to do otherwise would risk our relationships with others. When we are alone, even the most respectable of us act in ways we would not were anyone present. People who have no relationships with family or close friends, or whose relationships are with persons far away, are essentially alone all the time. They do not risk their attachments if they are detected in deviant behavior, because they have none to lose. Even in highly settled, stable communities some people are deficient in attachments, and it is they who are apt to engage in deviant behavior. In frontier areas, *most* people are deficient in attachments, and hence very high rates of deviant behavior exist.

Moreover, in areas where people are constantly passing through and where most people are strangers and newcomers, it is very difficult to sustain organizations of any kind, be they churches, fraternal lodges, or political clubs (Berry and Kasarda, 1978; Wuthnow and Christiano, 1979; Welch, 1983; Finke, 1989). People are recruited into and kept active in such organizations through social networks—through their attachments to others who also take part (Stark and Bainbridge, 1980, 1985). Where such networks are lacking, group actions are more apt to take the form of outbursts of collective behavior, such as riots or mob actions, than to be structured and directed by formal organizations.

As a result, frontiers will be short on churches, and long on crime and vice, simply because they *are* frontiers (Stark et al., 1983; Finke, 1989). And this imbalance will be greatly amplified because of *who* tends to migrate to frontiers.

## Who Migrates?

Studies of migration stress two factors: those that *push* people to leave a place and those that *pull* them to somewhere else. Among the major pushes are (1) lack of opportunity, (2) weak attachments, (3) fear of punishment, (4) disgrace, and (5) persecution. Of the five, only the last (and then only when groups are involved) is likely to cause "solid citizens" to migrate. Lack of opportunity can produce desirable migrants too, but the other three will tend to overproduce troubled and troublesome migrants. Those who lack attachments tend to be people who have difficulty forming and maintaining relationships. Those who fear punishment have usually offended, as have those in disgrace.

The major pulls are (1) economic opportunity, (2) anonymity and escape, and (3) greater freedom. Again, the last may attract very desirable migrants—as it did in the case of persecuted religious minorities who came to America. And economic opportunity can draw desirable migrants as well as undesirables.

When the total set of pushes and pulls is examined, however, two typical features of migrants to frontiers emerge. Many of them will be scoundrels, misfits, and others of dubious past and character, who are fleeing their pasts or seeking new opportunities to practice illegal or morally stigmatized activities. And most migrants will be men—some free of attachments, having no wife or family, some fleeing such responsibilities.

Thus we deduce the population of Dodge City, Tombstone, and Deadwood—towns filled with male drifters, gamblers, confidence tricksters, whores, and saloon keepers, and without churches, schools, or respectable women. Thus we also deduce many aspects of the American frontier when it was still back east. These deductions can be fleshed out with concrete facts about colonial America.

## Male America: Sex Ratios

The single best measure for locating frontiers is the sex ratio, usually calculated as the number of males per 100 females. The higher the ratio—the greater the imbalance of males to females—the more frontier-like the place. This is especially the case for highly imbalanced sex ratios among younger adults.

It is very significant, therefore, that, in his monumental study in progress[4] of people leaving for America from England and Scotland between December 1773 and spring 1776, Bernard Bailyn (1986) has found that almost four out of five (77.8 percent) were males; and they were mostly younger males. At a time when only 18 percent of the English and Scottish populations were in the 15–24 age group, half of those leaving for America were in this category. Bailyn's records of these people after their arrival here show that they typically did not linger in the settled areas along the coast, but headed to the frontier areas.

Given these patterns, it is no surprise that in the nation as a whole there were substantially more men than women in the eighteenth century. But it is the variation across colonies that is most instructive (see Table 2.4). On the eve of the Revolution, while in the other colonies men outnumbered women, in Massachusetts and Rhode Island, the women had already come to outnumber the men, a sure sign that the frontier had moved inland. Indeed, these data indicate that the nation was already beginning to split into male and female sections: a settled East, lacking men (especially men in the most marriageable age groups), and a western frontier, lacking women. This regionalization of gender became extremely pronounced in the nineteenth century, as we shall see in later chapters.

TABLE 2.4
Males per 100 Females by Colony or State

|  | Colonial census | 1790 U.S. Census |
| --- | --- | --- |
| Maine | 103 (1764) | 104 |
| New Hampshire | 104 (1775) | 101 |
| Vermont | 117 (1771) | 113 |
| Massachusetts | 97 (1764) | 96 |
| Rhode Island | 97 (1774) | 97 |
| Connecticut | 102 (1774) | 98 |
| New York | 107 (1771) | 107 |
| New Jersey | 107 (1745) | 105 |
| Pennsylvania | n.a. | 106 |
| Delaware | n.a. | 109 |
| Maryland | 111 (1755) | 106 |
| Virginia | n.a. | 106 |
| North Carolina | n.a. | 104 |
| South Carolina | n.a. | 109 |
| Georgia | n.a. | 104 |

SOURCE: Calculated from population totals reported by the Bureau of the Census (1975, vol. 1, pp. 24–37; vol. 2, pp. 1169–71).

The second column of sex ratios in Table 2.4 comes from the first U.S. Census, conducted in 1790. The westward drift of males and of the frontier comes into even sharper focus. Aside from Maine, New York was the only state for which earlier data exist in which the sex ratio had not declined. By 1790 Connecticut had joined Rhode Island and Massachusetts as states in which the women outnumbered the men. Where were the men of New England going? A glance at a map will provide an answer and will also explain why New York's ratio did not fall.

Because New England is north of New York City, many Americans have the impression it is also north of New York State. But New Englanders heading due west are soon in New York. And by 1790 that is where the western frontier was located, and where the young, migrating males from Massachusetts, Rhode Island, and Connecticut were to be found.

It was long a favorite theme of western movies that when the "nice" women arrived, it was time to build a church, a school, and a good jail. The part about churches was most certainly true. The higher the male to female sex ratio, the lower the rate of religious adherence. In fact, in colonial America an extremely high negative correlation of − .95 exists (− 1.0 is a perfect negative correlation) between the sex ratios and rates of religious adherence.

The immense importance of women for church life shows up very strongly when actual membership roles are scrutinized. In a study based on 97 Congregational churches in Massachusetts and Connecticut, Richard D. Shiels (1981) found that 64 percent of all new members were women—a fact he described as the "feminization of American Congregationalism" (p. 46). Recall from chapter 1 that the 1926 census of religious bodies showed the national Methodist membership included but 66.8 males per 100 female members. Similar sex imbalances in church membership, both here and abroad, turn up in study after study (Shiels, 1981; Stark and Bainbridge, 1985; Butler, 1990), thus confirming Cotton Mather's observation in 1691 that "there are far more Godly Women in the World than there are Godly Men" (in Cott, 1977, p. 127). One barrier to the churching of colonial America, and especially the frontier areas, was the lack of women.

## Scoundrels and Knaves

Substantial numbers of those who embarked for colonial America were of solid farmer and merchant stock, coming in hopes of greatly improving their lot through honest means. But it is also true, as Bailyn has described, that among them were "many hardened criminals—thieves, blackmailers, pimps, rapists, embezzlers, and thugs available for hire" (1986, p. 295). It is estimated that from 1718 to 1775 at least 50,000 persons, most of them convicted of capital crimes, were forcibly transported to America by order of English courts. Another 16,000 or so were sent over by the courts in Ireland (Bailyn, 1986).

Transported convicts were not the only source of scoundrels and knaves in the colonies. Many immigrants of seemingly highly respectable backgrounds were nothing of the sort. This seems to have been especially true of the clergy. Unlike the Congregationalists, who were soon producing their own clergy at Harvard and Yale, many of the denominations active in colonial America were dependent on clergy sent from overseas. The Episcopal Church, as the American branch of the Church of England, was served by clergy from the mother country. Many of the Presbyterian clergy were supplied by the Church of Scotland. And the Lutherans, German and Dutch Reformed, and the Roman Catholics depended on Europe for their pastors.

But who would come? Few were willing, and so these denominations always were short of clergy—a fact that hindered the churching of the colonies. Worse yet, in light of the constant complaints from their parishioners, we must suspect that many if not most who did come seemed lacking in energy, morals, or even authentic credentials.

Edwin S. Gaustad (1987, p. 15) has reported frequent grumbling by Anglican vestrymen "about clergy that left England to escape debts or wives or onerous duties, seeing Virginia as a place of retirement or refuge." In 1724 Giles Rainsford, an Anglican clergyman in Maryland, sent this dispatch concerning three of his colleagues to the Bishop of London: "Mr. Williamson is grown notorious and consumate in villainy. He really is an original for drinking and swearing. Mr. Donaldson is so vile that the other day, being sent for to a dying person, came drunk, and the poor expiring soul, seeing his hopeful parson in that condition, refused the Sacrament at his hands and died without it. Mr. Maconchie is a mere nuisance, and makes ye church stink. He fights, and drinks on all occasions, and as I am told *alienas permolet uxores* [forces his attentions on the wives of others]" (in Ritchie, 1976, p. 145).

Later in the century George Whitefield ([1756] 1969) noted in his journal that the Church of England might "flourish" in the colonies "were her ministers found faithful" (p. 386). Having heard of plans by the Society for the Propagation of the Gospel in Foreign Parts to send more missionaries to America, Whitefield noted in his journal that it would be better "that people had no minister than such as are generally sent over" (p. 387). In response to his own rhetorical question regarding why the Church of England was doing so poorly in America, he blamed the missionaries "who, for the most part, lead very bad examples" (p. 387).

Rainsford's and Whitefield's accusations were echoed later in the century by Thomas Coke (1793), the first Methodist bishop in America. After kind words for the Quakers and praise for the zeal of the Baptist clergy, Coke wrote: "But what shall we say for the Clergy of the Church of *England* in these states. . . . We would fain draw a veil over them, if

the truth of history would permit it . . . they were, with a few exceptions to the contrary, as bad a set of men as perhaps ever disgraced the
Church of God . . ." (in Powell, 1967, p. 37).

There also seem to have been frequent instances of people pretend-
ing to be clergy or falsely confessing to faiths they did not hold. In 1742,
when Henry Melchior Muhlenberg arrived in Pennsylvania, having
been sent from Germany to take charge of the Lutherans, his worst initial problem was with self-appointed and venal clergymen. Muhlenberg's *Notebook* (1959) is filled with complaints against greedy scoundrels
posing as legitimate Lutheran clergy, many of them ordained by Valentine Kraft, whose claims to official standing were fraudulent.[5]

> December 1, 1742. I learned forthwith that Mr. Kraft had traveled
> through the whole province of Pennsylvania, appointed deacons and el-
> ders here and there, and established a general presbytery in the whole
> country. . . . And besides all this, he had organized a consistory of which
> he was the president. . . . The purpose of the presbytery was to make it
> possible for Valentine Kraft and his assessor to travel around the country
> and carry on their trade with the holy sacraments. The consistory served
> the purpose of letting him ordain a few more lazy and drunken school-
> masters and place them as preachers in vacant places.
>
> January 4, 1743. Mr. Kraft now took off his hypocritical mask. . . . He
> became the boon companion of some worthless, drunken schoolmasters
> who wander about the country as preachers and make money with the
> Lord's Supper, baptism, and weddings. He got drunk with these fellows
> and carried on high.
>
> January 9, 1743 . . . Because the schoolmasters, already described, in-
> tended to establish opposition congregations in various places and thus
> vex me, I made two announcements to the congregation: (1) They were
> not to pay anything when they had their children baptized, and (2) at the
> Lord's Supper there was to be no offering of money at the altar for the
> pastor. Since these vagabonds are concerned only to get a few shillings for
> a baptism and the offerings at the Lord's Supper . . . I have abolished this
> abominable custom. (pp. 10–14)

Perhaps the most notorious case of all involved the Catholics. Antonio
de Sedella claimed to be a Capuchin friar when he appeared in New
Orleans in 1781, and he may have been. Whatever the case, Sedella
rapidly became superior of the Capuchins in New Orleans and vicar-
general and pastor of St. Louis Cathedral. Père Antoine, as he soon

came to be called, was popular in the city because of his reputation for being indulgent of moral weakness. But even the most lukewarm Catholics in New Orleans were humiliated and shocked when Père Antoine died in 1829 and, in accord with his will, was buried with Masonic rites (Hennesey, 1981).

## Establishment

Thus major impediments to the churching of colonial America are common features of all frontier settings: transience, disorder, too many men, too many scoundrels, and too few effective and committed clergy. But there were other important factors as well. Writing in 1776, Adam Smith noted how legal establishment of the church saps the clergy of their "exertion, their zeal and industry." He concluded, in a passage quoted at the end of this chapter, that when clergy do not need to depend upon their parishioners for their employment and pay, they neglect their duties and do not develop the skills required to stir up commitment. Taking a similar position, Colonel Lewis Morris, former governor of the New Jersey Colony, wrote from New York to a friend about the impact of establishment upon the Episcopal Church: "If by force the salary is taken from [the people] and paid to the ministers of The Church, it may be a means of subsisting those Ministers, but they wont make many converts. . . . Whereas [without establishment] the Church will in all probability flourish, and I believe had at this day been in a much better position, had there been no act [of legal establishment] in her favor; for in the Jersies and Pennsylvania, where there is no act, there are four times the number of church men than there are in this province of N. York; and they are soe, most of them, upon principle, whereas nine parts in ten, of ours, will add no great credit to whatever church they are of; nor can it well be expected otherwise" (in O'Callaghan, 1855, pp. 322–323). Morris may have slightly exaggerated the statistics, but New York did have an unusually low adherence rate, 15

When Henry Muhlenberg (1711–1787) first arrived in 1742 he found his pastorate occupied by a vagabond preacher, Valentine Kraft, and his pulpit was located in barns (top) and private homes. By 1745, however, Kraft was gone and the Augustus Lutheran Church at Trappe, Pennsylvania, was dedicated (bottom). (Courtesy of the Concordia Historical Institute, St. Louis, Missouri.)

percent, compared with New Jersey's rate of 26 percent and Pennsylvania's 24 percent (see Table 2.2).

In any event, it must be noted that the two potentially most powerful religious bodies in colonial America, the Congregationalists and the Episcopalians, rested upon legal establishment. The Episcopalians enjoyed legal establishment in New York, Virginia, Maryland, North and South Carolina, and Georgia; the Congregationalists were established in New England.

In Chapter 3 we will trace the slow process of disestablishment during the first part of the nineteenth century and examine how having been established helped to block the growth and westward expansion of both denominations. But even in 1776 the effects of establishment show up strongly in the geography of Congregationalism. Where it could rely on taxpayer support, the Congregationalist Church dominated the religious landscape, albeit this feat is made much less impressive by its very low rate of market penetration (see Table 2.5). In Massachusetts, Congregationalists made up 71.6 percent of adherents, in Vermont 65 percent, in Connecticut 64.2 percent, and in Maine 60.9 percent. But aside from a weak 17.2 percent in Rhode Island, Congregationalism was effectively nonexistent in the rest of the colonies, having not even one congregation in five colonies. Neither the Congregationalists nor the Episcopalians were long on clergy strongly motivated to pursue church growth.

## The Sect-Church Process

At this point in our examination of colonial religion, it is necessary to distinguish two primary forms of religious organizations—*churches* and *sects*. These are best conceptualized as the end points of a continuum made up of the *degree of tension* between religious organizations and their sociocultural environments (B. Johnson, 1963). To the degree that a religious body sustains beliefs and practices at variance with the surrounding environment, tension will exist between its members and outsiders. In the extreme case, well illustrated by the sad tales of Quakers persecuted in the Massachusetts Bay Colony, tension is so high that the group is hunted down by outsiders. When a religious body has no beliefs or practices setting it apart from its environment, no tension will exist. *Churches* are religious bodies in a relatively low state of tension

TABLE 2.5
Percentage Congregationalist by Colony, 1776

| Colony | Percentage Congregationalist |
|---|---|
| Massachusetts | 71.6 |
| Vermont | 65.0 |
| Connecticut | 64.2 |
| New Hampshire | 63.2 |
| Maine | 60.9 |
| Rhode Island | 17.2 |
| Georgia | 4.3 |
| New York | 1.8 |
| South Carolina | 1.2 |
| New Jersey | 0.4 |
| Pennsylvania | 0.0 |
| Delaware | 0.0 |
| Maryland | 0.0 |
| Virginia | 0.0 |
| North Carolina | 0.0 |

SOURCE: See Table 2.2.

with their environments. *Sects* are religious bodies in a relatively high state of tension with their environments.

There are intimate connections between churches and sects within any given religious economy. These were first noted by H. Richard Niebuhr in his celebrated book *The Social Sources of Denominationalism*, published in 1929. He sought to explain why Christianity was fractured into so many competing denominations. Why weren't Christians content with one church? Why did they constantly form new ones? Niebuhr might as well have asked why *all* religious groups are subject to constant schism, for all the world's faiths come in endless and disputatious variety and the answer he proposed can be generally applied.

In any event, Niebuhr's explanation of religious schism is elegantly simple. Churches and sects differ greatly in their ability to satisfy different human needs, needs that are always reflected in distinct segments of the religious market. As noted in the discussion of pluralism in Chapter 1, it is very difficult for any single religious organization to be at once very worldly and very otherworldly or both strict and permissive. Churches serve the segment of the market with less need for a strict and otherworldly faith; sects serve the segment seeking those features.

The sect-church process concerns the fact that new religious bodies nearly always begin as sects and that, if they are successful in attracting a substantial following, they will, over time, almost inevitably be gradually transformed into churches. That is, successful religious movements nearly always shift their emphasis toward this world and away from the next, moving from high tension with the environment toward increasingly lower levels of tension. As this occurs, a religious body will become increasingly less able to satisfy members who desire a higher-tension version of faith. As discontent grows, these people will begin to complain that the group is abandoning its original positions and practices, as indeed it has. At some point this growing conflict within the group will erupt into a split, and the faction desiring a return to higher tension will leave to found a new sect.[6] If this movement proves successful, over time it too will be transformed into a church and once again a split will occur. The result is an endless cycle of sect formation, transformation, schism, and rebirth. The many workings of this cycle account for the countless varieties of each of the major faiths.

More recently, the process by which sects are transformed into churches has been equated with the process of secularization. Social scientists have long used the term "secularization" to identify what was regarded as the master religious trend in modern times: a decline in the plausibility of supernatural beliefs that would culminate in the disappearance of religion. For years, every retreat from a vivid, active conception of the supernatural by major Christian bodies was greeted as another confirmation of the secularization thesis. All contrary signs of continued religious vigor were dismissed as one last hurrah—a dying gasp.

Eventually, however, the pile of contrary evidence became so immense that even most social scientists could no longer believe that religion was on the wane. At that point it was noticed that the idea that secularization would wipe out religion rested on a very narrow grasp of the sect-church process, one limited to the transformation of sects into churches. Social scientists had correctly observed the movement away from traditional Christian teachings by some of the most prominent denominations. But they had failed to observe the response to these changes elsewhere in the religious economy. Secularization *is a self-limiting process that leads not to irreligion, but to revival* (Stark and Bainbridge, 1985, 1987). As religious bodies become increasingly churchlike they not only lose their vigor but give rise to sects that revitalize the religious tradition in new organizations. As we shall see, the result is not a decline in religion, but only a decline in the fortunes of specific religious organizations, as they give way to new ones.

It is clear that, as products of the Reformation, the primary faiths of colonial America began as sect movements. By the Revolution, many of them had become much more churchlike than sectlike. A fuller understanding of the state of religion in colonial times, therefore, requires an assessment of the secularization process and a search for signs of its self-limiting consequences—revival.

## Secularization in Colonial America

What transforms sects into churches? Cotton Mather put it succinctly: "Religion brought forth prosperity, and the daughter destroyed the mother." He went on to explain that prosperity was a major threat to piety among Congregationalists, for the *"enchantments* of this world make them forget *their errand into the wilderness"* (in Ahlstrom, 1975, vol. 1, p. 215).

Two centuries later, Niebuhr (1929) gave the same answer. Sects arise to satisfy the needs of those less fortunate in pursuit of the world's goods: "In Protestant history the sect has ever been the child of an outcast minority, taking its rise in the religious revolts of the poor" (p. 19). That religion can make life bearable, even for those in extreme misery, is a central theme of traditional Christian doctrine, including the promise that faith will be rewarded in the world to come, where "the first shall be last, and the last, first." But to offer solace to the poor and downhearted, a religious body must resist many of life's "temptations." An organization filled with members or leaders who have unrestricted access to the "enchantments of this world" is severely handicapped in its capacity to serve the religious needs of the less successful.

In time, however, successful sects come to be dominated by the more successful[7]—those for whom life's pleasures are options. And thus begins the gradual accommodation to the world. Niebuhr (1929, p. 20) explained, "Rarely does a second generation hold the convictions it has inherited with fervor equal to that of its fathers. . . . As generation succeeds generation, the isolation of the [sect] from the world becomes more difficult."

Affluence rapidly became a threat to many American sects, because by the middle of the eighteenth century per capita wealth in the larger colonies was far higher than anywhere else in the world. There was an abundance of fertile land and natural resources available for the taking, and the immigrants took.

In 1756 Samuel Fothergill described the situation of his fellow Pennsylvania Quakers: "Their fathers came into the country, and bought large tracts of land for a trifle: their sons found large estates come into their possession, and a profession of religion that was partly national, which descended like a patrimony from their fathers, and cost as little. They settled in ease and affluence, whilst they made the barren wilderness as a fruitful field, suffered the plantation of God to be as a field uncultivated, and a desert . . . with the bent of their spirits to this world, could not instruct their offspring in those statutes they had themselves forgotten" (in Tolles, 148, p. 4). Fothergill's perceptions were fully vindicated in 1827 when a sect movement erupted among the Philadelphia Quakers. In his remarkable study of this schism, known as the Hicksite separation, Robert W. Doherty (1967) offered solid data that the Quakers who followed Elias Hicks and left the main body were much less well-to-do than were those who remained in the more worldly church. Doherty's data also show that the Philadelphia Quakers in general were far more affluent than their non-Quaker neighbors. Comparing the assessed value of the real estate owned by Quakers and non-Quakers, Doherty found that 30 percent of the former and only 9 percent of the latter owned property worth more than $4,000 (a huge sum at the time). Conversely, 66 percent of the non-Quakers and 43 percent of the Quakers had less than $2,000 worth of real estate. As to occupation, Doherty found that 13 percent of the Quakers in Philadelphia, in contrast with 2 percent of non-Quakers, were identified as "Gentlemen"—men who lived off investments and rents. An additional 45 percent of Quakers were merchants, businessmen, or professionals, compared with 28 percent of non-Quakers. Only 33 percent of Quakers were ordinary workers, while 64 percent of non-Quakers held such jobs. The same contrasts existed among farmers in Chester County, Pennsylvania. The average Quaker farmer had more acres, more cattle, and a higher assessed farm value than did his non-Quaker neighbors.

It was this affluence that encouraged the worldly Quakerism that Elias Hicks condemned.

In New England, in similar fashion, affluence was eroding the fervor of the descendants of the Mayflower voyagers and of the many other Puritan immigrants to the Bay Colony. Moreover, the flowering of intellectual life in New England, nurtured by clergy trained at Harvard and Yale, soon gave added impetus to secularization.

In his volume on the colonial clergy of New England, Weis (1936) reported that of the 1,586 men who had ever served as pastor of a Congregational church, 1,507, or 95 percent, were college graduates. Of these more than 60 percent went to Harvard and 29 percent went to Yale.

It may be that secularization ensues whenever religion is placed within a formal academic setting, for scholars seem unable to resist attempting to clear up all logical ambiguities. Rather than celebrate mysteries, religious scholars often seek to create a belief system that is internally consistent. Finding that things do not fit exactly, they begin to prune and revise and redefine.[8] Whether or not this corrosive effect of scholarship on religion is inevitable, this is what went on at Harvard and Yale, starting well before the Revolution. Ahlstrom (1975, vol. 1, p. 483) characterized Harvard late in the eighteenth century as "essentially and conscientiously Unitarian." And as Harvard's divinity school took shape "its faculty and students were Unitarian and remained so with few exceptions during the entire nineteenth century" (p. 483). As for Yale, in 1778 it appointed as its new president Ezra Stiles, who was of the opinion that revivals such as those led by George Whitefield depended upon driving people "seriously, soberly, and solemnly out of their wits" (p. 490).

Given the virtual monopoly on the "manufacture of ministers" enjoyed by Harvard and Yale, it is hardly surprising that the views of their faculty were shared by the Congregational clergy. The liberal faction dominated the desirable Congregationalist pulpits, from which they expressed their agreement with Stiles's views about revival and religious emotionalism. As Ahlstrom (1975, vol. 1, p. 474) reported, "A firm opposition to revivalism and the whole pietistic emphasis on a religion of the heart was a settled conviction with the liberals." Moreover, as the efforts by these liberals to adjust doctrine to Reason led rapidly to Unitarianism and Deism, their opposition to emotionalism transformed their preaching style. Exhortations to repent and to be saved gave way, as Ahlstrom put it, to "a well-styled lecture, in which the truths of religion and the moral duties of man were expounded in as reasonable a manner as possible. Sermons thus became a species of polite litera- ture. . . . Reviews of published sermons frequently were critiques of syntax and style rather than content" (pp. 474–475). The Puritan sect had given way to the Congregationalist Church.

## Sect Formation and Revival

If the leading religious bodies of colonial America were eroded by sec- ularization, and if secularization is self-limiting, where were the reviv- als? In several places. First of all, in the so-called Great Awakening. Second, and more significant, in the explosive successes of two classic sect movements, the Baptists and the Methodists. How these two up- start sects took center stage soon after the Revolution will be the subject of Chapter 3. But it is useful here to reflect very briefly on the nature of what later came to be called the Great Awakening, but which was actu- ally nothing more (or less) than George Whitefield's well-planned, well- publicized, and well-financed revival campaign. In Chapter 3 we will look more closely at the issue of "Great Awakenings" and examine the methods used by Whitefield and other revivalists. But for now we will simply focus on the story itself.

### America's First Great Revivalist

As the Congregational clergy began to substitute lectures on theology for heartfelt sermons of conviction, their flocks began to shrink. Some drifted away to the Baptists, where they could hear preachers who still preached; others probably just drifted. Into this inviting vacuum came the Grand Itinerant, George Whitefield.

Whitefield was an Englishman and belonged to the Holy Club at Ox- ford along with John and Charles Wesley, the eventual founders of Methodism. After Oxford, Whitefield did some preaching in England and then felt called to Georgia. There he met with considerable success before having to return to England in order to be ordained a priest in the Church of England. In England, like the Wesleys, Whitefield was barred from many pulpits because of his enthusiastic revivalist ap- proach. And like the Wesleys, he often preached in open fields or from the steps of buildings fronting on public squares. Soon he returned to America.

That George Whitefield (1714–1770) was cross-eyed, as shown in this 1742 engraving, can hardly have detracted from his extraordinary rhetorical skills. Benjamin Franklin, who reported so fully on Whitefield's visit to Philadelphia, did not think this worth noting. Instead, he stressed how Whitefield changed the city: "In 1739 arrived among us ... the Rev. Mr. Whitefield. ... The multitudes of all sects and denominations that attended his sermons were enormous. ... It was wonderful to see the change soon made in the manners of our inhabitants; from being thoughtless or indifferent about religion, it seemed as if all the world were growing religious, so that one could not walk through the town in an evening without hearing psalms sung in different families of every street" ([1868] 1916, pp. 191–192). (Courtesy of the Massachusetts Historical Society, Boston.)

# George Whitefield's Journal:
# Visit to Boston, October 1740

Sunday, October 12: Spoke to as many as I could, who came for spiritual advice. Preached, with great power, at Dr. Sewall's meeting-house, which was so exceedingly thronged, that I was obliged to get in at one of the windows. . . . Went with the Governor, in his coach, to the common, where I preached my farewell sermon to near twenty thousand people,—a sight I have not seen since I left Black-heath,—and a sight, perhaps never seen before in America. It being nearly dusk before I had done, the sight was more solemn. Numbers, great numbers, melted into tears, when I talked of leaving them. I was very particular in my application both to rulers, ministers, and people, and exhorted my hearers steadily to imitate the piety of their forefa-thers; so that I might hear, that with one heart and mind, they were striving together for the faith of the Gospel. . . .

Boston is a large, populous place, and very wealthy. It has the form of religion kept up, but has lost much of its power. I have not heard of any remarkable stir for many years. Ministers and people are obliged to confess, that the love of many is waxed cold. Both seem to be too much conformed to the world. There is much of the pride of life to be seen in their assemblies. Jewels, patches, and gay apparel are commonly worn by the female sex. The little infants who were brought to baptism, were wrapped up in such fine things, and so much pains taken to dress them, that one would think they were brought thither to be initiated into, rather than to renounce, the pomps and vanities of this wicked world. There are nine meeting-houses of the Congregational persuasion, one Baptist, one French, and one belonging to the Scots-Irish. There are two monthly, and one weekly lectures; and those, too, but poorly attended. I mentioned it in my sermons, and I trust God will stir up the people to thread more frequently the courts of His house. One thing Boston is very remark-able for, viz., the external observance of the Sabbath. Men in civil offices have a regard for religion. The Governor encourages them; and the ministers and magistrates seem to be more united than in any other place where I have been. Both were exceedingly civil during my stay. I never saw so little scoffing, and never had so little opposi-tion. Still I fear, many rest in a head-knowledge, are close Pharisees, and have only a name to live.

Whitefield was quite simply one of the most powerful and moving preachers ever to hold forth. His voice and style were so potent that David Garrick, the most famous English actor of the time, claimed that Whitefield could seize the attention of any crowd merely by pronouncing "Mesopotamia," (W. W. Sweet, 1944). He could be heard and understood by very large crowds, even outdoors. In his *Autobiography,* Benjamin Franklin reported that Whitefield:

> had a loud and clear voice, and articulated his words and sentences so perfectly that he might be heard and understood at a great distance. . . . He preached one evening from the top of the courthouse steps, which are in the middle of Market Street and on the west side of Second Street, which crosses it at right angles. Both streets were filled to a considerable distance. Being among the hindmost in Market Street, I had the curiosity to learn how far back he could be heard by retiring backwards down the street toward the river, and I found his voice distinct till I came near front street. . . . This reconciled me to the newspaper accounts of his having preached to twenty-five thousand people in the field. . . . By hearing him often I came to distinguish easily between sermons newly composed and those which he had often preached in the course of his travels. His delivery of the latter was so improved by frequent repetition that every accent, every emphasis, every modulation of voice was so perfectly well turned and well placed that, without being interested in the subject, one could not help being pleased with the discourse, a pleasure of much the same kind with that received from an excellent piece of music. This is an advantage itinerant preachers have over those who are stationary, as the latter cannot well improve their delivery of a sermon by so many rehearsals. ([1868] 1916, pp. 196–198)

Wherever Whitefield preached, whether in the Middle Colonies or in New England, pandemonium broke loose. Whitefield's crusade for Christ, as it no doubt would be called today, had been preceded by some effective local revivals, especially that led by Jonathan Edwards. But these were sideshows compared with the outburst generated by Whitefield. In Philadelphia, huge crowds gathered—attracting even skeptics like Franklin. In Boston, large numbers were turned away every time Whitefield preached, so he moved outdoors—especially after the tragedy in Reverend Checkley's Meeting House. And when Whitefield finally departed Boston by ship, after a whirlwind visit up the coast, a crowd perhaps as large as 30,000 turned out on the Common to bid him farewell. The magnitude of Whitefield's reception can be more fully appreciated by noting that in 1740 the total population of Boston was only about 20,000 (Chandler and Fox, 1974).

*Benjamin Franklin L.L.D. F.R.S.*

Among Benjamin Franklin's most famous aphorisms is "A fool and his money are soon parted." These views give added zest to Franklin's confession of how Whitefield's preaching in behalf of funds for the orphanage he founded in Georgia opened his purse: "I happened soon after to attend one of his sermons, in the course of which I perceived he intended to finish with a collection, and I silently resolved he should get nothing from me. I had in my pocket a handful of copper money, three or four silver dollars, and five pistoles in gold. As he proceeded, I began to soften and concluded to give him the coppers. Another stroke of his oratory made me ashamed of that and determined me to give the silver; and he finished so admirably that I emptied my pocket wholly into the collectors dish, gold and all" ([1868] 1916, p. 194). (Courtesy of the National Portrait Gallery, Smithsonian Institution, Washington, D.C.)

Crowds didn't just come to listen to Whitefield. Moved by his extraordinary power, thousands fell to the ground and cried out to God when Whitefield thundered, "Are you saved?"—and then explained why the answer was "No!" Whitefield was not satisfied to indict only his crowds for their sins. He attacked the local clergy for the predicament of their flocks: "I am persuaded, the generality of preachers [in New England] talk of an unknown and unfelt Christ. The reason why congregations have been so dead, is because they have had dead men preach to them" (Oct. 9, 1740; [1756] 1969, p. 471).

Visits to Harvard and Yale convinced him that they were places where "Light is become darkness." Thousands wept at each place Whitefield departed, but most of the local clergy remained dry-eyed.

With Whitefield gone, the fires soon died down. But several primary results lived on to shape American religion. First, Whitefield demonstrated the immense market opportunity for more robust, less secularized religion. In doing so he provided the model for itinerancy. If you have no pulpit, what does it matter? Preach anywhere people will gather. Soon scores, then hundreds, and eventually thousands followed in his footsteps, ministering to the nation. Second, it was not the "mainline" denominations of the colonies that gathered the primary fruits of Whitefield's awakening of religious sentiments. After all, many of their clergy agreed with Ezra Stiles that Whitefield's results were gained by driving his crowds into madness. Many of those brought shivering and trembling to salvation by Whitefield ended up in Baptist congregations, causing a sudden spurt of growth that carried them past the Episcopalians to become the third largest American denomination by 1776. Not only did many of Whitefield's converts end up Baptists, but his revival methods also took root among the Baptists and subsequently were adopted by the sect movement developing within the Church of England, nourished by Whitefield's old friends, the Wesley brothers. Although Whitefield himself steadfastly refused to become a Methodist, he was in many ways the man who did most to launch the Methodist movement in America.

To conclude this chapter and to set the appropriate stage for the next, let us return to Adam Smith and his analysis in *The Wealth of Nations* of why denominations that have been established faiths are so weakened as to be swept away when and where an unregulated religious economy comes into being.

> [Clergy] may either depend altogether for their subsistence upon the voluntary contributions of their hearers; or they may derive it from some other fund to which the law of their country may entitle them; such as a landed estate, a tythe or land tax, an established salary or stipend. Their exertion, their zeal and industry are likely to be much greater in the former situation than in the latter. In this respect the teachers of new religions have always had a considerable advantage in attacking those ancient and established systems of which the clergy, reposing themselves upon their benefices, had neglected to keep up the fervour of faith and devotion in the great body of the people; and having given themselves up to indolence, were altogether incapable of making vigorous exertion in defence even of their own establishment. The clergy of an established and well-endowed religion frequently become men of learning and elegance, who possess all the virtues of gentlemen; but they are apt gradually to lose the qualities, both good and bad, which gave them authority and influence with the inferior ranks of people, and which had been the original causes of the success and establishment of their religion. . . . in general every religious sect, when it has once enjoyed for a century or two the security of a legal establishment, has found itself incapable of making any vigorous defence against any new sect which chose to attack its doctrine or discipline. Upon such occasions the advantage in point of learning and good writing may sometimes be on the side of the established church. But the arts of popularity, all the arts of gaining proselytes, are constantly on the side of its adversaries. In England those arts have been long neglected by the well-endowed clergy of the established church, and are at present chiefly cultivated by the dissenters and by the methodists. The independent provisions, however, which in many places have been made for dissenting teachers, by means of voluntary subscriptions, of trust rights, and other evasions of the law, seem very much to have abated the zeal and activity of these teachers. They have many of them become very learned, ingenious, and respectable men; but they have in general ceased to be very popular preachers. The methodists, without half the learning of the dissenters, are much more in vogue. ([1776] 1937, pp. 740–741)

Thus Smith noted in 1776 that in England the Anglican establishment slept, the Calvinist dissenters dozed, and only the "methodists" had fire in their bellies and brimstone on their minds. On this side of the Atlantic it was much the same. Established faiths had drawn such a tepid response from the population that few Americans were churched.

Many of their clergy had indeed become "men of learning and elegance," who flocked to Harvard and Yale, scorning the "arts of gaining proselytes."

But upstart forces stirred. Rough and ready itinerants were on the prowl, men who firmly believed that the whole world was to be saved.

# Chapter 3

# The Upstart Sects Win America, 1776–1850

In 1776 the Congregationalists, Episcopalians, and Presbyterians seemed to be *the* colonial denominations. Of Americans active in a religious body, 55 percent belonged to one of the three. And at the time it seemed certain that these groups would continue to be the "mainline" for the foreseeable future. Indeed, in 1761 Ezra Stiles using a demographic projection technique taught him by Benjamin Franklin, proclaimed that one hundred years hence there would be seven million Congregationalists in the colonies and fewer than four hundred thousand Baptists. But by 1860 there were actually fewer than five hundred thousand Congregationalists in America, while the Baptists numbered nearly two million. What happened?

In this chapter we argue that, perhaps ironically, the decline of the old mainline denominations was caused by their inability to cope with the consequences of religious freedom and the rise of a free market religious economy. But before taking up these matters, it will be helpful to examine the great shift in religious fortunes that occurred between 1776 and 1850.

If we compare the "market share" of major bodies in 1776 and 1850 (see Figure 3.1), we see that in 1776 the Congregationalists, Episcopalians, and Presbyterians dominated—although their overall market penetration was very poor. Then, in just seventy-four years, the combined market total of these three bodies shrank to only 19.1 percent of reli-

FIGURE 3.1 Religious Adherents by Denomination, 1776 and 1850 (as percentage of total adherents)

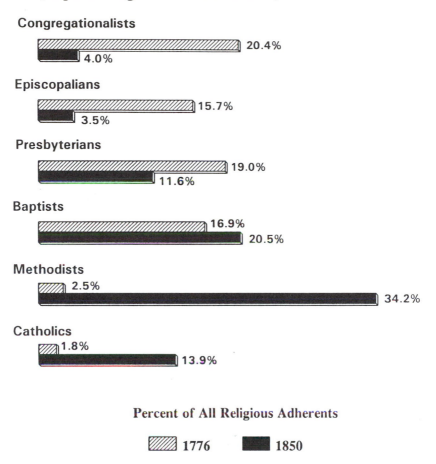

**Congregationalists**
20.4%
4.0%

**Episcopalians**
15.7%
3.5%

**Presbyterians**
19.0%
11.6%

**Baptists**
16.9%
20.5%

**Methodists**
2.5%
34.2%

**Catholics**
1.8%
13.9%

**Percent of All Religious Adherents**

1776     1850

gious adherents, even though the proportion belonging to churches had about doubled, to 34 percent.

For Congregationalism, the shift approached total collapse. The major denomination in 1776, it can only be described as a minor body less than eight decades later—falling from more than 20 percent of total adherents to but 4 percent. Despite this extraordinary shift in their fortunes, Congregationalist leaders during this era expressed surprisingly little concern, aside from complaints about a general decline in religion during the late eighteenth century. Perhaps they didn't think in terms of rates, and instead took pride in the fact that their number of members had more than tripled. It was not until the 1960s, when the failures of the Congregationalists first turned into losses in actual numbers rather than just in market share, that serious expressions of alarm were heard.[1]

The Episcopalians also fared badly in terms of their share of the religious market, falling from a strong second to last place among leading denominations—from 15.7 percent to 3.5 percent of all church adherents.

The Presbyterians' share of the religious market also declined, from 19 percent to 11.6 percent. But the Presbyterians' growth in actual numbers, unlike that of the Congregationalists and the Episcopalians, did keep pace with the growth of the population. The Presbyterians fared better because they were able to achieve some growth on the new American frontiers. Their share declined, however, because their growth failed to match the expansion of the proportion who were churched.

During this same period the Baptists achieved very substantial growth, primarily through conversion, and the Catholics grew rapidly, through immigration. But the major shift in the American religious market in this period was the meteoric rise of Methodism. In 1776 the Methodists were a tiny religious society with only 65 churches scattered through the colonies. Seven decades later they towered over the nation. In 1850 there were 13,302 Methodist congregations, enrolling more than 2.6 million members—the largest single denomination, accounting for more than a third of all American church members. For such growth to occur in eighty years seems nearly miraculous. But the general histories of American religion would make it even more of a miracle. Because all agree that religion fell into a state of sad neglect in the wake of the American Revolution, they would confine the rise of Methodism to less than fifty years.

## Ebb Tide or Torrent?

We noted in Chapter 1 the nearly uniform language used by historians to claim that American religion collapsed to the point of near-invisibility during and immediately after the Revolution, a period that Williston Walker (1894, p. 319) described as "the epoch of the lowest spiritual vitality that our churches have ever experienced." Or, to quote Leonard Woolsey Bacon (1897, p. 230): "The closing years of the eighteenth century show the lowest low-water mark of the lowest ebb-tide of spiritual life in the history of the American church." William Warren Sweet ([1930] 1950, p. 223) called the last fifteen years of the eighteenth century "the period of the lowest ebb-tide of vitality in the history of American Christianity." Winthrop S. Hudson (1965, pp. 115–116) agreed that this same period "witnessed that ebb tide of religious life which often characterizes post-war eras." Sydney Ahlstrom (1975, vol. 1, p. 442) reported, "The churches reached a lower ebb of vitality during the two decades after the end of hostilities than at any other time in the country's religious history."

Douglas H. Sweet (1976, pp. 346–347) noted that this belief about an ebb tide seems to have derived from the singular dependence of general religious historians on the accounts of Lyman Beecher and some of his colleagues: "The writings of Lyman Beecher may have exerted a greater influence over twentieth-century historiography than those of almost any other early commentator. As evidence of this, one need consider no more than the frequency with which Beecher's description of Yale in the 1790s is quoted in text upon text. In their search to find an explanation, and perhaps, even a narrative filler, for the period between the American Revolution and the Second Great Awakening, modern church scholars have written an account based largely on the hyperbolized observations and conclusions of clergymen and clerical historians [belonging to] . . . the established order."[2]

We shall have occasion toward the end of the chapter to discuss Lyman Beecher's views on many matters. Here it suffices to note that Beecher's claims about religious decline were as much a reflection of his contempt for Methodists and Baptists and their style of worship as they were a reflection of his awareness of the problems besetting Congregationalists and Episcopalians in this era, including attacks upon their legal establishment. In an 1814 address to a charitable group that funded seminary scholarships, Beecher, a prominent Congregational minister and later the president of Lane Theological Seminary, condemned the preaching of "ignorant and unlettered men." Such men are "utterly unacquainted with theology" and do far more harm than good as far as Christian faith is concerned: "Illiterate men have never been the chosen instruments of God to build up his cause" (in Hatch, 1989, p. 18). Having delivered this line, Beecher seems to have had a jarring second thought—as Nathan O. Hatch has so perceptively noted—for he was prompted to add that the twelve disciples were tutored by Jesus for three years "to supply the deficiency of an education." In any event,

Lyman Beecher (1775–1863). (Courtesy of the Billy Graham Center Museum, Wheaton, Ill.)

Beecher felt entirely justified in calling an area religiously "destitute" as long as it was without educated, mainline clergy, no matter how many Methodist and Baptist churches it might sustain; he regarded the latter two as "worse than nothing."

For better or worse, any accurate characterization of religion in this era must confront statistics on rapid Baptist and Methodist growth, and these are far more compatible with the image of a torrent than with that of a low ebb. The Methodists reported 4,921 members in 1776. By 1800, at the end of the period that Marty (1975, p. 82) has called the "big sleep" in American religious life, the Methodists had grown to 64,894, and by 1806 they numbered 130,570—hardly a "sleepy" performance, given that the nation's population did not even double during this interval.[3] As for the Baptists, they claimed to have numbered 35,101 in 1784, to have grown to 65,345 by 1790, and then to 172,972 by 1810.

The sources of these statistics are neither obscure nor recent. The Methodist data come from the *Minutes* of their annual conferences, which were published yearly. They can also be found in the *Methodist Centennial Yearbook* (1884), which is widely available. The Baptist data were also published in church reports, but we found them in the *American Quarterly Register* (1841), which may still be found in virtually any major university library. Had the "ebb tide" writers made use of the available sources and determined the true state of affairs, the received wisdom concerning this period would be that the colonial mainline bodies began their long slide toward obscurity by the end of the eighteenth century, but that at the same time those feisty upstart sects, the Baptists and the Methodists, had begun a period of torrential growth. Thus the central questions come into clear focus. *Why* did the leading denominations of 1776 crumble in a free market religious economy? What did they do wrong? Or what did the Methodists and the Baptists do right?

## The Rise of a Free Market Religious Economy

By the start of the Revolution, the era of harsh religious persecution in the colonies had ended. Religious toleration prevailed in fact, if not yet in statute. And in the immediate post-war period, toleration slowly gave way to religious freedom. In the eyes of the newly established federal government, not only would all faiths be permitted to worship, all would be given equal opportunity. There would be no established church, and the state would be separated from all religious entanglements.

But the religious situation looked quite different when examined at a more local level. The Congregationalists were established in New England, while the Episcopalians, as the Church of England, were established in some of the Middle and Southern colonies. The Episcopal establishments fell quickly after the British defeat. But in New England, the Congregationalists (including their emergent Unitarian division) clung to taxpayer support. Eventually they were beaten by a rather unlikely alliance: the rationalists and freethinkers, on the one hand, and the upstart, aggressive, evangelical Protestant sects, on the other. The freethinkers resented having their taxes go to any religion; the sectarians resented their taxes going to false religions. Given that each of the religious groups wanted religious freedom for itself, even if few of them really wanted religious freedom for all, there was no other safe way to proceed but to create an unregulated, free market, religious economy.[4]

But disestablishment didn't happen overnight, and even then de facto establishment persisted long after the official sanctions had been withdrawn. Connecticut disestablished the Congregationalist Church only in 1818, followed by New Hampshire in 1819. And it was not until 1833 that Massachusetts ceased to collect "church taxes" on behalf of the Congregationalists.

After the battle to disestablish Congregationalism was won, it turned out that the other "mainline" bodies only opposed favoritism that was exclusively for the Congregationalists. They welcomed favoritism as long as it included themselves. And so it came to be that the Congregationalists, Episcopalians, and Presbyterians frequently engaged in collective efforts to benefit from many forms of official support at the local level and formed cartels aimed at preventing free market forces from developing.

The efforts to impose de facto establishment were vigorous, but they failed dismally. Similar efforts to use "nondenominational" front organizations to channel public donations for home missions into narrowly denominational benefits eventually failed too. But we must pause to examine these maneuvers, for in and of themselves they reveal many aspects of the fatal flaws the old "mainline."

## Cartel Agreements and Local Privilege

When George Whitefield brought his itinerant ministry to town, many local ministers found him a dangerous challenge to their privileged position and denied him their pulpits. Whitefield was not forestalled; thousands flocked into fields and public squares to hear him, as we have seen. But when many others began to take up itinerancy in the aftermath of Whitefield's tours, the local clergy and political elites moved against them, especially in New England.

Late in 1743, only three years after Whitefield had captivated the city, the president and faculty of Harvard gathered to issue a unanimous *Testimony against the Reverend Mr. George Whitefield and His Conduct*. Published in 1744, the *Testimony* began: "In regard of the Danger which we apprehend the People and Churches of this Land are in, on the Account of the Rev. Mr. George Whitefield, we have tho't ourselves oblig'd to bear our Testimony in this public Manner, against him and his Way of Preaching. . . . And we do therefore and hereby declare, That we look upon his going about, in an Itinerant Way, especially as he hath so much of an enthusiastic Turn, utterly inconsistent with the Peace and Order, if not the very Being of the Churches of Christ" (p. 3). Next, the Harvard faculty complained:

> the People, many of them, are strongly attach'd to him (tho' it is most evident that he hath not any superior Talent at instructing the Mind, or shewing the Force and Energy of those Arguments for a religious Life which are directed to in the everlasting Gospel). . . .
>
> First then, we charge him, with *Enthusiasm*. . . . we mean by an *Enthusiast*, one that acts, either according to Dreams, or from sudden Impulses and Impressions upon his Mind, which he fondly imagines to be from the Spirit of God, persuading and inclining him thereby to such and such Actions, tho' he hath no Proof that such Perswasions or Impressions are from the holy Spirit. . . . (pp. 3–4)

Shortly thereafter, on January 22, 1744, the Congregational clergy of Boston and of Bristol County gathered in Boston to see what could be done to stop itinerant preachers. "Ministers do not invade the Province of others," they proclaimed, in the familiar tones of those who want regulated, not free, markets. The group subsequently published *The Testimony of the Association of Ministers against the Reverend Mr. George Whitefield and His Conduct*, in which they recorded their "most solemn Testimony against . . . Mr. Whitefield in Person" and "against Itinerant Preaching, as practiced of late among us."

What were Whitefield's sins? That he had traveled "from Town to Town preaching," although God has "no where in the Gospel appointed any such Officer in his Church, where the Officers are already settled in it, and the Gospel fully and faithfully preached; as also directly tending to destroy the Peace and Order of these Churches, and to throw them off from the good Foundation upon which they were settled by our wise and pious *Ancestors*" (1745, p. 4). Worse yet, Whitefield had "used his utmost Craft and Cunning, to strike the Passions and engage the Affections of the People." And finally these angry clergymen cited scripture to prove that God "hath enjoined our Ministers, that they be not Busy-Bodies in other Men's Matters; i.e., don't play the Bishop in another's Charge" (1745, pp. 6–7).

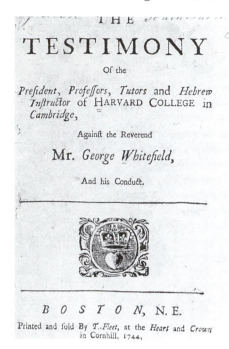

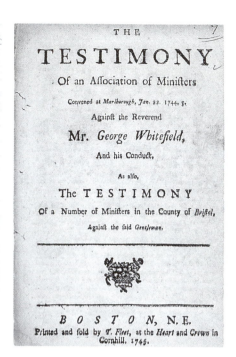

The Harvard faculty and the Congregational clergy of New England argued that it was their "duty" and "obligation" to provide testimony against the "enthusiasm" and "Itinerant Way" of George Whitefield. In other words, they were protesting his emotional message of salvation for the masses and his complete disregard for the cartel agreements of local clergy. (Courtesy of the Billy Graham Center Museum, Wheaton, Ill.)

Meanwhile, clergy in Connecticut appealed to the Assembly for protection against the "disorderly intruding" of clergy into other men's parishes. They were rewarded with a statute requiring itinerants to secure written consent from local clergy before doing any preaching and providing for constables to escort offenders out of the colony (Marty, 1984, p. 120).

Nearly a century later and far to the west, efforts persisted to maintain "gentlemen's agreements" whereby pastors would not poach on one another's flocks. In his autobiography (1856), the great Methodist itinerant Peter Cartwright offered this example of a phenomenon he often encountered. Arriving in a new community, he was approached by the local Presbyterian minister, who did not object to his preaching, but requested that he make no effort to form a church in this neighborhood because it was within the "bounds of his congregation." Cartwright responded: "I told him that was not our way of doing business; that we seldom ever preached long at any place without trying to raise a society. He said I must not do it. I told him the people were a free people and lived in a free country, and must be allowed to do as they pleased. . . . He said that was true; but if we raised a society it would diminish his membership, and cut off his support" (p. 123). Cartwright explained that he had no option but to continue and that if any cared "to join our Church I shall take them in." He then announced that when he returned in a month he would organize a class, because several local people had requested that he do so. The Presbyterian clergyman responded that he would "openly oppose" Cartwright.

Over the next three Sundays the local minister preached against Methodism and itinerancy. According to Cartwright, these attacks simply produced "a vast crowd" for his return visit, and twenty-seven people joined the Methodists that day. This was only the beginning: "Public opinion was in my favor, and many more of this preacher's members came and joined us, and the minister sold out and moved to Missouri, and before the year was out I had peaceable possession of his brick church" (1856, p. 125).

The most ambitious effort to create a religious cartel was no doubt the 1801 Plan of Union between the Presbyterians and the Congregationalists. Recognizing their mutual Calvinism, the plan called for unified, noncompeting missionary efforts to the western frontier, meanwhile dividing the settled areas into exclusive "markets," the Presbyterians to stay south of New England, the Congregationalists to stay north of the old Middle Colonies. In the end the plan harmed them both, in large part because it reduced their competitive capacities without restricting the efforts of their most serious challengers. The Methodists and Baptists were not in the Union.

An additional source of efforts at de facto establishment came from the fact that local political and economic elites were usually aligned with the colonial mainline bodies. Thus in many communities, especially toward the frontier, the mainline bodies received "use" subsidies in the form of being allowed to hold their services in schools and other public buildings without charge. Whitney R. Cross ([1950] 1982, p. 45) reported: "In Buffalo during 1818, Presbyterians monopolized the court house and Episcopalians, the school house. Methodists could only meet in the latter place at sunrise or sunset."

Peter Cartwright (1785–1872) described his younger self as a "wild, wicked boy [who] delighted in horse-racing, card-playing, and dancing" and "made but small progress" with his formal education (1856, pp. 27–28). Yet he went on to become one of the most famous and respected Methodist itinerants. Twice a member of the Illinois legislature, he lost in his bid for Congress to another famous frontiersman—Abraham Lincoln. (Courtesy of the Billy Graham Center Museum, Wheaton, Ill.)

## "Nondenominational" Front Groups

In 1798 the General Association of Connecticut voted to become an agency "to Christianize the Heathen in North America, and to support and promote Christian knowledge in the new settlements, within the United States" (in Ahlstrom, 1975, vol. 1, p. 513). Soon other such groups appeared—voluntary associations of private citizens devoted to "interdenominational" efforts to sustain home missions. In 1826 many of these groups were consolidated by the founding in New York of the

American Home Missionary Society (AHMS). For many decades this organization appeared to dominant efforts to convert the godless frontier; it collected and spent large sums annually to support clergy and build churches in the "wilderness," where other means to sustain organized religion were lacking.

The AHMS journal was widely distributed in the cities of the eastern seaboard, and its appeals for funds were carefully nondenominational. For example, in 1827 the journal asked for funds to support a mission to Niagara County in the far western corner of New York State on grounds that the area was almost entirely "destitute of the stated ministry of the gospel of every denomination." At the same time nearby Monroe County was classified as a "moral waste," and "destitute of both religious and moral principles" (in Cross, [1950] 1982, p. 48).

In truth, there were many churches and many ministers of the gospel active in both these counties at the time—but they all were Baptists or Methodists.[5] And that was precisely the rub. The Congregationalists, Presbyterians, and Episcopalians could not sustain churches in these areas without home mission subsidies, if for no other reason than that they depended on a well-educated and well-paid clergy. But as Horace Galpin wrote to Miles Squier at AHMS headquarters, in the West the people could "have the preaching of . . . the Methodists for nothing, to the subversion of the regular ministry" (in Cross [1950] 1982, pp. 45–46). To raise the money needed to offer "free" religion out west, the mainline denominations conspired for decades to deceive the public about why funds were needed and who received them. Clergymen who were willing to claim that places abounding in Baptists and Methodists were unchurched could have no qualms about not sharing "nondenominational" contributions with such outsiders and upstarts.

Indeed, an AHMS missionary to Arkansas wrote back to his superiors in 1846 that the Baptists, Methodists, and other sects were "standing in the way" of the work of the society: "After a minute examination and mature and prayerful deliberation I have come to the settled conviction that it would be decidedly for the religious interests of Arkansas if every minister and preacher of the above denominations were out of the State" (in W. W. Sweet, 1964b, p. 698).

But wishing couldn't make it so. The Methodists and the Baptists were there to stay. And if the Methodists were excluded from using the court house or the school house in Buffalo to hold their services, they were not prevented from building a church. Several years later, after a very successful "revival" led by a circuit rider, they did just that. The same pattern occurred again and again. Even with their AHMS subsidies, the colonial mainline could make only feeble efforts at moving west. Yet somehow sufficient local funds could always be found to build churches out west, if they were Methodist and Baptist churches. Before we try to say why this was the case, let us first look more closely at the religious situation in 1850.

## Religion in 1850

In 1850 the West "Coast" was not along the shores of the Pacific. That year there were all of 13,294 people in the Oregon Territory, which included what was yet to become the Washington Territory, and of the 92,597 residents of California, 85,578 were men—many of whom were forty-niners who had come there during the gold rush that began the previous year. Elsewhere, what is today regarded as the Far West was essentially unsettled. Even in Utah, the Mormon migration had added up to only 11,380 people by the time the 1850 census was taken. In 1850 the west had barely crossed the Mississippi River—Iowa, Arkansas, Missouri, and Texas were the only places across the Mississippi having any substantial population (the Minnesota Territory was still the "North Woods," having but 6,077 residents, two thirds of them men). In effect, the West "Coast" in 1850 was lapped by the waters of the Mississippi.

For this reason we will examine the religious situation of 1850 in an America of thirty states as mapped in Figure 3.2, which shows how well the sex ratio identifies the frontier. The states farthest west had substantially more males than females. In contrast, New England had more females than males.

Recall that in 1776 there was a huge negative correlation between the sex ratio and religious adherence—frontiers always are deficient in churches. Thus Figure 3.3 is no surprise. The frontier states along the Mississippi had noticeably lower rates of religious adherence. Iowa was lowest, with only 138 adherents per 1,000 population. Arkansas, Michigan, and Texas were the other three states below the 200 level. Notice, however, that New England was not the most churched area in 1850: Maryland, Indiana, and Ohio were the states with the highest adherence rates.

However, if New England was not outstanding in terms of religious participation, it was exceptional for its high ratios of clergy to population (see Figure 3.4). In Vermont and New Hampshire there were two

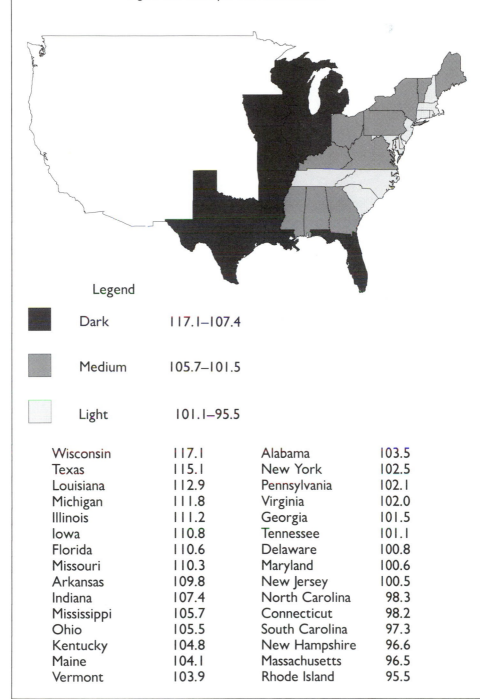

Figure 3.2. Males per 100 Females, 1850

Legend

| | | |
|---|---|---|
| ⬛ | Dark | 117.1–107.4 |
| ◼ | Medium | 105.7–101.5 |
| ◻ | Light | 101.1–95.5 |

| Wisconsin | 117.1 | Alabama | 103.5 |
|---|---|---|---|
| Texas | 115.1 | New York | 102.5 |
| Louisiana | 112.9 | Pennsylvania | 102.1 |
| Michigan | 111.8 | Virginia | 102.0 |
| Illinois | 111.2 | Georgia | 101.5 |
| Iowa | 110.8 | Tennessee | 101.1 |
| Florida | 110.6 | Delaware | 100.8 |
| Missouri | 110.3 | Maryland | 100.6 |
| Arkansas | 109.8 | New Jersey | 100.5 |
| Indiana | 107.4 | North Carolina | 98.3 |
| Mississippi | 105.7 | Connecticut | 98.2 |
| Ohio | 105.5 | South Carolina | 97.3 |
| Kentucky | 104.8 | New Hampshire | 96.6 |
| Maine | 104.1 | Massachusetts | 96.5 |
| Vermont | 103.9 | Rhode Island | 95.5 |

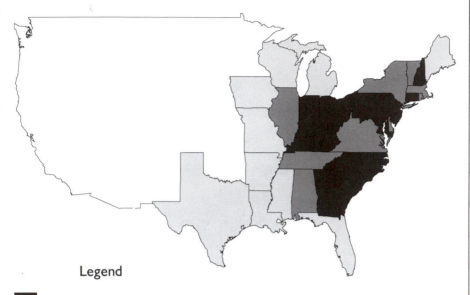

Figure 3.3. Religious Adherents per 1,000 Population, 1850

Legend

| | | |
|---|---|---|
| ■ | Dark | 422–352 |
| ▨ | Medium | 347–296 |
| ▢ | Light | 288——138 |

| | | | | |
|---|---|---|---|---|
| Maryland | 422 | | Massachusetts | 327 |
| Ohio | 420 | | Delaware | 326 |
| Indiana | 416 | | Vermont | 322 |
| Georgia | 392 | | Virginia | 314 |
| Kentucky | 388 | | New Hampshire | 296 |
| New Jersey | 378 | | Florida | 288 |
| South Carolina | 367 | | Mississippi | 275 |
| Pennsylvania | 366 | | Maine | 255 |
| Connecticut | 360 | | Missouri | 241 |
| North Carolina | 352 | | Louisiana | 218 |
| Tennessee | 347 | | Wisconsin | 216 |
| Rhode Island | 346 | | Texas | 199 |
| Illinois | 340 | | Michigan | 187 |
| New York | 331 | | Arkansas | 166 |
| Alabama | 329 | | Iowa | 138 |

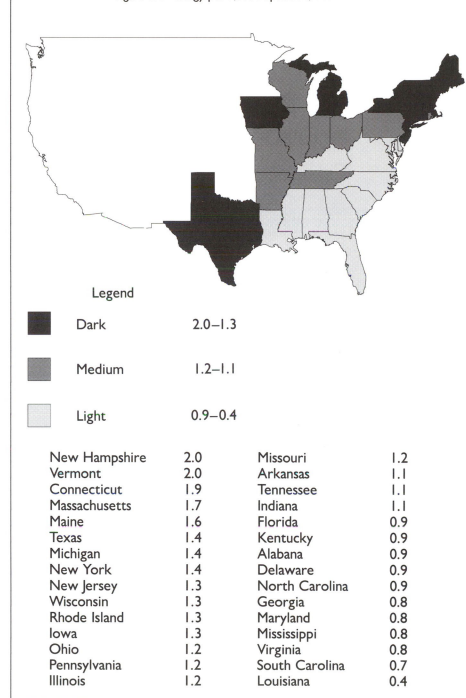

Figure 3.4. Clergy per 1,000 Population, 1850

Legend

| | | |
|---|---|---|
| ■ | Dark | 2.0–1.3 |
| ■ | Medium | 1.2–1.1 |
| ☐ | Light | 0.9–0.4 |

| | | | |
|---|---|---|---|
| New Hampshire | 2.0 | Missouri | 1.2 |
| Vermont | 2.0 | Arkansas | 1.1 |
| Connecticut | 1.9 | Tennessee | 1.1 |
| Massachusetts | 1.7 | Indiana | 1.1 |
| Maine | 1.6 | Florida | 0.9 |
| Texas | 1.4 | Kentucky | 0.9 |
| Michigan | 1.4 | Alabana | 0.9 |
| New York | 1.4 | Delaware | 0.9 |
| New Jersey | 1.3 | North Carolina | 0.9 |
| Wisconsin | 1.3 | Georgia | 0.8 |
| Rhode Island | 1.3 | Maryland | 0.8 |
| Iowa | 1.3 | Mississippi | 0.8 |
| Ohio | 1.2 | Virginia | 0.8 |
| Pennsylvania | 1.2 | South Carolina | 0.7 |
| Illinois | 1.2 | Louisiana | 0.4 |

clergy for every 1,000 inhabitants. In Maryland, with its high adherence rate, there was less than one pastor to serve every 1,000 persons.

Appendix Table A.2, containing the adherence rate per 1,000 population for the three denominations of the old colonial mainline and the two upstart sects, allows us to see in detail where the upstart sects won America. In Maine, for example, of every 1,000 inhabitants, 48 were affiliated with the Congregationalists, 2 with the Episcopalians, 3 with the Presbyterians, 89 with the Baptists and 58 with the Methodists. The "upstart ratio" shows that for every person in Maine affiliated with an old colonial mainline body, 2.8 were affiliated with the Baptists or the Methodists.

Even in New England the mainline denominations had crumbled badly in the face of aggressive Methodist and Baptist activity. Only in Connecticut did the old mainline still outnumber the upstarts. Outside New England, it wasn't even close. Indeed, the bitter fruits of the 1801 Plan of Union between the Presbyterians and Congregationalists come into dramatic focus. For reasons we assess in detail later, the Congregationalists were unable to minister to the West and hence failed to grow with the nation, but the Plan of Union caused them to make no efforts to spread their ministry into the cities and settled areas south of Connecticut, where conditions were much more favorable to their organizational abilities. Moreover, the Plan kept the Presbyterians from mounting efforts to missionize in New England, and because the Presbyterians were the only one of the three mainline faiths that showed any ability to compete with the upstart sects, their absence left the door to New England wide open for the Methodists and the Baptists. If the Presbyterians were left out of the calculations of the upstart ratios for all thirty states, the presence of the colonial mainline could hardly be detected in most of the nation.

To grasp more fully what had happened by 1850, and as a useful glimpse of why it had taken place, we may contrast the biggest loser with the biggest winner (see Table 3.1). The correlations compare the social geography of the old number one faith, the Congregationalists, with that of the new number one, the Methodists.

Where the Methodists were stronger, church adherence was higher (.66)—hardly surprising, because Methodist membership gains were the primary cause of the rise in the adherence rate. Variations in the strength of Congregationalism, however, were not correlated with the adherence rate. But Congregationalism was stronger where there was a more ample supply of clergy—the correlation is a huge .81. In contrast,

TABLE 3.1

Comparisons of Congregationalists and Methodists, 1850

|  | Correlations with Congregationalists per 1,000 | Correlations with Methodists per 1,000 |
|---|---|---|
| Religious adherents per 1,000 | .05 | .66** |
| Clergy per 1,000 | .81** | − .51** |
| Residents born in state per 1,000 | .53** | .03 |
| Sex ratio | − .39* | − .25 |

Level of significants: ** < .01; * < .05.

the Methodists tended to do best where clergy were in short supply, hence the minus sign before the correlation coefficient (− .51). The Congregationalists had retained their greatest strength in the most settled areas, where the highest proportion of residents had been born in-state (.53). The Methodists were not affected by this factor, doing equally well where there was much migration as where there was little. Finally, the Congregationalists did poorly where men outnumbered women (− .39), and although the correlation between the sex ratio and Methodism also is negative, it is not statistically significant.

The Methodists could function everywhere—on the frontier or in the city. The Congregationalists could function only in "civilized" areas, but even there they could not hold their own against the upstarts. In fact they could not even withstand Methodist and Baptist competition on their home ground of New England.

## Why the Upstarts Won

Where there are winners there are losers. Much can be learned from a comparison of the two primary winners in the American religious economy between 1776 and 1850, the Methodists and Baptists, with the two primary losers, the Congregationalists and Episcopalians. There also is much to be gained from examination of the "also-ran" Presbyterians, whose growth kept pace with the population, but not with the increase in the proportions active in churches.

## Organizational Structures

Social scientists agree that the structure of an organization can have tremendous impact on its efficiency and success. This has been especially stressed in studies of religious organizations (Harrison, 1959; Wood and Zald, 1966; Szafran, 1976). Nevertheless, it would appear at first glance that variations in denominational polity played little or no part in who grew and who did not.

The two most successful denominations, the Baptists and the Methodists, seem to be polar extremes in terms of polity. Historians have often cited the democratic structure of the Baptist church as an attractive feature to the people of the early frontier (W. W. Sweet, 1952; Ahlstrom, 1975; Hudson, 1981), but the Methodist Church was even more successful on the frontiers, and everyone knows the Methodists have a hierarchical structure with strong, centralized authority placing control firmly in the hands of the clergy. Similar variation would seem to exist among the losers. The Protestant Episcopal Church and the Congregational Church seem at opposite extremes, with the Presbyterians falling somewhere in between.

When we look more closely at these denominational organizations, however, we find that historians were correct to stress the way in which the democratic congregational life of the Baptists helped them church the frontiers. But with the exception of Hatch (1989), historians have failed to note that this applied to the Methodists as well. For in those days the Methodists were about as democratic *locally* as were the Baptists. The local congregations were divided into small, close-knit groups called classes. Each class met on a weekly basis and was composed of approximately a dozen members. Here is where the zeal of camp meetings was maintained, intimate fellowship was achieved, and the behavior of the faithful was monitored. But the class also helped to select potential leaders. Exhorters and local preachers were frequently recommended by their class, and each was subject to an "annual examination of character in the quarterly conference" (in Gorrie, 1852, p. 295). And although class-leaders, who were deemed responsible for the "moral and Christian conduct" of members, were appointed by the itinerant in newly established missions, the more common practice was for the local (unpaid) preacher to appoint and supervise their activities. As a result, the average Methodist congregation was a model of "congregationalism," in the sense that control actually resided in the hands of the adult membership.

In this era the actual pastoral functions were performed in most Methodist churches by unpaid, local "amateurs" just like those serving the Baptist congregations up the road.[6] A professional clergy had not yet centralized control of the Methodist organization. True, the circuit-riders were full-time professionals vested with substantial authority. But they only visited a congregation from time to time and played the role of visiting bishop[7] and evangelist more than the role of pastor. It was only when the circuit riders dismounted and accepted "settled" pastorates that the "episcopal" structure of Methodism came to the fore. Indeed, it may well be that to the extent that the Methodists were able to create a national organization based on the circuit riders, they had the best of both worlds—centralized direction and local control (Miyakawa, 1964). In any event, despite apparent differences in polity, both the Methodists and the Baptists were surprisingly democratic and thus able to respond to the actual desires of the market.

In contrast, the Congregationalists were not nearly so "congregational" as either of the upstart sects. That Congregationalism was dominated by a highly professional clergy was the result of two interrelated factors. First, as we take up in detail below, the Congregationalists had opted for a highly educated clergy. This led to a chronic shortage of clergy and maximized their bargaining power, both individually and collectively. A second factor was establishment. As the established church of most New England colonies, Congregational churches were organized at town meetings, were supported by the town's "religious taxes," and "the towns played the customary role in concurring in the choice of the minister" (McLoughlin, 1971, p. 795). This system made the clergy influential in local governmental affairs. Moreover, establishment allowed the Congregationalists to depend on secular organizational structures to provide central coordination of their religious affairs within New England and left them with no alternative model for coordination among congregations. Whereas the Baptists would form regional associations whenever four or five Baptist churches were established, Congregational churches established outside of the New England region were often isolated units, lacking any regional support.

In fact, to be untied with churches beyond the local state line was contrary to the organizational plan of the early Congregational churches (Atkins and Fagley, 1942).

The 1801 Plan of Union with the Presbyterians illustrates the organizational problems of the early Congregationalists. Although the Plan, first supported by the Congregational General Assembly of Connecticut and later approved by the General Associations of Massachusetts, New Hampshire, Vermont, and Maine, was designed to unify the two denominations' frontier missionizing efforts, it resulted in the Congregationalists' being swallowed up by the Presbyterians. This was in large measure because the latter had established presbyteries, in addition to congregations, on the frontier. Because there was no alternative Congregational central structure, the Plan of Union led whatever individual Congregational churches that did arise to end up joining a presbytery and thus effectively to switch denominations (W. W. Sweet, [1930] 1950). Although as Williston Walker (1894) claimed, the Plan of Union was a "wholly honorable arrangement, and designed to be fair to both sides," it inadvertently favored the Presbyterians because only they had a structure sufficient to sustain congregations in less settled areas. As "their Presbyteries were rapidly spread over the missionary districts," Walker continued, "the natural desire for fellowship . . . led Congregational ministers to accept the welcome offered therein" (pp. 317–318). The Congregational associations in the individual New England states were simply not able, or not willing, to support the national expansion of their church. In the end, the Plan slowed the decline of the Presbyterians and confined the Congregationalists to New England.

The Episcopalians and the Presbyterians did have national and regional organizations, but each was beset with organizational problems. The Revolution did great damage to the Episcopalians. Many members supported the Crown and fled at war's end. Sweet (1952) reported that the majority of Virginia's 100 Anglican parishes were defunct by the end of the war and that the number of active Anglican clergy had dropped from 91 to 28. Sweet also estimated that North Carolina, Georgia, and Pennsylvania each had only one active Anglican priest by the end of the Revolution. In addition to these disasters, the Episcopalians lost their formal connection with the Church of England, thus ending their supervision by the Bishop of London and the substantial flow of subsidies and mission clergy provided by the Society for the Propagation of the Gospel in Foreign Parts. Although the process of national reorganization began in 1783, effective new central authority was lacking for several more decades. Thus in a critical time, when rapid growth was shaping a new nation, the Episcopal Church was struggling to support its remaining churches and to recover from the war. It lacked the resources to expand its share of the religious market.

In contrast, the Presbyterians were well organized and emerged from the Revolution with enhanced prestige. Sweet (1964b, p. 3) suggested that "no church in America, at the close of the War for Independence, was in a better position for immediate expansion than was the Presbyterian." The Presbyterians had established strong presbyteries throughout the nation, and, as we have seen, they fared much better than did the Congregationalists or the Episcopalians during this era. Their growth, however, was constantly plagued by divisions within their organization. Although the Plan of Union contributed to their increases, the new "Presbygational" churches also contributed to doctrinal and polity controversies. Holding camp meetings similarly contributed to Presbyterian growth in rural and frontier areas, but this practice aroused disapproval "back east," leading to sharp regional and doctrinal controversy. The Presbyterians worked tirelessly for unity, which they understood to be rooted in uniformity. Through their efforts to enforce strict national standards on polity and doctrine, they frequently shattered the very unity they sought and prompted regional schisms.

It appears that the situation facing the churches in this period placed very stern demands on denominations to become competitive organizations prepared to seek souls to the ends of civilization and beyond. Polity alone would not achieve this, but organizational structures that prevented a *nationwide* effort were a fatal flaw.

It may be pertinent here to note that though it is convenient to speak of organizations doing this or that, organizations per se never do anything. Only people ever act. Who was representing these denominations in the religious marketplace? What was their background and training and how were they recruited and deployed? And what were their motives?

## Ministers

The organizational forms used by the Baptists and the Methodists were quite different, but their clergy were nearly interchangeable. In both denominations, ministers primarily came from the ranks of the common folk and, to a very important extent, remained common folk. Unlike the Congregational, Presbyterian, and Episcopalian ministers, who typically were of genteel origin and were highly trained and well educated, the Baptist and Methodist clergy were of the people. They had little education, received little if any pay, spoke in the vernacular, and preached from the heart.

The local preacher for either of the upstart sects was a neighbor, friend, or relative of many of the people he served. Although this may have meant that the clergy held the same prejudices as did their flocks— and thus hampered the prophetic role of religion—it fostered a close relationship between the minister and the people in the pews. The minister shared the wants, needs, and desires of the people, and he made every effort possible to share the same religion too.

One of the most striking differences between the clergy of the upstart sects and those of the colonial mainline, and the easiest to document, was in their education. It was no secret that the great majority of Baptist and Methodist ministers had little education. The 1853 *Baptist Almanac* estimated that in 1823 only about 100 of the 2,000 Baptist clergy had been "liberally educated." The famous Methodist itinerant Peter Cartwright estimated that at the General Conference of 1844 fewer than 50 (of approximately 4,282 traveling ministers) "had anything more than a common English education [grade school], and scores of them not that." But neither denomination was apologetic for this lack of training. Cartwright went on to boast that these uneducated clergy "preached the Gospel with more success and had more seals to their ministry than all the sapient, downy D.D.'s in modern times" (Cartwright, 1856, p. 408).

As was true of most Methodist leaders of the time, including Bishop Asbury, Cartwright was opposed not to higher education but, rather, to the use of theological schools for the designing of "man-made" ministers.[8] Nevertheless, the Methodists were in no hurry to found colleges. Between 1780 and 1829, forty colleges and universities were successfully founded in the United States. Of these, 13 were Presbyterian, 6 were Episcopalian, 4 were Congregational, 3 were Baptist, 1 was Catholic, 1 was German Reformed, 1 was a joint effort by the Congregationalists and Presbyterians, and 11 were public (W. W. Sweet, 1964b). None was Methodist.[9] Indeed, just prior to the founding of Indiana Asbury University in 1837, a committee of the Indiana Conference gave reassurance that it would never be a "manufactory in which preachers are to be made." Thus the founders kept faith with the bishop's memory as well as with the spirit of American Methodism as expressed in the *Discipline* of 1784, which advised preachers never to let study interfere with soul-saving: "If you can do but one, let your studies alone. We would throw by all the libraries in the world rather than be guilty of the loss of one soul."

As noted in Chapter 2, Weis (1936), in his invaluable work on the colonial clergy, tabulated data on the educations of all men who held a pulpit in New England from the first settlement through 1776. Of the 1,586 who had ever been pastor of a Congregational church, 1,507, or 95 percent, were college graduates. Of the 127 Anglicans and 51 Presbyterians, all were college graduates. But of the 217 Baptists, only 25 (or 11.5 percent) had a college degree. Weis listed no Methodists. Our data locate only two Methodist congregations in New England as of 1776, and these had probably just appeared.

Somewhat later statistics on seminary enrollments also display the vast educational differences among Protestant clergy. In 1831, according to the *American Almanac* (1833), Congregational seminaries enrolled 234 students, the Presbyterian seminaries 257, Episcopalian 47 (they still drew on men educated in England), and the Baptists 107. The Methodists had none; they were not to found their first seminary until 1847. By 1859, according to the *American Almanac* (1861), the Congregationalists had 275 seminarians, the Presbyterians had 632, the Episcopalians had 130, the Baptists had 210, and the Methodists had 51. The Congregational, Episcopalian, and Presbyterian seminaries had educated over 6,000 ministers before a single student graduated from a Methodist seminary. Even when the first Methodist seminary was established, it has been estimated that "at least two thirds of the ministers were in opposition" to seminary education for ministers (Clark, 1952, p. 296). Moreover, in founding a Methodist seminary, the stated intent was "not to call young men to the ministry, but to prepare . . . young men who have previously been called by God and his church" (in Clark, 1952, p. 344). A student was not allowed admission to the seminary unless he could provide a certificate demonstrating that he was a licentiate, a church member who had been granted the right (licensed) to preach, but who was not ordained.

Although the Baptists opened theological schools long before the Methodists, seminary-trained Baptist ministers were always a small minority and largely confined to the northern states—even though the South was the Baptist stronghold. The position of the Baptists was that

"God never called an unprepared man to preach."[10] Thus even by the middle of the nineteenth century, the Baptists and the Methodists still relied on an uneducated clergy.

But if the Baptist and Methodist ministers lacked education in comparison with the other leading Protestant bodies, they were not less educated than the people they served. In 1870, for example, only 2 percent of seventeen-year-olds graduated from high school (Bureau of the Census, 1975). The Methodist bishop Francis Asbury argued, "a simple man can speak and write for simple, plain people, upon simple truths" (in Miyakawa, 1964, pp. 90–91). On the frontier or even in New England, the Baptist and Methodist clergy held the same level of education as the population in general. Although their lack of education is often viewed with scorn (Sweet was clearly eager to show how his Methodist forebears had made up for this later in the nineteenth century by founding many colleges), it was, in fact, the education of the clergy of the colonial mainline denominations that was truly unusual. These men were recruited from and moved most comfortably within "society"—the social and financial elite. Robert Baird noted in 1844 that many ministers of these denominations "belong to families of the first rank in the country; and as they can at least give their families a good education, with the advantages of such an education, as well as a good character, and the good name of their fathers, their children are almost invariably prosperous and often form alliances with the wealthiest and most distinguished families in the country" (p. 306).

Genteel social origins, combined with advanced levels of education, often increased the social distance between the minister and many of his congregants, to say nothing of the barriers raised between clergy and the vast unchurched population. As democratic convictions grew, many Americans began to detect objectionable attitudes among the highly educated, often regarding them as snobs who thought they were better than ordinary folks. This was particularly true in the growing frontier areas and in the South, where many people retained bitter memories of having been looked down upon by the educated and salaried clergy of the established churches of the past. And in New England, where battles were being waged over religious taxes and disestablishment, the privileges of the highly educated and well-paid clergy were widely questioned. One Connecticut dissenter provided this succinct critique: "Preachers that will not preach without a salary found for them by law are hirelings who seek the fleece and not the flock" (in McLoughlin, 1971, p. 927). The highly educated minister might have enhanced the "respectability" of religion, but he did little to gather the flock.

In addition to influencing patterns of interaction between minister and flock, an educated clergyman had expanded career opportunities. For many, teaching at a seminary or college, rather than being a famous preacher or serving as a leader in the local association or conference, represented the pinnacle of success. Once again, Cartwright provided a pithy summary: "Multiply colleges, universities, seminaries and academies; multiply our agencies, and editorships, and fill them all with our best and most efficient preachers and you localize the ministry and secularize them, too; then farewell to itinerancy" (1856, p. 81). In short, well-educated clergy entered a prestigious full-time profession with a variety of career opportunities, whereas the uneducated clergy answered a call from God and the people to serve the local church in saving souls.

Reliance on well-educated clergy also created a serious practical problem for the colonial mainline: a constant shortage of clergy. This shortage in turn allowed clergy to be very selective in their placement, and nearly all chose to serve a well-established congregation rather than to pioneer a new one. In contrast, the Baptists and the Methodists had a surplus of available clergy and thus could find plenty of pastors to move west with the people. As a result, the Baptists and the Methodists were usually the only churches operating in the newer market areas. In contrast, the constant shortage of educated clergy for the Congregational, Episcopalian, and Presbyterian churches limited their range to established markets.

But why did the Baptists and the Methodists have an abundance of clergy? Both denominations developed systems that made it easy for gifted laymen to enter the ministry. Among the Baptists the local preacher, or farmer-preacher, was often a man of local origins whose call was ratified by his fellow congregants. It was not uncommon for more than one member of a congregation to receive "God's call." Those not selected to fill the local pulpit had to seek one elsewhere, typically by starting a new congregation. The result was free market competition among Baptist preachers and a generous supply of clergy to fill any available slot. The Baptist farmer-preachers came with the people because they *were* the people.

Although the Methodist literature is filled with concerns over a shortage of itinerant clergy, the circuit rider was only the most visible and

# What? Have You Found Me Already?

*In a feature article on the "Circuit Preacher" in the October 12, 1867, edition of* Harper's Weekly, *the following story was offered to illustrate the persistence and determination of circuit riders in the early nineteenth century.*

Richard Nolley was one of the most famous circuit heroes of the South, and is now venerated as a martyr. He labored sturdily against fierce persecution. Fire-crackers were often thrown upon him in the pulpit, and while he was upon his knees praying;.... His voice was a trumpet, and no man of the Southwest proclaimed the Gospel with greater energy. He penetrated to the newest settlements on the Tombigbee, Alabama, where he was beset with Indian perils.... It was in this wild region that happened the fact often cited as an illustration of the energy of the primitive circuit preacher. Nolley came to a fresh wagon track in the woods and soon found an emigrant family, which had just pitched on the ground of its new home. The man was unlimbering his team and the wife was busy about the fire. "What," exclaimed the settler, on hearing the salutation of the preacher and glancing at his unmistakable appearance, "have you found me already? Another Methodist preacher. I left Virginia to get out of their reach; I went to Georgia and thought to have got a long whet, but they got my wife and daughter into the church; then in this purchase (Choctaw Corner) I found a piece of land and was sure I should have some peace of the preachers, and here is one before my wagon is unloaded!" Nolley gave him small comfort. "My friend," he said, "if you go to heaven you will find Methodist preachers there; if you go to hell you will find some there, I fear; and you see how it is in this world, so you had better make terms with us and be at peace."

romantic element of the Methodist system for serving sparsely settled areas. The itinerants would organize and coordinate the activities of the local churches, and their visits provided variety, excitement, and supervision. But much of the responsibility was delegated to the locals. Class-leaders, for example, were charged with the "duty" of inquiring into the "spiritual state of each member . . . to reprove, comfort, or exhort them as occasion may require" (in Gorrie, 1852, p. 206). And it was the ex-horters, stewards, and local preachers who carried on the day-to-day functions of the local church.

Not only could the Baptists and the Methodists generate surplus clergy, both denominations operated with incredibly low overhead. The Baptists typically paid their preachers nothing at all; most earned their living with a plow just like other members of the congregation. Local Methodist church leaders also received little, if any, pay. Even the circuit riders, who faced constant danger from the elements and spent most of their days in the saddle, received only the most meager wages. Their official salary was $100 per year in 1834, but the western circuit riders were often granted only a small percentage of this sum (Miyakawa, 1964). If itinerant ministers were married, which was strongly discouraged,[11] the official policy was to grant an additional $100 for the wife, $16 for each child under seven, and $24 for each child from seven to fourteen years of age. These additional stipends, however, were almost never granted to the western circuit riders. The report of the *Methodist Western Conference Committee of Claims* for 1803, considering the circuit rider Jesse Walker's claim for back pay, noted: "It appears to us that $76 are for children. It is our judgment that the demand for children be deducted, and then he is deficient [owed] $89.37." In similar fashion the board noted that of Benjamin Young's claim of $28.95, "$4.75 is for Doctor's bills, which we judge an improper charge and therefore allow him but $24.14" (in W. W. Sweet, 1920, p. 87).

Even after applying such rules of frugality, the committee could only make partial payments. In the end Walker got $61.56 and Young received $10.14. And Francis Asbury, the famous Methodist bishop in America, was owed $20.36 and was actually paid $10.00. The 1808 report shows that Peter Cartwright received $65 from the committee, of which he donated $25 back to the church. That same year Asbury was paid $25 and donated $5 of it to the church. Little wonder that Asbury, despite his power and fame,[12] hardly ever had more than a dollar and was utterly dependent upon small donations from those he encountered along the road to sustain him. When a friend once asked to borrow $50, Asbury reflected, "He might as well have asked me for Peru" (in Marty, 1984, p. 172).

Like the Methodists, Baptist clergy received little, if any, pay outside the settled areas of the East. The Long Run Association *Circular Letter* of 1838 reported that only 6 of nearly 600 Baptist churches in Kentucky attempted "to support their ministry; and of those, only two could be

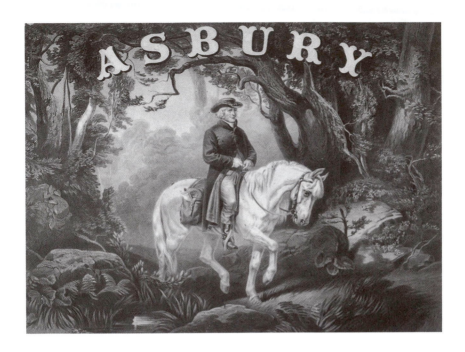

Francis Asbury (1745–1816). (Courtesy of the Billy Graham Center Museum, Wheaton, Ill.)

said to do it" (in Shurden, 1980, p. 53). And even in the settled areas, salaries of only $60 to $100 a year are frequently reported in biographical accounts (W. W. Sweet, 1964a).

In comparison, the average yearly income for Presbyterian and Congregational ministers at this time was estimated at between $1,000 and $3,000 in large towns and between $400 and $1,000 in small country towns (Hayward, 1836, p. 155). Indeed, in his *Autobiography* (1910), Barton W. Stone, the young organizer of the Cane Ridge camp meeting, reported that when he gave up his Presbyterian congregation in rural Kentucky "I sacrificed . . . an abundant salary for the support of myself and family" (1910, p. 171).

Vivid proof of the economic chasm separating the upstarts from the old mainline is found in Table 3.2. The 1850 census noted the value of all church property, which consisted of the church building and, sometimes, a parsonage. The average value of local church property was very low for the Methodists and Baptists compared with that of the Congre-

**TABLE 3.2**
Value of Church Properties, 1850

| Denomination | Average value of local church property |
|---|---|
| Methodists | $1,174 |
| Baptists | $1,244 |
| Presbyterians | $3,135 |
| Congregationalists | $4,763 |
| Episcopalians | $7,919 |
| Unitarians | $13,449 |

SOURCE: Bureau of the Census (1854).

gationalists, Presbyterians, and Episcopalians. The figure for the Congregationalists, moreover, ought to be considered in light of the fact that many of their most affluent, urban congregations had defected to the Unitarians prior to 1850. Given the huge average value of Unitarian property, the Congregational average before these defections would have been up around that for the Episcopalians. The incapacity of the old mainline denominations to move west seems evident in the material comforts they provided for clergy who stayed put.

The uneducated and often unpaid clergy of the Baptists and Methodists made it possible for these denominations to sustain congregations anywhere a few people could gather, for it was the pursuit of souls, not material comfort, that drove their clergy forth. Indeed, it would be hard to imagine that any sum of money could have motivated Bishop Asbury to travel nearly 300,000 miles on horseback, disregarding weather and chronic ill-health, to supervise his far-flung network of itinerants and circuit riders. It was thus that the upstarts swept over the nation. Just like the Confederate general Nathan Bedford Forrest, they always got there "fustest with the mostest." Moreover, they knew what to do when they got there: preach!

## The Message

The education and background of the ministers influenced the message they brought and how they delivered it. Perhaps the contrast between

How the West was won: a Methodist circuit-rider, determined to reach the next congregation in time for services, pushes on through a stormy night. (Courtesy of the Billy Graham Center Museum, Wheaton, Ill.)

faith and theology best conveys the vivid differences between "called" and educated clergy. Does the religious message address matters of faith that are directly relevant to the experience and concerns of the laity, or is it a discourse on abstruse theological matters? Put another way, is it a message of conversion or a message of erudition?

We should point out, however, that it is not education in general that leads to secularization. Clearly, religious participation did not decline as the education of the population increased. Instead, we are suggesting that the message becomes more worldly, and is held with less certainty, as religion becomes the focus of scholarly critique and attention.

Neither the Baptists nor the Methodists set forth their confessions in complex theological writing that required extensive instruction or teaching. The Baptists had traditional ties with Calvinism, whereas the Methodists emphasized Arminian views, but both denominations stressed spiritual conversion and a strong individual responsibility to God. For both denominations the power of God was experienced as well as taught, and their message seldom excluded the topics of sin and salvation, or hellfire and redemption. Their emotion-packed messages centered on experience with the sacred and warned of the evils of the secular. Writing in 1792, Jedidiah Morse, the "father of American Geography," described Methodist preachers thus: "Their mode of preaching is entirely extemporaneous, very loud and animated. . . . They appear studiously to avoid connection in their discourses, and are fond of introducing pathetic stories, which are calculated to affect the tender passions. Their manner is very solemn, and their preaching is frequently attended with surprising effect upon their audiences" (in Gaustad, 1982, p. 308).

In contrast, the denominations of the colonial mainline offered a message that was literate and intellectual, but one that increasingly said less about salvation, hellfire, or the other principal themes of the Baptist and Methodist sermons.

The Presbyterians of Kentucky, Tennessee, and other frontier areas, where they placed more emphasis on religious experience, are somewhat of an exception; but even there an introduction to Presbyterianism often required an instructional approach that was attractive to the well-educated but was often viewed as overly formal by the average farmer.

It is not only content that is involved here, but the style of delivery—Marshall McLuhan might have suggested that in some ways the minister was the message. The Baptist and Methodist preachers looked like ordinary men, because they were, and their sermons could convert and convince ordinary people because the message was direct and clear and the words were not read from notes, but seemed (to both speakers and hearers) to issue directly from divine inspiration. No wonder that Baptist and Methodist services could so often become outbursts of emotional participation. Peter Cartwright recalled, "while I was preaching, the power of God fell on the assembly, and there was an awful shaking among the dry bones. Several fell on the floor and cried for mercy" (1856, p. 65). We must never underestimate the impact of humble and ardent preachers on the spread of faith.

Charles Grandison Finney, one of the greatest preachers of the era (despite being a highly educated man and a Congregationalist), put the matter clearly in his *Lectures on Revivals of Religion*, published in 1835 (1960): "Many ministers are finding it out already, that a Methodist preacher, without the advantages of a liberal education, will draw a congregation around him which a Presbyterian minister, with perhaps ten times as much learning, cannot equal, because he has not the earnest manner of the other, and does not pour out fire upon his hearers when he preaches" (pp. 273–274).

If the goal was to arouse faith, the carefully drafted, scholarly, and often dry sermons of the learned clergy were no match for the impromptu emotional pleas of the uneducated preacher. Theology has its place, but it does not save souls in the way that the Methodists and Baptists understood the task at the turn of the nineteenth century. What saved souls, they had discovered, was a heartfelt message of conversion.

The Harvard and Yale divinity schools did not train their students to earn their own livings behind a horse and plow or prepare them to spend half their days in the saddle going from one rural hamlet to another. As George Whitefield charged, the primary impact of these schools on many of their students, then as now, may have been to replace faith with theology and belief with unbelief. Indeed, it was in the religion departments and divinity schools, not in the science departments, that unbelief was formulated and promulgated in American intellectual life. As James Turner (1985, p. xiii) concluded, "In trying to adapt their religious beliefs to socioeconomic change, to new moral challenges, to novel problems of knowledge, to the tightening standards of science, the defenders of God slowly strangled Him. If anyone is to be arraigned for deicide, it is . . . not the godless Robert Ingersoll but the Godly Beecher family."

As we shall see, the opposition by Lyman Beecher and other pillars of the Congregationalist establishment to their co-religionist Charles Finney's immensely successful revival campaigns along the frontier displayed their strong preferences for intellectualized and "reasonable" religion, whatever the cost in terms of the failure to convert or mobilize support. Had they been able to embrace Finney and use his methods, it might have been the Congregationalists who towered over the nation in 1850. But as described in Chapter 2, they were already too far down the path of secularization—the faith of the Puritans had been so accommodated that it no longer could inspire or sanctify.

## Awakenings and Routine Revivalism

"Great Awakenings" are perhaps the most dominant theme in all general histories of American religion. The underlying thesis is that the nation has been subject to periodic paroxysms of public piety. There has been near unanimity across the theological spectrum that something extraordinary happened during the period approximately from 1739 through 1742 that is worthy of the name Great Awakening. From the early 1800s through the early 1830s there was apparently a second outbreak of religious excitement, especially along the western frontier, that eventually became known as the Second Great Awakening. Many distinguished historians, among them William G. McLoughlin (1978, 1983), have identified several later awakenings and argue in favor of a cyclical theory of American religious expression.

The primary grounds for dispute have, from the beginning, been about the causes of these awakenings—about why the intensity of public religious expression waxes and wanes. For many evangelical Christians, revivals are simply sent from heaven and reflect a literal outpouring of the Holy Spirit. Many social scientists have been equally certain that revivals are caused by such things as the business cycle and various social and natural disasters (McLoughlin, 1978; J. F. Wilson, 1983; Gordon-McCutchan, 1983; Barkun, 1986). Others have echoed the charges by Ezra Stiles that awakenings are interludes of widespread hysteria and attribute them to various psychic insecurities (Gordon-McCutchan, 1981).[13]

Recently, both kinds of explanations have been questioned by scholars who suggest there *never were any awakenings,* or least none that took the form of huge spontaneous outbursts. Jon Butler (1982, 1990) has noted that contemporaries did not use the words "Great Awakening" and did not lump various local outbursts of enthusiasm into a more general phenomenon. Butler shows that to link these events "distorts the extent, nature and cohesion of the revivals that did exist" (1982, p. 306). Suggestions such as these have generated the academic equivalent of shouts of "heresy." When Timothy L. Smith (1983) claimed that nothing really unusual was going on in the so-called Burned-Over District of Western New York and Ohio in the 1820s, critics rushed to "prove" that in fact hundreds of local revivals occurred at that time. Of course they did. Smith's point is not that these events didn't occur, but that they were neither spontaneous outbreaks nor unusual. Rather, they were planned well ahead and conducted according to the routine methods by which clergy of many denominations sought periodically to energize commitment within their congregations and also to draw in the unchurched.

Smith identified revivalism as a method involving "special efforts to secure conversions amidst excited group emotions," which:

> had begun to permeate American Protestant movements during the last two decades before 1825. They persisted, year in and year out, in urban even more than in rural settings, throughout the next forty years and dominated America's religious life during the last half of the nineteenth century. Unusual religious revivals received widespread public attention only when a vision of a national awakening captured the imagination of a particular city or section of the country. Thus the unusual character ascribed to events [in the Burned-Over District and elsewhere, later] represents far more a cycle of some sort in the attention of secular writers than in the extent of actual religious excitement. (1983, p. 98)

To say that Smith is correct may put us in opposition to most social scientists who address the topic, but it puts us in agreement with the people who actually produced these so-called awakenings.

Let us begin with George Whitefield. Everyone seems to agree that if there was a First Great Awakening it consisted primarily of his enormously successful revivals during 1739 and 1740 (cf. Ahlstrom, 1975). Many scholars committed to the Great Awakening thesis stress how the times were right for the man. Indeed, Stout (1986, p. 189) marveled at how the "crowds materialized out of nowhere" wherever Whitefield went. To this, Whitefield would have said "Nonsense." He knew that crowds never materialized out of nowhere, nor was he prepared to wait for a cultural crisis to make America ripe for revival. He believed that he had been charged by God to *cause* a spiritual awakening. To this end he and a group of assistants invested great effort and money to attract crowds ready to receive Whitefield's message.

In his extraordinary study based on Whitefield's records, Frank Lambert (1990, p. 813) remarked: "What was new about Whitefield was the skill as an entrepreneur, an impresario, that made him a full-fledged forerunner of evangelists like Charles Grandison Finney and Billy Graham." Lambert noted that Whitefield was a master of advance publicity who sent out a constant stream of press releases, extolling the success of his revivals elsewhere, to cities he intended to visit. These advance campaigns often began two years ahead of time. In addition, Whitefield had thousands of copies of his sermons printed and distributed to stir up interest. He even ran newspaper advertisements announcing his impending arrival. When Benjamin Franklin became Whitefield's publisher, sales of the Great Itinerant's journals and sermons soon amounted to a very large proportion of Franklin's gross receipts. In some cities, according to Lambert, Franklin sold more copies of Whitefield's works than he did of his own popular *Poor Richard's Almanac*. It was from these efforts that the crowds "materialized." When Whitefield returned to Georgia, the so-called Great Awakening ended (although sustained for a few months by various imitators).

As for the Second Great Awakening, it was no more (or less) than a series of local revival meetings, organized and led by professional evangelists. It is true that these revival meetings were frequent and that church membership was rising. But the revivals were not spontaneous. Nor did their frequency fluctuate in response to "crises" such as financial panics: as far as we can tell, the rate of revivals held steady throughout the period.

It is perhaps even more telling that Charles Finney, who was the moving force behind much of the revival activity that caused outsiders to perceive western New York as the Burned-Over District, stressed that revivals did not simply happen, but had to be carefully staged. Although Finney ([1835] 1960, p. 13) often felt the Holy Spirit within him when he preached, he flatly denied there was anything miraculous about revivals: "[A revival of religion] is not a miracle. . . . It is a purely philosophical result of the right use of the constituted means." As for the "constituted means," Finney published lengthy instructions explaining just what to do and how to do it, if one wanted to hold a successful revival meeting. A key passage makes the point:

> Ministers ought to know *what measures* are best calculated to aid in accomplishing . . . the salvation of souls. Some measures are plainly necessary. By measures I mean what things ought to be done to get the attention of the people, and bring them to listen to the truth. Building houses for worship, and visiting from house to house, are all "measures," the object of which is to get the attention of the people to the gospel. . . .
>
> What do the politicians do? They get up meetings, circulate handbills and pamphlets, blaze away in the newspapers, send their ships about the streets on wheels with flags and sailors, send coaches all over town, with handbills, to bring people up to the polls, all to gain attention to their cause and elect their candidate. All these are their "measures," and for their end they are wisely calculated. The object is to get up an excitement,

and bring the people out. They know that unless there can be an excitement it is in vain to push their end. I do not mean to say that their measures are pious, or right, but only that they are wise, in the sense that they are the appropriate application of means to the end.

The object of the ministry is to get all the people to feel that the devil has no right to rule this world, but that they ought all to give themselves to God, and vote in the Lord Jesus Christ as governor of the universe. Now what shall be done? What measures shall we take? Says one, "Be sure and have nothing that is new." Strange! The object of our measures is to gain attention, and you *must have* something new. (Finney, [1835] 1960, p. 181)

Finney went on at length to advise that good ventilation was important, that too much singing could be a distraction, that prayers should be intense but short, that dogs and young children should be left at home, that ministers should not be reluctant to confront sinners and reprobates in the audience by name, and that conversions made while the convert was under the influence of liquor seldom took.

Finney's actions were as direct and rational as his advice. He mounted his revivals with careful plans and preparations. Large numbers of lay workers were recruited ahead to make preparations, and both local clergy and laity were trained to minister to sinners as they came forward: "The whole process was carefully planned and organized to reach out as widely as possible. Urban revivalism required extensive financing from well-to-do lay leaders. In later years professional urban evangelists improved on Finney's techniques, but they did not fundamentally alter his approach" (McLoughlin, 1978, p. 128).

Finney well knew that to remain healthy, all organizations, be they churches, fraternal lodges, or corporations, must have some means for periodically renewing commitment and that the key to such renewal lies in a sudden intensification of the perceived benefits of belonging. The primary benefits of religious membership come in both worldly and otherworldly forms. Hence, Christian evangelists seek to revive among their listeners gratitude for the benefits of salvation. The primary worldly benefits of religion derive from human relations, from the attention, respect, and affection members bestow on one another. And there is nothing like taking part in a revival to strengthen the flow of affect among members. Finney explained that a primary purpose of a prayer meeting is to let everyone take part in order to "diffuse union, confidence, and brotherly love through the whole."

Charles Grandison Finney (1792–1875) and his second wife, Elizabeth Atkinson, posed for this daguerreotype during an evangelistic tour of Britain in 1850. (Courtesy of the Oberlin College Library, Oberlin, Ohio.)

Application of the right methods produces a great sense of rededication and strengthened interpersonal ties among participants in revival meetings, feelings they perceive as true blessings. Usually the meetings have been scheduled for months or even years. Most people have done it before. No one was shocked when Finney ([1835] 1960, pp. 9–10) told his listeners: "Religion is the work of man. It is something for man to do. . . . [But] Men are so spiritually sluggish, there are so many things to lead their minds off from religion, and to oppose the influence of the gospel, that it is necessary to raise an excitement among them, till the tide rises so high as to sweep away the opposing obstacles."

However, although all organizations need renewals or revivals of member commitment, it also is true that these must be episodic. People can't stay excited indefinitely. Here too the itinerant revivalist offers the perfect solution. When he or she leaves, the revival is concluded, leaving local pastors to consolidate the gains made during the revival.[14]

## Camp Meetings: Revival and Recreation

Both Whitefield and Finney held their revivals in towns and cities, and revivals remain primarily an urban phenomenon. But at the turn of the nineteenth century, rural America developed an equally potent counterpart, the camp meeting.

It is uncertain just where or when camp meetings originated. One of the first camp meetings took place at the Gasper River Church in Kentucky during July 1800. There James McGready, a Presbyterian, aided by several other ministers, scheduled several days of religious services to be held outdoors and suggested that people come prepared to camp over. This "camp meeting" drew farm families from substantial distances and was a huge success. A year later, a similar meeting was held in the spring in Logan County, Kentucky. Barton W. Stone, a newly ordained Presbyterian minister from Concord, Kentucky, attended this meeting in order to see for himself how these open air revivals were conducted:

> Having heard of a remarkable religious excitement in the South of Kentucky . . . I was very anxious to be among them, and early in the spring of 1801 went there to attend a camp-meeting. There, on the edge of a prairie in Logan County, Kentucky, the multitudes came together, and continued a number of days and nights encamped on the ground, during which time worship was carried on. . . . The scene to me was new and passing strange. It baffled description. Many, very many, fell down, as men slain in battle, and continued for hours together in apparently breath-

less and motionless state—sometimes for a few moments reviving, and exhibiting symptoms of life by a deep groan, or piercing shriek, or by a prayer for mercy most fervently uttered. After lying thus for hours, they obtained deliverance. The gloomy cloud, which had covered their faces, seemed gradually and visibly to disappear, and hope in smiles brightened into joy—they would arise shouting deliverance, and then would address the surrounding multitude. (in Rogers, 1910, pp. 153–154)

Upon his return, Stone stopped at the Cane Ridge Meeting House, where he gave an enthusiastic account of the Logan County meeting: "The whole country appeared to be in motion to the place, and multitudes of all denominations attended. All seemed heartily to unite in the work and in Christian love. Party spirit, abashed, shrunk back. To give a true description of this meeting can not be done; it would border on the marvelous. It continued through five days and nights without ceasing. Many, very many, will through eternity remember it with thanksgiving and praise" (in Rogers, 1910, p. 157).

Stone immediately began to prepare for a similar meeting scheduled to begin on August 6, 1801, at Cane Ridge, in Bourbon County, Kentucky. He saw to it that the Cane Ridge meeting was "given full publicity at the first great meeting in Logan County" and also was "proclaimed from the pulpits throughout Kentucky" (Rogers, 1910, p. 55). When the day arrived a very large crowd gathered—at least 10,000 and perhaps as many as 20,000. Considering that at this time, nearby Lexington, then the state's largest city, had barely 2,000 inhabitants, this was a huge turnout. During the course of the next week an estimated 3,000 were converted. The camp meeting was marked by multitudes writhing on the ground—a form of worship then referred to as "muscular"—in response to nonstop preaching by scores of ministers. Stone (1910) describes the scene:

Four of five preachers were frequently speaking at the same time, in different parts of the encampment, without confusion. The Methodist and Baptist preachers aided in the work, and all appeared cordially united in it—of one mind and one soul, and the salvation of sinners seemed to be the great object of all. We all engaged in singing the same songs of praise—all united in prayer—all preached the same things—free salvation urged upon all by faith and repentance.

. . . Many things transpired there which were so much like miracles that, if they were not, they had the same effect as miracles on infidels and unbelievers; for many of them were convinced that Jesus was Christ, and bowed in submission to him. This meeting continued six or seven days and nights, and would have continued longer, but provisions for such a multitude failed in the neighborhood. (in Rogers, 1910, pp. 157–158)

Cane Ridge holds such a central place in histories of American religion because it, unlike previous meetings that may have been as large and that certainly produced as much emotional response, came to the attention of the eastern press. These press reports about Cane Ridge seem initially to have caused a joyful response from mainline church leaders, for the meeting was everywhere hailed as a miracle and the "greatest outpouring of the Spirit since Pentecost" (Ahlstrom, 1975, p. 525), though ultimately the methods were condemned.

Unfortunately, most of the writing about Cane Ridge fails to penetrate beneath the surface of the crowd's emotional involvement and the apparent spontaneity of the affair. But as in the case of urban awakenings, the facts support a much more reasonable interpretation of what people were really doing and why.

Like Whitefield and Finney's urban meetings, the meeting at Cane Ridge was carefully planned: "The grounds were prepared for the vast throng. For several hundred yards an oblong square with [a] temporary pulpit in the center made of split boards with [a] handrail for its protection, and rough hewn logs at regular intervals for seats. The surrounding grounds were filled with tents in regular street order. From five to seven ministers were speaking at one time. The church-building was set apart as a lodging place for the preachers. Every obstacle seems to have been surmounted, that all might be present" (Rogers, 1910, p. 56). As already noted, vigorous efforts were made to attract a crowd. Moreover, those in charge intended to stir up intense, emotional outbursts during the services. Those who came knew what to expect (many had been to camp meetings before) and if they responded with unusual enthusiasm this could be explained by their lack of regular access to worship services and by the duration of the event. Finally, if the size of the crowd that showed up amazed the eastern press, city folks failed to grasp that camp meetings provided the ideal religious and social solution to the isolated circumstances of American farmers.

Unlike European peasants who huddled together in villages from which they went out to the fields each morning, American farmers lived on their individual farmsteads. Even in the more densely settled areas, the next farm was a goodly distance away. It was hard to sustain rural churches because so few families lived within reasonable travel distance of one another. Indeed, this is one reason why the Methodist circuit

# Barton Stone Explains
# Religious Exercises

*The old colonial mainline issued many objections to the uncontrolled religious fervor of revival meetings such as Cane Ridge, especially the unexplainable "bodily agitations." In contrast, the upstart sects viewed these bodily agitations as proof of "spiritual outpouring." Barton Stone gives the following account of these "bodily agitations" known as "religious exercises" (in Rogers, 1910, pp. 159–162).*

The falling exercise was very common among all classes,.... The subject of this exercise would, generally, with a piercing scream, fall like a log on the floor, earth or mud, and appear as dead. I have seen very many pious persons fall in the same way from a sense of the danger of their unconverted children, brothers or sisters.... I have heard them agonizing ... and speaking like angels to all around.

The jerks can not be so easily described. Sometimes the subject of the jerks would be affected in some one member of the body, and sometimes in the whole system. When the head alone was affected, it would be jerked backward and forward, or from side to side,.... When the whole system was affected, I have seen the person stand in one place and jerk backward and forward in quick succession,.... I have inquired of those thus affected. They could not account for it; but some have told me that those were among the happiest seasons of their lives.

The dancing exercise. This generally began with the jerks.... The subject, after jerking awhile, began to dance, and then the jerks would cease. Such dancing was indeed heavenly to spectators;.... While thus exercised, I have heard their solemn praises and prayers ascending to God.

The barking exercise (as opposers contemptuously called it) was nothing but the jerks. A person affected with the jerks, especially in this head, would often make a grunt, or bark, if you please, from the suddenness of the jerk.

The laughing exercise ... was a loud, hearty laughter, but one *sui generis;* it excited laughter in none else. ... and his laughter excited solemnity in saints and sinners. It is truly indescribable....

I shall close this chapter with the singing exercise. ... The subject in a very happy state of mind would sing most melodiously, not from the mouth or nose, but entirely in the breast, the sounds issuing thence. ... It was most heavenly. None could ever be tired of hearing it.

riders and the Baptist farmer-preachers so dominated these areas. Similarly, many farm families suffered greatly from loneliness. Wives often went months without seeing another adult woman and their husbands seldom saw other adult men.

The camp meeting made it possible for farm families to take part in revival campaigns just like those going on in cities and towns. It offered them a legitimate reason to take a vacation, and one that involved intense socialization. Within a few years, farm families all across the nation looked forward to spending a week to ten days at a camp meeting as soon as their spring planting was complete, or later after the fall crops were in. They came seeking not only to renew their faith and ensure their salvation but also to visit with old friends and make new acquaintances, and to rest from their daily toils.

A persistent problem for camp meeting organizers was intrusive outsiders who came only for the "mammoth picnic" or social holiday, and not for religion. Cartwright's (1856) autobiography is filled with scenes of confrontations with "drunken rowdies" who sought to disturb the camp meetings. He proudly recounted the time he took whips away from some young men sitting with the ladies, and the time he knocked down drunken "Philistines" who attempted to ride through a Tennessee campground. Drunks and vendors of various vices became so common on the periphery of camp meetings that several states passed laws against the sale of liquor within a mile or two of a camp meeting (C. A. Johnson, 1955, p. 224).

A friendly critic of the camp meeting noted, "Take away the worship, and there would remain sufficient gratifications to allure most young people" (in C. Johnson, 1955, p. 208). Camp meetings not only satisfied the soul, they were fun. It was widely said along the frontier that during camp meetings as many souls were conceived as were saved.

## Choosing to Lose

It was abundantly clear to all parties that enthusiastic preaching, revival campaigns, and camp meetings were potent methods for mobilizing religious participation. Thus it was well known, even among professors at Harvard and Yale, that the Baptists had benefited greatly from Whitefield's crusade, and even the popular press recognized the rapid growth of Methodism following the Revolution. Moreover, because 94 percent of Americans lived on farms in 1800, the camp meeting was even more important for church growth than were urban revivals. None of this,

A Methodist camp meeting, where men and women in front of the covered speaker's platform gesticulate, shout, dance, and swoon in response to the preacher's exhortations, while many others look on and four more preachers await their turn. Notice the large number of women in the crowd. Notice too that everyone is dressed up. Besides their obvious religious function, camp meetings had social and recreational aspects as well. (Courtesy of the New-York Historical Society, New York City.)

however, prompted the colonial mainline denominations to adopt similar "marketing" tactics. To the contrary, their leading lights condemned all such methods while ridiculing Methodist and Baptist preachers as ignorant, and even dangerous, fools.

Indeed, when Finney began setting revival fires in western New York, as a Congregationalist minister operating under the 1801 Plan of Union, he was quickly condemned by Congregationalist and Presbyterian leaders. Asahel Nettleton thundered that Finney and his revivalists are doing the "cause of Christ great mischief" (Beecher and Nettleton, 1828, p. 11). How? First, by invading towns without invitations from local pastors. Nettleton explained: the settled pastor "has a right to pursue his own measures, within his own limits . . . no itinerant has any business to interfere" (p. 20). Second, by "the practice of females praying with males," in public assemblies—"some of my brethren have been absolutely insulted by females on this subject" (pp. 10, 15). Third, by preaching in the vernacular, using excessive informality and "passion." Nettleton cautioned against kindling "fires where there was not some spiritual watchman near, to guard and watch against wildness" (p. 16). Worst of all, Nettleton charged, Finney's revivals aroused the riffraff against their betters—referring to Finney's followers as "the *ignobile vulgus*" (p. 15).

Soon the most famous religious intellectual of the time also came down against Finney. Lyman Beecher boldly predicted that this "mode" of revivalism "threatens to become one of the greatest evils which is likely to befall the cause of Christ" and threatens the new nation by throwing it "back in civilization, science, and religion, at least a whole century" (Beecher and Nettleton, 1828, pp. 80, 99). Beecher was appalled that Finney and his followers displayed little respect for the settled and learned ministry, allowed "female prayer" in mixed assemblies, and used a "language of unbecoming familiarity with God" (p. 91). Moreover, Beecher too was greatly concerned that Finney's message would cause common people to lose proper respect for their betters. If Finney followed the belief that "all men, because sinners, are therefore to be treated alike by the ministers of the gospel, without respect to . . . station in society," the result would be "anarchy and absolute destruction" (p. 89).

Ironically, Beecher was one of the few Congregationalist leaders who recognized the competitive threat posed by the Baptists and Methodists, even in New England, and he proposed Congregationalist revivals as the best defense against them. But these revivals must not use vulgar methods, must not cause "muscular" reactions, must not infringe on local cartel arrangements, and must not give the lower classes the idea that all are equal in the eyes of God. That is, revivals were fine as long as they weren't very successful.

Finney defended himself against Beecher and Nettleton's charges, meanwhile continuing his campaigns. But the opposition made local mainline clergy less willing to be linked to his efforts. Hence it was the Baptists and Methodists who gained most from the fires that Finney set. Some years later, Finney and Beecher came to an understanding, but only after Finney had adopted a much more cautious approach to revival preaching and had ceased his campaigns in western New York. By then revival meetings were virtually monopolized by the Baptists and Methodists.

The same thing had happened to camp meetings. Originated by

Presbyterians in Kentucky, concern was soon expressed that these meetings would lead to excesses and to disregard for ministerial authority. That Methodist and Baptist preachers were usually given time in the pulpit during the many days of services also raised serious objections. According to Barton Stone (1910, pp. 166–167): "At first they were pleased to see the Methodists and Baptists so cordially uniting with us in worship, no doubt hoping that they would become Presbyterians. But as soon as they saw these sects drawing away disciples after them, they raised the tocsin of alarm—the Confession is in danger!—the church is in danger!"

Several years after the Cane Ridge meeting, the Presbyterian Synod of Lexington, Kentucky, suspended Barton Stone and four of his friends for "insubordination" because they refused to affirm their commitment to strict Calvinist doctrines. For Stone and his associates, these doctrines were at odds with the fundamental theological basis of camp meeting revivals: that all could be saved. He later complained: "Calvinism is among the heaviest clogs on Christianity . . . discouraging . . . sinners from seeking the kingdom of God" (1910, p. 153). Stone observed that the strict Calvinist doctrines (reserving salvation for the elect few) could not cause the kind of fervent faith and changed life that Methodists and Baptists sought from their hearers. Hence, Stone offered pragmatic as well as theological grounds for preaching that all could be saved, and that salvation goes to all who "believe in Jesus and come to him." As he put it:

> When we began first to preach these things, the people appeared as awakened from the sleep of ages—they seemed to see for the first time that they were responsible beings, and that a refusal to use the means appointed was a damning sin.
>
> The sticklers for orthodoxy amongst us writhed under these doctrines, but, seeing their mighty effects on the people, they winked at the supposed errors, and through fear, or other motives, they did not at first publicly oppose us. (1910, p. 166)

If the Presbyterians thought they could silence Stone and his four associates through suspension, they had misread them. Upon notification of their suspension all five young preachers "forever dissevered the ties which bound them to the mother church" (Rogers, 1910, p. 64). But they kept right on preaching and eventually joined with the Campbellites to form the Christian Church.

Thus did the old mainline cease participating in the camp meetings,

FRANK LESLIE'S
ILLUSTRATED
NEWSPAPER

No. 1,406.—Vol. LV]     NEW YORK—FOR THE WEEK ENDING SEPTEMBER 2, 1882.     [Price 10 Cents.

AN OLD-FASHIONED CAMP-MEETING—AN EXHORTER PRAYING FOR THE FAMILY OF A CONVERT.
FROM A SKETCH BY A STAFF ARTIST.—SEE PAGE 23.

One of the objections to revivals and camp meetings was that women were allowed to pray with men. These charges were often directed against the Methodists, because women took an active role in their prayer meetings and served as exhorters at camp meetings, as here. By the 1850s, however, Cartwright (1856, p. 517) reports that there were "fashionable objections to females praying in public." (Courtesy of the Billy Graham Center Museum, Wheaton, Ill.)

thereby surrendering all of the pulpit time to the Baptists and the Methodists. With Bishop Asbury leading the way, the camp meeting soon became a Methodist institution. Only several months after attending his first camp meeting in 1800, Asbury ([1852] 1958) notified his itinerants of the "pleasing, growing prospect" of this new method. By January 1801 he proudly reported: "I have received great news from Vermont, of a work of God equal to that in Cumberland. Good appearances in Massachusetts, and in the State of [New] York, in Philadelphia and Baltimore, Maryland, Delaware and some places in poor, rich, dry, barren, formal, Pennsylvania. . . . God hath given us hundreds in 1800, why not thousands in 1801, yea, why not a million if we had faith. 'Lord increase our faith' " (vol. 3, p. 196). He followed this with letters to those circuit riders who had yet to organize a camp meeting. Asbury's letter to Thornton Fleming in South Carolina in 1802 is characteristic: "I have heard of two men that preached against the work [holding camp meetings], one in particular, that was suddenly called away by death. If a man should thus sin against God by opposing his work, who shall entreat for him? . . . I wish you would also hold campmeetings; they have never been tried without success. To collect such a number of God's people together to pray and the ministers to preach, and the longer they stay, generally, the better—this is field fighting, this is fishing with a large net" (vol. 3, p. 251). Nor was Asbury's letter without success. Less than a year later, Asbury and Fleming jointly conducted a camp meeting attended by several thousand. Through the years Asbury's enthusiasm for camp meetings continued to grow. In 1807 he noted a "reputable report" of from 2,500 to 3,000 converts gained in a single, ten-day camp meeting in eastern Maryland and added "campmeetings are as common now, as quarter meetings were 20 years back, in many districts, happy hundreds have been converted; in others happy thousands! Glory! Glory! Glory!" (vol. 3, pp. 380–381).

But if the old mainline denominations would not take part in camp meetings or hold their own, they were not unaware of the immense gains that the Methodists and the Baptists were making through these means. In keeping with their monopolistic thinking, mainline clergy began to inspire local officials to define camp meetings as disturbances of the peace or as violations of other statutes. This subject seems to have been ignored by church historians, but turns up in sources such as Asbury's letters and journals. For example, Asbury wrote to Stith Mead, presiding elder of the Richmond Virginia District: "A spirit of persecution is waked up over the whole continent. All earth and hell is roused

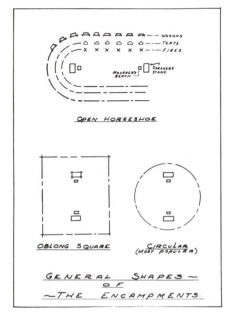
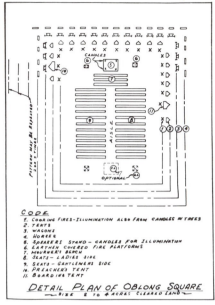

Even the shape of the camp meeting grounds was carefully planned. To the left are three of the most common encampment shapes, and to the right is a more detailed outline of the "oblong square" encampment shape. Regardless of the shape used, the "Speaker's Stand" and "Mourner's Bench" held center stage. (From C. A. Johnson, 1955, pp. 43, 47.)

against field meetings, but we will endure fines, imprisonment, and death sooner than we will give them up. We have 25.00 dollars [a fine] to pay, on the Eastern shore of Virginia, no law, or justice for Methodists" (Asbury, [1852] 1958, vol. 3, pp. 380–381).

It wasn't just enthusiasm and dedication that made the Methodists the masters of the camp meeting. Their system of circuit riders was ideal for organizing a number of neighboring communities to hold a camp meeting. When they gathered for their annual conferences, moreover, the circuit riders were able to share techniques and methods for holding successful meetings. In 1854 the Reverend B. W. Gorham distilled fifty years of Methodist experience with camp meetings into a massive *Camp Meeting Manual*, containing "practical observations and directions."

In his manual, Gorham explained how to select and prepare a site for the meeting and provided detailed plans for building the preaching

## Camp Meeting Schedule

*The Reverend B. W. Gorham's* Camp Meeting Manual *(1854, pp. 155–156) offered the following schedule as one that "worked well."*

1. Rise at five, or half-past five in the morning.
2. Family prayer and breakfast from half-past six to half-past seven.
3. General prayer meeting at the altar, led by several ministers appointed by the Presiding Elder, at half-past eight, A.M.
4. Preaching at half-past ten, followed by prayer meeting to twelve, P.M.
5. Dine at half-past twelve, P.M.
6. Preaching at two, or half-past two, P.M., followed by prayer at the altar till five.
7. Tea at six, P.M.
8. Preaching at half-past seven, followed by prayer meeting at the altar till nine or ten.
9. All strangers to leave the ground and the people to retire at ten, or immediately thereafter.

stand, the altar, and the benches. He also explained how to make and set up the tents. He advised that the meeting should last from five to eight days, stressed the importance of proper policing, and suggested a schedule that "worked well."

Finally, Gorham noted that no matter how well planned, the success of a camp meeting depended on effective preaching: "*Preaching;* not dry, dogmatic theorizing; not metaphysical hair splitting; not pulpit bombast; but plain, clear, evangelical Bible truth, uttered with faithful, solemn, earnestness, and with the Holy Ghost sent down from heaven" (1854, p. 163).

How did the upstart sects win America? Partly by default. As free market conditions increasingly prevailed in the religious economy, the old mainline denominations failed to meet the competitive challenges and eventually abandoned the marketplace to the upstarts.

Comfortable, well-paid mainline clergy rarely desired to go West and had no taste for ministering to the *ignobile vulgus.* They earned more esteem from publishing their sermons in books than from bellowing them to multitudes in open fields. In any case, clergy flirting with Unitarianism or who thought Methodists and Baptists were literally "out of their wits" would have been of little worth out where the great harvest of souls was under way, even had they been willing to venture forth. It is impossible to imagine Lyman Beecher exhorting the "muscular" sinners at Cane Ridge.

Moreover, clergy accustomed to gentlemen's agreements limiting competition and who thought good manners forbade recruiting from a colleague's flock were ill-equipped to hold their own in a free market. In contrast, when Baptists and Methodists collided in pursuit of flocks no holds were barred and no quarter was asked or given. For example, no sooner had the Methodist Peter Cartwright left a stop on his circuit after having made twenty-three converts, when nearby Baptists responded by sending three preachers to recruit them. Word was sent to Cartwright (1856, p. 66) "for fear these preachers would run my converts into the water before I could come round." Arriving in the nick of time, with his converts standing on the bank of the creek, Cartwright managed to recover them to the fold of those who believed in "infant sprinkling."

## The Design of Victory

The victory of the upstarts was a matter not only of what the mainline did wrong, but of what the Methodists and the Baptists did right. Just as revivals aren't simply spontaneous, happenstance events, but require careful planning and the application of appropriate methods, so too with church growth—the Methodist "miracle" of growth between 1776 and 1850 didn't just happen, either. The Methodists knew perfectly well what they were up to, what worked and didn't work in gaining and holding members, and why. It therefore is instructive to consult a remarkable book, published on the occasion of the "first century of American Methodism," by the Reverend C. C. Goss (1866). In it, the design for the Methodist "miracle" is presented in detail. There could be no better summary of the arguments we have developed in this chapter than these excerpts from Goss's neglected analysis.

> This poor despised people, called Methodists, celebrating their first centennial, head and shoulders above the older denominations of the country, the question naturally arises, What has conduced to such a rapid growth? . . .

## ITS MODE OF PREACHING

When compared with most of the leading denominations, the style of the Methodist preacher is peculiar, both as to matter and manner. Although it is not quite as marked as in days gone by, yet it is sufficiently discernable at the present. . . . As a rule, a Methodist addresses himself directly to the heart, while many others appeal to the intellect. . . . Methodist preachers never converted the pulpit into a professor's chair; but with earnestness have urged and beseeched men to flee the wrath to come. . . . To [the Methodist preacher] the mathematical, or dry Scotch mode of working out the problem of salvation, is too slow a process. . . .

As a general rule, a Methodist preacher comes directly from the people. His former life was spent in the workshop, or in some other way where he was called to mingle with his fellow-man. . . .

The sermons, too, of these men have been mostly extemporaneous. . . . These sermons also have been delivered in plain, simple language—the language of the people. . . . Book language has not been so much used as the common language, hence the people have known where to say Amen. . . .

## SELF-SACRIFICING SPIRIT OF ITS MINISTRY

. . . As no class is more identified with Christ in effort for the salvation of the lost than the ministry, so no class are called upon to make greater sacrifices. The Methodist ministry are perhaps sharers with Christ in this respect to a greater degree than others. It is a part of the system with which they are identified. As they have no certain dwelling-place, they are rightfully styled itinerants. . . .

## SYSTEM OF FREE CHURCHES

This system was not only necessary in the outset, in order to secure an attendance, but it was as providential as it was necessary. As Methodism was raised up to meet the spiritual wants of a large class, not blessed with an abundance of this world's goods, it was important that they not be debarred by any financial considerations. Beside there is somewhat of a connection between a "free gospel" and "free seats." . . .

The system of renting pews in the house of God, or of selling them, is very deleterious to the spread of the gospel. . . .

A subdued and orderly camp meeting, pictured on the front page of the Reverend B. W. Gorham's *Camp Meeting Manual.* Writing in 1854, when camp meetings were in decline, Gorham was trying to promote their use and to disarm critics, who charged they were a source of "wickedness" and "undue excitement." (Courtesy of the Billy Graham Center Museum, Wheaton, Ill.)

## ITS FREQUENT REVIVALS

Methodism originated with revivals; its lifepower has been drawn from them, it can only exist by their continued use. Scarcely a Methodist minister passes a winter without a revival. Camp-meetings also tend to keep the revival spirit alive during the summer. . . .

## ITS LAY EFFORTS

That every member of the Methodist Episcopal Church is a working member we do not pretend; that there are many such also in other Churches we admit; but what is asserted is, that the growth of the denomination has been in proportion to its activity, and, in a special sense, may be attributed to its efficient system of lay operations.

When a person unites with the Church he is immediately placed in one of the classes, under the care of a person of experience and discrimination. . . . The Methodist Episcopal Church is not a spiritual lounging place, in which members can simply take comfort, it is not a spiritual restaurant, where persons enter to feast upon the good things of the kingdom; but it is a spiritual workshop, where persons who enter are expected to work for Christ. It would be a fatal day for Methodism if its members ever get too proud or too indolent to work for Christ. Its activity has been its life, the law of its growth, and it can only exist and prosper by its continued operation. . . .

### ITS MISSIONARY SPIRIT

. . . Methodist preachers have always acted on the presumption that they were included in the call, to "go and preach the Gospel to every creature," hence they have gone whether invited or not; and sometimes have gone when they were invited in a very emphatic manner to leave. This missionary spirit has given to the Church the epithet, "the pioneer Church," and to its ministry, "the circuit-riders."

While the mission of some other churches may be to settle, the peculiar prerogative of the Methodist Episcopal Church is to push out into destitute regions, to break new ground, to urge upon the masses generally the saving truths of the Gospel.

### DOCTRINE OF SANCTIFICATION

In Methodism this doctrine has occupied a prominent place. . . . No matter what the terms used, whether sanctification, perfection, consecration, resignation, or any other, the meaning was "holiness of heart, without which no man shall see the Lord.". . . This is not needed simply as a doctrine believed and preached, but *inwardly experienced;* then it will be preached both in the pulpit and in the life.

. . . It is this spiritual essence that satisfied the spiritual nature, for which thousands are hungering and thirsting. And with inward spiritual power and outward aggressive effort to meet this felt want, Methodism may be the means under God, during this second century, of lifting this wicked disquieted world into a purer, serener, and diviner region. (Goss, 1866, pp. 162–186)

By the time Goss wrote these insightful lines, however, they no longer applied. Most congregations were no longer the province of local class-leaders and exhorters—the amateurs had been replaced as the circuit riders dismounted and settled into comfortable parsonages. The professional clergy now ran the Methodist Church in a fully realized episcopal fashion. Many Methodist clergy had begun to *read* their sermons, and many of the younger ministers now came to the pulpit from

Methodist seminaries. In an astonishing reversal of their original principles, some Methodist congregations had begun to rent their pews,
and the word "sanctification" was appearing far less frequently in Methodist publications. Gorham devoted the entire first half of his *Camp
Meeting Manual* to a defense of the camp meeting and to an expression
of deep regret that each year fewer Methodist camp meetings were
being held. We shall return to the Methodist story in Chapter 5.

# Chapter 4

# The Coming of the Catholics, 1850–1926

Until recently, the history of the Roman Catholic Church in the United States has been told briefly and badly by Protestants. Quite aside from the patronizing and even hostile tones they have too often employed, Protestant authors have been remarkably ignorant of elementary facts. But the most serious failure of these historians has been to regard the growth and vigor of American Catholicism as simply a matter of immigration. To hear them tell it, all the priests had to do was to stand at the gangplanks and enroll the faithful as they disembarked—a task made all the easier because these newcomers were people accustomed to "blind obedience."

In truth, most of the millions of immigrants from "Catholic" nations who flowed into the United States in the latter part of the nineteenth century were at best *potential* American Catholic parishioners. To tap this potential, the Roman Catholic Church had to counteract the vigorous efforts of Protestant sects to recruit these immigrants, and it had to inspire them to entirely new levels of commitment and participation. For the fact is that the great majority of people in "Catholic" nations are not very good Catholics, in that they seldom attend mass, rarely participate in the sacraments, and do not contribute money to the church (Martin, 1990; Stark, 1990). Ironically, it is only where the Catholic Church is in the minority and is somewhat embattled that it can generate the vigorous participation we have come to associate with American Catholicism (Stark and McCann, 1989). In the United States, the Roman

Catholic Church became an extremely effective and competitive religious firm when forced to confront a free market religious economy.

## Catholic Membership Statistics

Estimates of the Catholic population in the United States during the nineteenth century were incredibly inflated. *The American Almanac* for 1826 stated that there were 1,071,000 Roman Catholics in the nation. Hayward (1836) estimated that there were from 800,000 to 1.2 million American Catholics in 1835, and 1.2 million is the number given by Bishop John England in 1836 when asked the number of Catholic church members. These totals rose rapidly. In the 1856 revised version of his book *Religion in America,* Robert Baird set Catholic membership at 3.3 million for 1855. The report of the 1906 census of religious bodies cites A. J. Schemm as having established that there were a total of 4.5 million American Catholics in 1860.

To the extent that these numbers were based on anything but pure guesswork (and Bishop England said he was only guessing), they were the result of a great fallacy. People simply added all immigrants from all "Catholic" countries to the previous Catholic total and then factored in a high rate of natural increase. Ford claimed that Irish immigration and fertility alone should have produced 24 million Catholics by 1870, to say nothing of the millions more that should have been produced by immigrants from elsewhere. A more cautious estimate was offered by Abbé Villeneuve, who added together the Irish, German, French, Belgian, and Italian immigrants and claimed there ought to have been at least 20 million American Catholics by 1890 (Shaughnessy, 1925).

Because these overcounts were taken for fact, the results of the religious census of 1890 seemed to ratify the proposition (long advocated by both Protestants and Catholics) that, when presented with the opportunity to *choose,* millions of immigrants had deserted the faith. This census, the first to ask each congregation for its membership totals, reported only slightly more than 7 million Catholics. If millions more "Catholics" had entered the nation, where were they? Defection seemed the only possible conclusion. Bishop England estimated that more than 3 million Catholic immigrants had defected by 1836, and throughout the rest of the century the American Catholic hierarchy grew increasingly upset about the church's terrible losses. In a memorial presented to the Pope in 1910, the loss of members was estimated to be 10 million. Others placed it at 20 million. "What, then, has become of the other twenty millions?" Villeneuve asked. "They have turned Protestant or have become indifferent," he answered (in Shaughnessy, 1925, p. 233).

But it wasn't true. In 1925 Gerald Shaughnessy published a quantitative study, notable for its sophistication and careful scholarship, entitled *Has the Immigrant Kept the Faith: A Study of Immigration and Catholic Growth in the United States, 1790–1920*. What Shaughnessy demonstrated should have been obvious all along. The "missing" millions had never existed, because the millions of immigrants from "Catholic" nations weren't Catholics. Consider the Irish. Weren't nearly all Irish immigrants at least nominally Catholic? Of course not. Very substantial proportions of Irish immigrants were ardent Protestants from the North. As Andrew Greeley (1979) has shown, even today the majority of Americans of Irish descent are Protestants, and the same is true for those of French descent.

By factoring all the immigration statistics to reflect the actual Catholic composition of the nations from which immigrants came, Shaughnessy estimated the Catholic population in 1850 as 1.6 million, not 3.5 million. Even this figure is high. For one thing, Shaughnessy assumed that immigrants accurately reflected the religious composition of their homeland. But that often was not true—French immigrants, for example, seem to have been disproportionately Protestant. For another, Shaughnessy knew that there would be vigorous efforts to refute his findings and so he was always careful to select the most conservative assumptions. Nevertheless, his estimates for 1850–1880 are far closer to our estimates than they are to the figures used by earlier writers.

Many leading Protestant historians have ignored Shaughnessy's statistics. Even though he favorably cited Shaughnessy's statistics for 1880–1910, Sweet ([1930] 1950, p. 273) repeated errant estimates of 600,000 Catholics in 1830, 3.5 million in 1850, and 4.5 million in 1860. Olmstead (1961, p. 83) set the 1860 Catholic total at only 3.1 million, but still claimed that they "constituted the largest single denomination in the United States." Ahlstrom (1975, vol. 1, p. 633) wrote: "So incredibly large was the flow of immigrants that by 1850 Roman Catholics, once a tiny and ignored minority, had become the country's largest religious communion." He placed Catholic membership at 3.5 million in 1860, a million fewer than Sweet had claimed, but still far too high. Neither

Hudson (1981) nor Marty (1984) offers sources for his statistics, but each accepts Ahlstrom's conclusion. Hudson wrote that "by 1852 . . . the Roman Catholic Church had become the largest ecclesiastical body in the nation" (p. 128), and Marty offered Catholic membership figures for 1800 to highlight the growth by 1850: "In 1800 only 50,000 Catholics lived in the United States; by 1850 theirs was the largest church in America" (p. 272).

Even those few historians who accepted Shaughnessy's greatly reduced statistics mistakenly concluded that by 1850 the Catholics had surpassed all other Christian denominations (Dolan, 1978). The error lay in failing either to deflate the Catholic totals for members under age thirteen (Catholics count all baptized persons as members) or to inflate the figures for groups, such as the Methodists and the Baptists, who do not count children. Given that 39 percent of the nation's population in 1850 was age thirteen or under, failure to standardize produces very distorted comparisons—which is why we rely here on adherence rates that standardize definitions of membership.

When we use estimates based on census data (Finke and Stark, 1986) and standardize for denominations not counting children, the statistics reveal a very different profile (see Figure 4.1). In 1850, the year by which religious historians say Roman Catholicism had become the largest denomination in the country, Catholic totals are only slightly higher than those of the Presbyterians and fall far below those of the Baptists and the Methodists. It was another generation before Roman Catholics became the largest denomination in America.

But can it really matter that much just when the Catholics became number one? We think it does. As already noted, exaggerations of Catholic membership led to subsequent misapprehensions about huge rates of Catholic defection. In addition, as we see in Chapter 5, Catholic membership gains were incorrectly used to excuse the relative decline in many major Protestant bodies in the latter part of the nineteenth century.

In any event, Table 4.1 allows us to examine Catholic growth from 1850 through 1926. According to our calculations, in 1850 there were only slightly more than a million American Catholics, or 5 percent of the total population (14 percent of all church adherents). The massive waves of immigration during the 1850s more than doubled the Catholic total by 1860, to nearly 2.5 million adherents. But the substantial non-Catholic component of immigration in this decade limited the increase in the proportion of Americans who were Catholic to only 8 percent.

## FIGURE 4.1  Total Adherents by Denomination, 1850–1890

(in thousands; adherents include children and adults)

Year

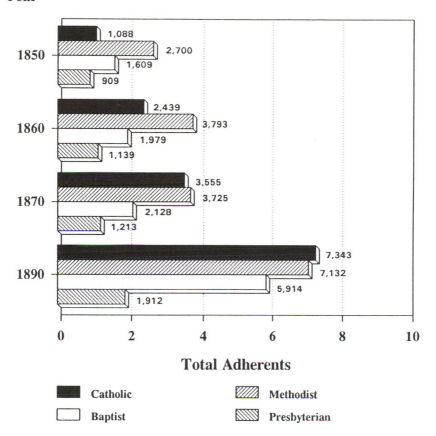

Total Adherents

■ Catholic          ▨ Methodist
□ Baptist           ▧ Presbyterian

Indeed, the largest increase in the proportion who were Catholic occurred between 1890, when the census recorded more than 7 million Catholics (making up 12 percent of the population), and 1906, when the census found more than 14 million Catholics (making up 17 percent of the population). From 1906 through 1926 the Catholic "market share" remained constant at 16 percent of the population.

If we examine the regional and ethnic dispersion of American Catholics in 1860, we find that Rhode Island was the most Catholic state. The Irish and the Italians were no doubt a major component of the 21.4 percent of Rhode Islanders who were Catholic. But Hispanics put California

TABLE 4.1

Catholics as Percentage of Total Population and
Church Adherents, 1850–1926

|  | 1850 | 1860 | 1870 | 1890 | 1906 | 1916 | 1926 |
|---|---|---|---|---|---|---|---|
| Catholic adherents | 1,088 | 2,439 | 3,555 | 7,343 | 14,211 | 15,722 | 18,605 |
| % of total population | 5 | 8 | 9 | 12 | 17 | 16 | 16 |
| % of total adherents | 14 | 21 | 26 | 26 | 32 | 30 | 28 |

SOURCE: The years 1850, 1860, 1870 are based on membership estimates (Finke and Stark, 1986). Other years from Bureau of the Census.

in second place with 19 percent Catholic. French Cajuns made up the bulk of Louisiana's 16.6 percent Catholic population; Germans (many of them living in St. Paul) were a major reason Minnesota was fourth, with 14.8 percent of its population enrolled in the Catholic faith.

In 1890, the impact of Hispanics on Catholic membership showed up clearly in New Mexico, where 77 percent were Catholic, and Arizona, where 37.5 percent were Catholic. Then came Rhode Island (33 percent), Massachusetts (32.3 percent), and Minnesota (24.5).

Notable is the tiny Catholic population in the South, where few immigrants settled. Even today, Catholics make up only a tiny proportion of the populations of southern states, other than Louisiana.

These statistics make it clear that the major growth in the proportion of Catholics in the United States took place much later than previous writers have claimed and that, when they finally did arrive by the millions, the immigrants kept the faith. Shaughnessy concluded: "There is no evidence of even an appreciable or measurable loss [of immigrant Catholics]. . . . It is very probable that there has been no loss at all, beyond that defection of Catholics which ordinarily takes place" (p. 221).

Faced with a free market religious economy with a full spectrum of denominational options, "Catholics" from Germany, Italy, and Poland, like Irish Catholics before them, chose Roman Catholicism. Indeed, to a substantial degree these immigrants chose to *become* Catholics, because their prior Catholicism often had been quite nominal. How did the Catholic Church become such an effective competitor when faced with a free market?

The basis of Catholic success is remarkably similar to that of the up-start Protestants—the Baptists and the Methodists. The Catholics aggressively marketed a relatively intense, otherworldly religious faith to a growing segment of the population. Besides offering familiar liturgy, symbols, and saints, the Catholic Church also emphasized personal renewal through devotional activities and in effect produced its own brand of revivalism. In terms of clergy, too, the Catholics were more like the upstarts than like the old mainline Protestant bodies. Whether they were sent from abroad or recruited locally, the Catholic clergy were not of genteel social origin, nor did they aspire to a comfortable salary. Priests, nuns, and brothers were ready to go wherever they were sent and to do what needed to be done. Locally, the parish church provided a secure haven for ethnic subcultures in which immigrant groups could retain aspects of their native culture—especially language, food, child-rearing practices, and styles of worship—while adapting to their new nation. A major achievement of the American Catholic Church was its ability, despite its overwhelmingly Irish hierarchy, to appeal to a broad spectrum of ethnic backgrounds and to prevent ethnic differences from producing major schisms. In addition, above the parish level the church created an encapsulated social structure—a kind of parallel Catholic America—that protected Catholics from the dominant and often hostile Protestant environment.

## Making American Catholics

At the end of the nineteenth century, the German sociologist Max Weber expressed amazement at the levels of voluntary financial support that Americans freely gave their churches: "church affiliation in the U.S.A. brings with it incomparably higher financial burdens, especially for the poor, than anywhere in Germany. . . . I have personally known of many burdened cases in a congregation in a city on Lake Erie, which was almost entirely composed of German immigrant lumberjacks. Their regular contributions for religious purposes amounted to almost $80 annually, being paid out of an average annual income of about $1,000. Everyone knows that even a small fraction of this financial burden in Germany would lead to a mass exodus from the church" (1946, p. 342).[1]

This situation was precisely what confronted the American Catholic Church. How could pastors convince European immigrants, accustomed to inexpensive religion from a church supported by lands, endowments, or government subsidy, to provide funding at a level that Weber thought would empty the churches of Europe? This task would have been impossible with parishioners who displayed the relatively low levels of commitment and participation typical in Europe. Indeed, to get immigrant Catholics to give as Methodists and Baptists did, it was first necessary to get them fired up with religious conviction in the same way that the Methodists and Baptists were.

Moreover, the local Catholic parish had to gather and motivate the faithful while fending off mission efforts by Protestant sects. Some went to amazing lengths in their efforts to gain Catholic adherents. Shaughnessy (1925, p. 221) reported: "Statues, altars, candles and similar appurtenances are used by certain sects, in their 'Italian missions,' to entrap the unwary and the ignorant." Here Shaughnessy raised a very sensitive matter. Over the decades many American Catholic leaders had complained of the religious ignorance and indifference of Italian immigrants. In 1888 Archbishop Corrigan of New York wrote to Cardinal Manning: "There are 80,000 Italians in this city, of whom only two percent have been in the habit of hearing Mass" (in Ellis, 1956, p. 483). In a similar vein, Bishop Thomas A. Becker of Wilmington wrote in 1883: "It is a very delicate matter to tell the Sovereign Pontiff how utterly faithless the specimens of his country coming here really are. Ignorance of their religion and a depth of vice little known to us yet, are the prominent characteristics. The fault lies higher up than the poor people. The clergy are sadly remiss in their duty" (in Hennesey, 1981, p. 174). Apparently someone was finally willing to mention this matter to the Pope, for on December 10, 1888, Pope Leo XIII wrote a special plea to the American hierarchy on behalf of Italian immigrants (as translated in Ellis, 1956, pp. 482–485). The Pope urged American priests to guard their flocks from the "ever present excitement of the passions, and the deceits practiced by the sects that flourish widely [in the United States]." The Pope's message also mourned the "wretched lot of so many whom we perceive to be wandering like sheep without a shepherd."[2] But the Pope took no notice of any shortages or shortcomings of shepherds back in Italy. The American hierarchy, however, continued to grumble about the problem. In 1913 Archbishop James Quigley of Chicago remarked: "the Italians who come from Southern Italy and Sicily are unexcelled in their ignorance of religion" (in Hennesey, 1981, p. 174).

Similar complaints were being made about French-Canadian immigrants. The Bishop of Burlington, Vermont, complained in 1886 of their "complete ignorance of religion . . . [and that they] knew not either confession or communion and many . . . have been invalidly married before Protestant ministers" (in Hennesey, 1981, p. 175).

To survive in America the Catholic Church had to overcome ignorance and apathy. Of course, this was precisely the task that had faced the Baptists and the Methodists as they confronted an overwhelmingly unchurched population following the Revolution. Even as the first large waves of Catholic immigrants began to arrive, American Protestantism had not yet enlisted the majority of the population in a local church. Given the similarity in the situations they faced, it is not surprising that Catholics and evangelical Protestants employed similar tactics.

## Revivalism and Personal Renewal

Revivals, miraculous cures, heartfelt religious experiences, and emotional spiritual renewal are activities usually associated with various sects of evangelical Protestantism. But each of these was also an important part of parish life in the immigrant Catholic church. By the middle of the nineteenth century, evangelism had come to the fore of parish life. In Dolan's (1978, p. 186) words, "the widespread neglect of religion [to which European immigrants had been accustomed] and the competitive spirit of the American religious environment demanded something more than ritual and ceremony." Led by the religious orders, especially the Redemptorists, Paulists, Jesuits, and Passionists, Catholic revivalism and devotionalism spread to every region of the nation. The primary objective was the renewal of Catholic parishes and the mobilization of the nominally Catholic population.[3]

At the center of this new evangelical surge was the Catholic revival campaign. American Catholics didn't call these revivals, nor did they label those who led them evangelists. These events were referred to as Catholic parish missions, and their origins were traced to the Jesuits in the sixteenth century. But revival meetings is what they were, and they occurred about as frequently and regularly in Catholic parishes as in Baptist and Methodist congregations.

In his authoritative study of Catholic revivalism from 1830 to 1900, Jay Dolan (1978, p. 44) reported that "as many as thirteen [religious orders] were conducting missions at any one time"—the Redemptorist Order alone conducted 3,955 local revivals from 1860 to 1890.[4] The Jesuit revivalists Father Arnold Damen and Father John Coghlan reported that during the mission season of 1876–77 they had given communion to 116,265 church members in various parishes scattered across the nation, received 484 Protestant converts in the faith, and had conducted 1,464 first communions and 2,056 confirmations (Garraghan, 1984, pp. 95–96). Despite these Herculean efforts, the orders could not meet the demand for parish missions. Father Damen wrote: "If I could double myself and give four missions at one and the same time, I could not satisfy all the requests with which they press me to come to their assistance" (in Garraghan, 1984, p. 101). During the late 1870s Damen's mission schedule was always filled at least two years in advance.

Even in 1906, when religious orders such as the Jesuits and the Passionists were beginning to shift their attention to retreats for the laity, the Census of Religious Bodies reported: "The home missionary work of the church, . . . is less an organized work for church extension than a series of evangelistic or revival services, which are called missions" (1910, p. 606). Though the census report was unable to offer statistics on the number of revivals conducted by five of the orders active in parish missions, including three of the most active orders (the Redemptorists, the Paulists, and the Passionists), it tallied 672 missions conducted by the remaining six orders in 1906. If the five uncounted orders conducted even another 600 parish missions in 1906, there would have been one mission for every ten parishes in existence that year, and there is good reason to suppose that these five orders actually conducted far more than 600 missions. The recommended interval between parish missions was no oftener than every three years and no less often than every ten years. It seems clear that most parishes conformed to this recommendation and that missions were a common feature in the parishes of the immigrant church.

Like Protestant revivals, the Catholic parish mission was not a spontaneous outburst of renewal. Dolan (1978, p. 60) noted: "Handbooks spelled out in detail the sermons that should be preached, the ceremonies that should be conducted and the atmosphere to be created." The famous Jesuit revivalist Francis X. Weninger published three books in which he attempted to share with other priests his insights about holding effective missions, and to explain "the matter of sermons, the instructions to the various classes of exercitants, the address, the solemnities to be observed, together with the whole conduct of the mission" (in Garraghan, 1984, p. 58).

Like the revivals of Whitefield and Finney, the parish missions of the religious orders were planned far in advance and required weeks or even months of preparation. At the appointed date one or more full-time traveling evangelists from one of the religious orders would arrive to conduct a series of services based on the same emotional dynamics as those held by their Baptist and Methodist counterparts—albeit the key symbols and rhetorical devices had a distinctively Catholic flavor. Beneath the references to saints and apart from the incense and the votive candles, the evangelistic concerns were the same: to stir the spirit and save the soul. Moreover, the fundamental message was the same: that the gates of hell are gaping and eternal fires await.

A popular manual on conducting parish missions suggested that one sermon should be devoted to death and advised that a catafalque be placed at the front of the church. Following a mournful hymn, the preacher should ask the people where their souls would be if they were today lying in state ready for burial. The manual noted: "This ceremony never fails to make a very deep impression" (Wissel, 1886, p. 115).

And just as Protestant evangelists often exhorted their audiences to tears and physical reactions, so too did Catholic preachers. Father Burtsell reported in his diary that during a revival preached by the famous Joseph Wissel in New York City in 1867, "one woman began to cry aloud; twenty others joined in as a chorus; and the whole congregation showed similar symptoms when the preacher said: 'Don't cry now but cry at your confession: then bewail your sins' " (in Dolan, 1975, p. 156). In 1848, as Charles Finney was preparing to take his evangelistic campaign to England, Francis X. Weninger conducted is first parish mission not far from Finney's home. The Cincinnati *Wahrheits freund* described Weninger's success: "Not a single Catholic who attended the mission failed to go to confession. . . . [Father Weninger] all along drew tears of repentance and consolation from the eyes of his hearers. Often there was general sobbing and weeping throughout the church" (translated in Garraghan, 1984, p. 54). The results of a parish mission in New York City in 1863 were quantified in the local Catholic paper: "fifteen to thirty

Im Kreuze ist heil!

Der Ertrag zum Besten der verlassenen Heidenkinder in China & Indien.

Francis Xavier Weninger (1805–1888). "I continually am giving Missions in the woods as well as in the metropolis going to every chapel, no matter how many families there are. In the course of the year I am preaching over 1,000 times every year" (in Garraghan, 1984, p. 57). (Courtesy of the Archives of the University of Notre Dame.)

priests were occupied without interruption from morning to night in hearing confessions [and] twenty-thousand persons approached the tribunal of penance" (Garraghan, 1984, p. 92).

A typical Catholic revival lasted for eight days, but many went on for two weeks. Jesuits such as Father Weninger preferred a two-week revival, because this allowed them to devote the first week to women and the second week to men—the idea being that initially it was easier to draw women to the services. Once the proper spirit had been established among them, they would "urge their husbands, sons, or brothers to avail themselves of its graces" (Garraghan, 1984, p. 96).

Gilbert J. Garraghan (1984, p. 96) has recorded a typical daily schedule for a parish mission:

> 5 A.M. Mass and sermon
>
> 8:30 A.M. Mass and sermon
>
> 3 P.M. Way of the Cross
>
> 7:30 P.M. Rosary, sermon and Benediction of the
>          Blessed Sacrament

Despite the many daytime activities offered, the main event was the evening service. As the audience gathered, songs and prayers were used to "warm up the audience" and then the preacher held sway for about an hour (Dolan, 1975).

A leaflet distributed to members of St. Paul's Parish in New York City in 1895 illustrates the similarities between the Protestant revival and the Catholic mission.

> A mission is a time when God calls with a more earnest voice than at other times all persons, but sinners especially, to work out their salvation with fear and trembling. It is an extraordinary time to make your friendship with God. It is a time when the greatest truths of religion—heaven, hell, the evil of mortal sin, the justice of God, his tender mercy—are preached to you. It is a time when priests from early morning till night wait in the confessionals for you, to absolve you from your sins, and restore you to God's favor. . . . It is a time when you are exhorted, by the cross and blood of Christ, if indeed you have a spark of gratitude or love towards God, to turn your face to him with contrition. (in Dolan, 1978, p. 58)

But this passage also makes it clear that the parish mission was embedded in a distinctively Catholic culture. The revivalists relied on Catholic rituals and sacraments. Spiritual renewal was completed with the sacraments of confession and communion. The revivalists used these sacraments, and others such as reciting the rosary, because their aim was to renew and reactivate the faith of parish members, not to convert Protestants. Although Catholic revivalists took pride in any Protestant converts they gained, attempts to increase the number of missions to non-Catholics seldom received strong support and often faced resistance or open hostility (Jonas, 1988). This no doubt reflected concern that such efforts played into the hands of those who stirred up public fears concerning Catholic intentions.

In any event, just as the aim of Methodist evangelists was to strengthen commitment to the local congregation, the aim of the Catholic evangelist was to animate the religious life of the parish. One of our colleagues, recalling several revivals held in his suburban Boston parish during the 1950s, reported: "Those guys [the visiting evangelists] said things to us that our local pastor couldn't ever say because he was a sweet man and besides it was his job to forgive us. They told us we were all sure to go to hell unless we went to confession and told the truth for a change." Dolan (1978, p. 181) summarized the benefits to the parish: "Personal conversion was completed through the sacraments of the church; parish schisms were healed; pastors were invested with godlike authority; orthodox religious behavior, centered around a new devotional piety, was promoted; and the organization of parish confraternities took place."

Confraternities are organized lay groups within a parish that meet regularly and pursue a special program of devotions. One of the oldest is the Archconfraternity of the Holy Rosary, whose specific purpose is to foster praying of the rosary. Confraternities are the Catholic analogue of prayer groups within evangelical Protestant congregations. Just as prayer groups were used to consolidate and sustain the religious enthusiasms stirred up by revivalists, Catholic confraternities were assigned that role in Catholic parish life. Father Weninger claimed that confraternities were necessary for "the continuance of the fruit of the mission after it has closed" (in Garraghan, 1984, p. 59). Moreover, just like Protestant prayer groups, the special devotional gatherings of the confraternities were the primary setting for unusually intense religious experiences such as "communion with the saints" and the reception of gifts and favors from God. According to Taves (1986, p. 62): "miraculous cures were usually associated both with devotional acts, such as novenas, confession, communion, or prayers to Mary and the saints, and with devotional objects that were believed to have or transmit supernatural power, such as eucharistic wafers, scapulars, or relics."

Thus we can begin to grasp how American Catholicism met the challenges of an unregulated religious economy. The parish pastors did not wait for immigrants to come to mass: they went out and rounded them up, often making effective use of revivalism and emotional worship services. During a parish mission held in St. Paul's Parish in New York City in 1859, a substantial number of young men received communion for the first time, many years past the normal age—and nearly all of them were immigrants of "Catholic" backgrounds. Nor was this limited to New York City. In his insightful history of American Jesuits in middle America, Garraghan (1984, p. 97) noted "a curious feature of these early parish-missions was the large number of adults who made their first holy communion on such occasions. This delay in receiving the sacrament was due in most cases to neglect on the part of the parents." And we have ample testimony that this neglect was the common "Catholic heritage" of the vast majority of immigrants as they came down the gangplanks. Thus, entirely dependent upon voluntary contributions from members for the support of the church, and facing vigorous competition from highly skilled, itinerant Baptist and Methodist evangelists who were ready to travel the nation exhorting the faithful, the Catholic religious orders quickly responded by sending forth equally skilled evangelists to ride many of the same trails.

## American Priests

Just as Francis Asbury was willing to ride nearly 300,000 miles up and down America to build Methodism, later in the century the Jesuit revivalist Francis X. Weninger was equally willing to travel more than 200,000 miles to preach more than eight hundred Catholic parish missions.[5] In similar fashion, no sooner had the Baptists put six railroad "chapel cars" into service to missionize in the western states,[6] than the Catholics responded by commissioning three of their own (Hooker, 1931; Mondello, 1987). Let us therefore look more closely at those primarily responsible for creating a church capable of meeting all these challenges—the clergy.

After an early period of "trusteeship," during which lay members asserted control over local congregations, the Roman Catholic Church emerged in America with a fully episcopal structure in which bishops

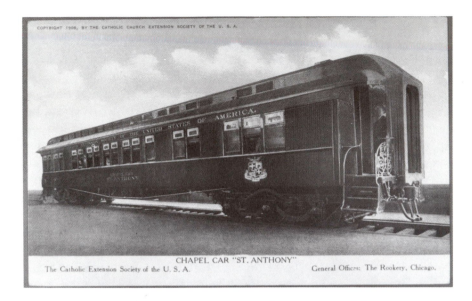

CHAPEL CAR "ST. ANTHONY"

The Catholic Extension Society of the U. S. A.   General Offices: The Rookery, Chicago.

SOLEMN HIGH MASS ON MOTOR CHAPEL "ST. PETER"
ON A RANCH NEAR BROWNSVILLE, TEXAS.

EXTERIOR VIEW OF MOTOR CHAPEL "ST. PETER" OWNED BY
THE CATHOLIC CHURCH EXTENSION SOCIETY OF THE U. S. A.
GENERAL OFFICES, McCORMICK BLDG., CHICAGO.

presided over their dioceses and pastors ruled their parishes. Moreover, the American Catholic Church was (and is) far more directly responsible to the Pope than is typical of national Catholic churches in Europe. Ironically, the reason for direct Roman control of the American church lies in the principle of the separation of church and state. The U.S. government has never negotiated any conditions for the appointment of bishops. Thus papal appointments within the American hierarchy are subject to no other authority, whereas in many parts of Europe the head of state holds veto power over such appointments.

Despite the strict authority held by a trained and professional clergy, however, American Catholicism has always been in very close touch with its laity (at least until recently). A major reason for this involves the recruitment, training, and placement of parish clergy.

There are two kinds of Catholic priests. The "religious" priests are members of religious orders, such as the Jesuits and the Paulists. "Secular" priests are those who serve the local parishes and staff the diocese. "Religious" priests typically take vows that are considerably more restrictive than those taken by secular priests—for example, secular priests do not take vows of poverty. Because the religious orders are of national and international scope, religious priests are trained in a few central seminaries and placed wherever they are needed, often far from home. Secular priests, however, are typically local Catholics, recruited from, trained by, and assigned to their home diocese. Most priests in Chicago are natives of the Chicago area. The secular priest usually works amid his relatives and life-long friends and serves a community with which he is utterly familiar and sympathetic. Although it is true that most priests do not come from lower-class backgrounds, neither do they tend to come from upper-status families. Most priests come from families typical of the parish in which they reside (Fichter, 1961). Hence, like Baptist and Methodist clergy during the nineteenth century, Catholic priests are "of the people."

As graduates of local seminaries secular priests are trained by other local secular priests, not by "learned professors," and their interpretations of Catholic doctrine will tend, therefore, to be quite orthodox and

Train and motor chapel cars, supported by the Catholic Extension Society in the early twentieth century, were used to initiate and support missions to the pastorless people of rural America. The mobile chapels would hold mass wherever Catholics could be found— or converted. (Courtesy of the Lake County, Ill., Museum, Curt Teich Postcard Archives.)

in keeping with local practices. Because all priests take vows of celibacy, moreover, the priesthood does not become a family occupation passed from father to son, as it so typically did among clergy in the old Protestant mainline denominations. Rather, priests are recruited in each generation from among young men with more intense personal religious convictions. The doctrine that a clergyman must be "called" by God has long been a central Catholic teaching.

The ordinary social origins and local training of secular priests were clearly displayed in the sermons given by nineteenth-century parish pastors. Dolan (1975) examined many surviving manuscripts of sermons given by parish priests in New York City during the nineteenth century and found them to be plain spoken and without literary pretensions. Even the sermons of Bishop John Hughes, whose preaching was widely admired, were phrased in colloquial language and aimed primarily to "attract the attention of his audience and awaken their emotions" (Dolan, 1975, pp. 147–148): "His style was simple and his argument plain, not theologically complicated . . . [his sermons] included doctrinal instruction as well as moral exhortation; one cannot escape the impression that Hughes always sought to instruct his listeners as well as move their wills."

Thus did local Catholic pastors hold their own against the powerful sermonizing of the Baptists and the Methodists. The Catholic clergy also understood that sermons were for saving souls and energizing the faithful. They exhorted sinners to confess and be saved, and they did so in the most direct and forceful language they could summon. But they did something more. Typically they preached to their immigrant parishioners in their native tongue and did so within the security of a familiar ethnic as well as religious community—a community that helped both to gain and to retain the active participation of the immigrants and their children.

## Ethnic Parishes

Because Catholic parishes are geographical units, they are often very homogeneous in terms of class or ethnicity. To the extent that a city has distinct rich and poor neighborhoods, this will be reflected in the makeup of parishes serving those neighborhoods. Similarly, cities having solidly ethnic neighborhoods will also tend to have parishes that are each dominated by one ethnic group. American Catholicism in the nine-teenth century was a mosaic of ethnic parishes. It would be hard to overstate their variety.

Consider that the 1916 census of religious bodies found that approx-imately half (49%) of all Catholics attended a parish where a language other than English was used in religious services. In those days, of course, the Mass was said in Latin in all Catholic parishes around the world. But the sermon was in the local language. In the United States the "local" language was what the people in a parish spoke. If we con-sider that the sermons in Irish-American parishes were given in English, it is even more powerful testimony to the recent immigrant status of Catholics that half of the parishes in 1916 had non-English services. In fact, 21 percent of Catholics in 1916 attended a parish where only for-eign languages were used, and the remaining 28 percent attended par-ishes where religious services were conducted in both English and a foreign language.

Foreign language services included a very broad range of languages (see Table 4.2). The five largest groups were the Germans, Italians, Poles, French (many of them Canadian immigrants), and Hispanics (in those days primarily persons of Mexican origin). The census listed twenty-four other languages being used for religious services in Catho-lic parishes. Despite the fact that the Irish dominated the ecclesiastical hierarchy of the American Catholic Church, sufficient non-Irish priests were available to staff an immense number of foreign-language par-ishes. It was not simply language, however, that told visitors that they were in an Italian or German parish. The Catholic Church may have presented itself as the guardian of the "one true and holy, Roman ap-ostolic faith," but the character of that faith differed greatly across the nations of Europe and therefore across the parishes of America. Mem-bers of a German parish might have been shocked to observe "tongue dragging" by women in Italian parishes, a feast day practice in which especially pious women dragged their tongues on the floor as they crawled or were carried down the aisle to the statue of the Madonna (Orsi, 1985). Italians, in turn, might have been puzzled as to the reli-gious significance of the huge, quasi-military pageants and processions held in German parishes to mark each of the major holy days. But a woman newly arrived from Germany commented happily, "Oh, so we find ourselves again in a new, holy Germany" (Dolan, 1975, p. 77).

For many American Catholics, preferences for versions of the faith

TABLE 4.2
Parishes Reporting Use of a Foreign Language for Services, 1916

| Language reported | Total using foreign lang. | | Use only foreign lang. | | Use English and foreign lang. | |
|---|---|---|---|---|---|---|
| | Parishes | Adher. | Parishes | Adher. | Parishes | Adher. |
| French | 699 (11.5%) | 1,026,966 (13.4%) | 200 (9.0%) | 478,255 (14.5%) | 499 (13.0%) | 548,711 (12.6%) |
| German | 1,890 (31.1%) | 1,672,690 (21.8%) | 206 (9.2%) | 191,347 (5.8%) | 1,684 (43.8%) | 1,481,343 (33.9%) |
| Italian | 476 (7.8%) | 1,515,818 (19.7%) | 149 (6.7%) | 420,511 (12.7%) | 327 (8.5%) | 1,095,307 (25.1%) |
| Polish | 735 (12.1%) | 1,425,193 (18.6%) | 466 (20.9%) | 1,165,604 (35.2%) | 269 (7.0%) | 260,129 (6.0%) |
| Spanish | 841 (13.8%) | 552,244 (7.2%) | 530 (23.8%) | 278,748 (8.4%) | 311 (8.1%) | 273,496 (6.3%) |

| | | | | | | |
|---|---|---|---|---|---|---|
| Bohemian | 178 (2.9%) | 133,911 (1.7%) | 76 (3.4%) | 67,827 (2.1%) | 102 (2.7%) | 66,084 (1.5%) |
| Indian | 100 (1.6%) | 26,402 (0.3%) | 39 (1.7%) | 5,839 (0.2%) | 61 (1.6%) | 20,563 (0.5%) |
| Lithuanian | 96 (1.6%) | 150,227 (2.0%) | 87 (3.9%) | 140,144 (4.2%) | 9 (0.2%) | 10,133 (0.2%) |
| Slavic | 113 (1.9%) | 118,264 (1.5%) | 98 (4.4%) | 106,927 (3.2%) | 15 (0.4%) | 11,337 (0.3%) |
| Slovak | 109 (1.8%) | 125,687 (1.6%) | 69 (3.1%) | 78,447 (2.4%) | 40 (1.0%) | 47,240 (1.1%) |
| Misc.* | 839 (13.8%) | 929,719 (12.1%) | 310 (13.9%) | 373,330 (11.3%) | 529 (13.8%) | 556,389 (12.7%) |
| TOTALS | 6,076 (100%) | 7,677,171 (100%) | 2,230 (100%) | 3,306,439 (100%) | 3,846 (100%) | 4,370,732 (100%) |

SOURCE: Bureau of the Census (1919, vol. 1, pp. 81–82).
*Many of the parishes included in this row reported the use of more than one foreign language for religious services. One parish reported the use of six different languages.

based on ethnicity persisted far beyond the first generation. When with the passage of time it proved impossible to continue to serve these desires through neighborhood parishes, the traditional territorial design was altered to allow the formation of "national parishes" that could be attended by members of a specific "nationality" from all across the city. These parishes, organized by nationality or language, became increasingly popular as the diversity and the number of non-English speaking immigrants increased. Joseph Casino (1987, p. 40) reported: "Whereas between 1850 and 1880 only 9% of the new parishes established in the Northeast were national parishes, between 1880 and 1930, 30% were national." He noted that in Manhattan and Philadelphia as much as 50 percent of all new parishes were national during the years 1902–1918 for Manhattan and 1897–1908 for Philadelphia. As a result of such growth, an urban neighborhood might have two Catholic parishes, one based on the neighborhood and the other on ethnicity. Typically there was very little interaction between such parishes (Gleason, 1987). In her study of five Slovak parishes in Pittsburgh, June Granatir Alexander (1987) found that in more than 90 percent of 1,316 marriages performed between 1895 and 1913, both bride and groom were from Slovakia, 65 percent from the same county in the old country and 38 percent from the same village.

The ethnic and social class homogeneity of most parishes allowed the Catholic Church to serve the specific needs of special segments of the religious market, while the diversity across the parishes allowed specialized appeals to the broad spectrum of immigrants. The national church (and numerous ethnic churches not established as national churches) gave ethnic groups local autonomy without sacrificing the unity of the larger whole. (In contrast, the Lutherans were fragmented into twenty-one different denominations in 1916—most of them created by rather modest linguistic and cultural differences.) At the very time when Protestants viewed the Catholic Church as a Roman monolith, the Irish hierarchy was painfully aware of the ethnic mosaic that lay within.

Many ethnic parishes were also partly sustained by mutual benefit

Postcards designed by Lithuanian (ca. 1919), German (ca. 1915), and Polish (ca. 1916) Catholic parishes in Chicago illustrate the importance of ethnicity. All clearly identify their nationality, but the Lithuanian and Polish parishes signify their Roman Catholic identity with only initials. (Courtesy of the Lake County, Ill., Museum, Curt Teich Postcard Archives.)

SV. JURGIO LIET. R.-K. BAŽNYČIA, MOKYKLA IR KLEBONIJA.

Rectory.

St. George's Lithuanian School.

ST. GEORGE'S LITHUANIAN R. C. CHURCH, CHICAGO, ILL.

St. Nicholas German Catholic Church,
Roseland, Chicago, Ill.

TYMCZ. KOŚCIÓŁ I SZKOŁA NAJŚ. SERCA JEZUSA W CHICAGO.

SACRED HEART OF JESUS, POLISH R. C. TEMP. CHURCH AND SCHOOL, SO. LINCOLN AND 48TH ST., CHICAGO, ILL.

societies, such as the Sons of Italy, that were brought over from the homeland. These societies provided members with insurance benefits in time of sickness or death, but they also provided the immigrant with a sense of ethnic identity. The mutual benefit society became the ethnic group's representative organization, and the immigrants turned to their society to initiate actions on behalf of their specific ethnic group. For this reason, the societies often served as the catalyst for establishing a parish and remained an active part of parish life once the parish was established (Dolan, 1984; Gleason, 1987). These societies, along with numerous publications and other organizations, helped to cement the bond between ethnicity and religion.

Up until 1880 the mutual benefit societies and the numerous devotional confraternities were the two main types of societies founded in the parish (Shaw, 1987). But Dolan (1985, p. 204) reports that after 1880 the parish "was transformed into a community institution." Suddenly there was a sharp increase in both the number of societies and in the stated purpose of the parish societies established. The societies now included social, recreational, and charitable groups as well as the long-standing devotional and mutual benefit societies. The parish was rapidly becoming the social and cultural center for the parishioners it served.

Perhaps the most visible institution in the Catholic subculture was the parish grammar school. This institution was so prized that in 1884, when approximately four out of every ten parishes had a grammar school, the Third Plenary Council of Baltimore decreed that within two years a parochial school should be erected near each church (Hennesey, 1981). As we shall see when we discuss Catholic schools more fully below, the goal of a school in every parish was never achieved. But even to have announced such an aim is indicative of the strong support of the bishops, as well as the parishes, for parochial school education. Because each school was created and sustained by the parish, Catholic education was greatly decentralized. Each school was a reflection of the parish itself (Shaw, 1987; Perko, 1988). If it was an ethnic parish, then the school could transmit the ethnic heritage as part of its curriculum—to say nothing of the informal transmission of ethnicity as part of the daily interaction of students with a common heritage.

The parish subculture as a whole passed on a culture that was different from the dominant culture. The Catholic parish could provide social, religious, and cultural supports that were simply not available from the Protestant churches. Catholicism and ethnicity were intertwined in

| | 1st Grade | 2d Grade | 3d Grade | 4th Grade | 5th Grade | 6th Grade | 7th Grade | 8th Grade |
|---|---|---|---|---|---|---|---|---|
| Catechism(Polish) | 135 | 135 | 135 | 135 | 135 | 135 | 90 | 90 |
| Bible History (Polish)....... | 90 | 90 | 90 | 90 | 90 | 90 | ... | ... |
| Church History (Polish)....... | ... | ... | ... | ... | ... | ... | 60 | 60 |
| Reading (Polish) . | 315 | 285 | 210 | 150 | 150 | 150 | 135 | 135 |
| Grammar & Composition (Polish) | ... | ... | 60 | 90 | 90 | 90 | 90 | 90 |
| History of Poland (Polish)........ | ... | 30 | 30 | 60 | 60 | 60 | ... | ... |
| Literature(Polish) | ... | ... | ... | ... | ... | ... | 90 | 90 |
| Arithmetic (Eng.) | 300 | 300 | 300 | 300 | 300 | 300 | 300 | 300 |
| Reading & Spelling (English).... | 360 | 300 | 210 | 150 | 150 | 150 | 150 | 150 |
| Grammar & Composition (Eng.).. | ... | ... | 60 | 90 | 90 | 90 | 90 | 90 |
| History of United States (Eng.) ... | ... | ... | 60 | 90 | 90 | 90 | 90 | 90 |
| Geography (Eng.) | ... | 60 | 60 | 60 | 60 | 60 | 60 | 60 |
| Penmanship. .... | 90 | 90 | 90 | 90 | 90 | 90 | 90 | 90 |
| Drawing......... | 60 | 60 | 60 | 60 | 60 | 60 | 60 | 60 |
| Vocal Music (Eng. and Polish)...... | 105 | 105 | 90 | 90 | 90 | 90 | 90 | 90 |
| Recess.......... | 150 | 150 | 150 | 150 | 150 | 150 | 150 | 150 |
| Total no. minutes per week.. | 1605 | 1605 | 1605 | 1605 | 1605 | 1605 | 1605 | 1605 |

A curriculum said to be "typical" for a Polish Catholic school in the early twentieth century. Approximately 40 percent of the first-grade curriculum was conducted in Polish. This was reduced only slightly, to 35 percent, by the eighth grade. (From J. A. Burns, [1912] 1969, p. 324.)

the local parish to provide the immigrants and their children a community unto themselves.

## Nuns

The key to the parochial school system, and, indeed, a central element in the life of the Catholic community, was the American nun.[7]

The American nun initially made the parish school possible. She was also responsible for the extensive network of Catholic hospitals, which, according to the census report, numbered 543, and for many of the 645 Catholic orphanages established by 1916 and providing a home for more than 130,000 children (Bureau of the Census, 1919). But the most frequent assignment given to American nuns was to form and maintain parish schools. Receiving salaries of less than a third of those paid to teachers in the public schools—and even substantially below the pay of Catholic brothers—nuns made is possible for even poor parishes to sustain parochial schools.

But it wasn't merely or even primarily the nuns' hard work for little pay that made them so central to Catholic life. What was most crucial was their direct role in shaping and passing on Catholic culture. "Sister said," became a key phrase in the conversation of Catholic children. The nuns were also frequently a direct link between an ethnic group and its country of origin. Each immigrant group supported religious orders of its own national background, and these orders in turn provided nuns familiar with the language, culture, and religious beliefs of the people. The more common problem was that many sisters coming over from the old country could not speak English (Dolan, 1985, p. 130). Writing in 1912, James A. Burns reported that "most new teaching orders came from abroad. . . . their first members—usually either French or German—were unable to speak English upon their arrival. . . . [when only one of eight nuns in a Cincinnati school could speak English] she went from class to class in order to help, until the teachers had acquired enough English to talk with their pupils."

Despite their lack of official authority, women religious essentially ran the local parish schools. The parish pastor was officially the principal of the parish school, but in practice he was too busy to oversee the day-to-day operations. And in any case, most pastors were fully aware that the sisters knew far more about schooling than they did. Bishops with big-city Catholic school systems to sustain expended great effort to attract communities of teaching nuns from Europe.

Fortunately, the American Catholic Church also proved very productive of nuns during the late nineteenth and early twentieth centuries, and soon nuns far outnumbered male religious. Unfortunately, no good nationwide data on nuns are available for this era. The census took pains, for example, to classify priests as religious and secular, to count churches, church members, seminaries, seminarians, schools, students, hospitals, patients, orphanages, and orphans—but not nuns. This omission probably reflected the state of Catholic statistics per se. The *Catholic Directory* lacks any data on nuns during this era, despite offering a detailed statistical portrait of most things Catholic—including the names of all Catholic players on major league baseball teams.

Catherine Ann Curry (1988) has attempted to reconstruct statistics on nuns from 1820 through 1900, assembling data from the records of the various orders (see Table 4.3). Curry warned that her national totals

TABLE 4.3

Number of Women Religious in the Immigrant Church, 1820–1900

| Year | Women religious | Priests | Women religious per priest | Women religious per 10,000 members |
|------|-----------------|---------|----------------------------|------------------------------------|
| 1820 | 270 | 150 | 1.8 | 13.8 |
| 1830 | 448 | 232 | 1.9 | 14.1 |
| 1840 | 902 | 482 | 1.9 | 13.6 |
| 1850 | 1,941 | 1,081 | 1.8 | 12.1 |
| 1860 | 5,090 | 2,235 | 2.3 | 16.4 |
| 1870 | 11,424 | 3,780 | 3.0 | 25.4 |
| 1880 | 21,835 | 6,000 | 3.6 | 34.9 |
| 1890 | 32,534 | 9,168 | 3.6 | 36.5 |
| 1900 | 49,620 | 11,987 | 4.1 | 41.2 |

SOURCE: Adapted from Curry (1988). "Women religious per 10,000 members" based on Shaughnessy's (1925) membership estimates.

must be "lower than reality," adding that she was confident that "these statistics are more accurate than anything at hand." We agreed. Even if the numbers are quite underestimated, they reveal that the rate of women religious per 10,000 Catholics hovered around 12 to 16 between 1820 and 1860 and then began a rapid climb to 41 per 10,000 by 1900. Thus women in religious orders outnumbered priests by two to one in the period 1820–1860, and by 1900 the ratio was at least four to one. This was the essential fact making Catholic education possible.

## American Catholicism as an Irish "Sect Movement"

Although the American Catholic Church was an amazing ethnic mosaic, the fundamental characteristics of American Catholicism, as it was taught, preached, and practiced, were Irish. The Irish predominated in the first great wave of Catholic immigration, had the added advantage of being English-speakers, and soon dominated the ecclesiastical hierarchy. In 1886 more than half of the American bishops were of Irish birth or descent, and by 1900 the proportion rose to two thirds (Hennesey, 1981; Dolan, 1985).

The *kind* of Catholic Church the Irish brought with them to America had much more in common with the upstart Protestant sects than it did with the Catholicism of the "Catholic" nations of Europe. This was not a low-tension Catholicism, on comfortable terms with its social environment, its bishops hobnobbing with the rich and powerful. It was a high-tension faith if only because it was the primary vehicle of political resistance by the poor Irish tenants and laborers against their English rulers and landlords. Transferred to the United States, where the Irish immediately encountered substantial prejudice and discrimination on both ethnic and religious grounds, the prickly stance toward the environment was maintained.

The Irish Catholic Church had not always been a model of zeal and commitment. Historians have paid considerable attention to the "devotional revolution" that transformed the church in Ireland beginning in 1850 (Larkin, 1972). During this era there was a very great increase in attendance at Mass, from perhaps 33 percent to more than 90 percent. The number of persons seeking ordination or enrolling in religious orders rose very rapidly—so much so that Ireland was able to export substantial numbers of priests and nuns to America until well into the twentieth century. Without these Irish "imports" it is hard to imagine how churches could have met their staffing needs. A letter penned by Father Eugene O'Connell from San Francisco in 1853 makes it clear how dependent the Catholic Church was on Irish priests to serve on the frontier. As recently as 1963, when a sample of parishes was selected from the Archdiocese of San Francisco, more than a third of the pastors had been born and ordained in Ireland.

---

# Father O'Connell's Letter Home

*Father Eugene O'Connell's letter home (in Ellis, 1956, pp. 312–314) was addressed to Father David Moriarty, president of All Hallows College of Dublin, Ireland, established in 1842. During its first sixty years All Hallows supplied the New World with 1,500 priests (Thernstrom, 1980).*

San Francisco
June 15th, 1853

My dear Father Moriarty

. . . How can I express to you my gratitude for your kind invitation to All Hallows after my wanderings in the Far West? I only await the arrival of one of the six missionaries whom Dr. Alemany [the Archbishop of San Francisco] expects from All Hallows previous to my departure. You would really pity the poor Bishop were you to see the fluctuating soldiers he has to fight his battle . . . he was obliged to make the two seminarians he has swear to remain with him. . . .

You must, I'm sure, have received letters from [the Archbishop] which shew you the urgent need he has of Irish clergymen and the provision he is making to secure a constant supply from All Hallows. . . . Since the Bishop transferred me from Santa Ynez to this city about three or four months ago, there has been a fire almost every month and the value of thousands of dollars consumed . . .

The temporal burnings of which I am speaking naturally remind me of the everlasting ones which they presage to thousands of the citizens of San Francisco, unless they stop in their career of iniquity. The rage for duelling, the passion for gambling and barefaced depravity prevail to a frightful degree. . . . Venus has numerous temples erected to herself in this city but, thank God, the Catholic church is not deserted all the while.

Without pausing to explore the causes of the Irish devotional revolution here, we may note that this revolution spread to America with successive waves of Irish immigrants (Larkin, 1972). And in combination with the immense predominance of Irish clergy, the sectlike qualities of Irish Catholicism predominated as well.

Once committed to the zealous conviction of the Irish brand of faith, the average American Catholic held as many moral reservations toward the general secular culture as did the average Baptist or Methodist. Granted, Catholics did not condemn drinking and dancing, for which they were constantly reproved by evangelical Protestants. But Catholics adhered to many moral and behavioral standards that were far stricter than those of secular society. Indeed, millions of evangelical Protestants took their cues about the moral suitability of movies from the ratings issued to guide Catholics by the National Legion of Decency. Like Baptists and Methodists, Catholics also stressed stricter sexual norms, greater modesty in dress, and were strongly opposed to "swearing" (as they defined it). Moreover, the Catholic Church required its members to make quite visible sacrifices, such as not eating meat on Friday and observing special restraints during Lent. Perhaps the most dramatic "sectarian" limits of Catholicism were its prohibitions on divorce and on contraception. These restrictions were the subject of constant comment among Protestants and stood as a very substantial barrier to intermarriage.

Within the context of American culture, the Catholic Church was thus far more sectlike than churchlike during the nineteenth and early twentieth centuries.

# A Separate Catholic America

Both authors of this book are members of a scholarly organization known today as the Association for the Sociology of Religion. Until 1970, however, this organization was known as the American Catholic Sociological Society, and because neither of us is Catholic, we would not have belonged back then.

It wasn't just Catholic sociologists who created their own separate organization. There also was an American Catholic Psychological Association, a Catholic Anthropological Conference, a Catholic Economic Association, an American Catholic Philosophical Society, and a United

States Catholic Historical Society. The Catholic Actors' Guild of America was founded in New York City in 1914 "for the spiritual and temporal welfare of persons in the theatre" (in Foy, 1965, p. 667). Catholics in most professional and semiprofessional occupations enrolled in local chapters of organizations such as the Catholic Accountants' Guild, the Catholic Lawyers' Guild, the Catholic Newsmen's Association, the Catholic Petroleum Guild, the Catholic Writers' Guild, the Catholic Broadcasters' Association, the Druggist Guild of St. James (founded to "promote high ideals among druggists; combat sale of contraceptive devices and drugs, and of indecent literature in drug stores" [in Foy, 1965, p. 622]), the Guild of Catholic Psychiatrists, and the National Federation of Catholic Physicians' Guilds.

The Catholic War Veterans duplicated the American Legion and the Veterans of Foreign War. From their founding in 1882 the Knights of Columbus provided a Catholic alternative to fraternal lodges such as the Masons, which Catholics were forbidden to join. And the Catholic Daughters of America were modeled on the Daughters of the American Revolution.

In these and countless other ways, American Catholics created a parallel society within which they were protected from Protestant insults as well as from Protestant influences. But the primary structure of a separate Catholic America was an immense system of schools and colleges.

## Catholic Schools

The 1916 Bureau of the Census report on religious bodies contained the following paragraph on Catholic education: "At the end of 1916 there were under the auspices of the Roman Catholic Church in United States 102 ecclesiastical seminaries, with 6,898 seminarians; 216 colleges for boys, with 49,813 students; 676 academies for girls, with 96,194 students; and 5,687 parochial schools, with an attendance of 1,537,644 children" (vol. 2, p. 652). These numbers represented a massive school-building effort begun by the Catholic Church in the 1840s. There was a consensus among American educators during the nineteenth century that it was a primary duty of the schools to give moral instruction. Horace Mann, the famous New York educator, wrote that public education "earnestly inculcates all Christian morals; it founds its morals on the basis of religion" (in Dolan, 1975, p. 101). Every priest in New York City agreed with him. But the trouble was, *which* Christian religion did Mann mean? The answer to that question was never really in doubt. In most places, the schools were frankly Protestant. As a result, in 1840 John Power, vicar general of the Diocese of New York, wrote in the Catholic newspaper: "How can we even think of sending our children to those schools in which every artifice is resorted to in order to reduce them from their religion?" (in Dolan, 1975, p. 103). His archbishop, John Hughes, said flatly, "the benefits of public education are not for us" (in Dolan, 1975, p. 104).

Thus American Catholics, though repeatedly denied any public funding or relief from public school taxes, set out to create a separate school system. The official aim was to provide a school in every parish, as we have seen. Many parishes found that they didn't really need to maintain a parochial school, however, because their community (or their neighborhood) was so overwhelmingly Catholic that the public school sufficed. In many small rural communities with significant Catholic populations, the school board hired nuns to staff the local public school. Eventually some states responded to this practice by passing "anti-garb" statutes, which prohibited teachers from wearing recognizable religious clothing in the classroom. Nevertheless, the Catholic school system was large. By 1916 more than a third of parishes (5,687) had schools. When the Catholic school system reached its peak in the mid-1960s, two thirds of American parishes did so.

In addition to parish schools, Catholic America created its own institutions of higher education, including such well-known institutions as Notre Dame, Fordham, Boston College, De Paul, Georgetown, Holy Cross, Loyola, Marquette, St. John's, Santa Clara, Seton Hall, and Villanova. The number of these institutions also peaked in the 1960s, at 295, and in the early 1990s there are 243 Catholic colleges and universities in the United States.

Although there is persuasive evidence that attending public rather than parochial schools has not appreciably reduced the commitment of Catholics, it is equally apparent that the Catholic educational system has provided the Catholic community with a social elite unified by "old school ties" as well as by religious affiliation (Greeley and Rossi, 1966).

# Westward with the Cross

We have seen that a major factor in the defeat of the colonial mainline denominations was their inability to move west with the nation. Educated clergy able to command well-paying pulpits were unwilling and unsuited to minister to the needs of rough-and-ready frontier communities. Because, by comparison with Protestants, Catholics today are so over-represented in the major cities of the United States, it can easily be overlooked that Catholic priests, monks, and nuns were very active along the frontiers. No one is surprised that in some counties in the Northeast, more than half of the population is enrolled in local Catholic parishes. But it is much less well known that there are many such counties scattered across the agricultural midwest.

It wasn't simply the Catholic capacity to dispatch missionaries westward that built these large Catholic settlements. Midwestern bishops, especially Bishop John Ireland of St. Paul, Minnesota, were effective in working with the railroads to attract Catholic homesteaders (J. P. Shannon, 1957). In this way very substantial Catholic settlements sprang up, not only in Bishop Ireland's Minnesota, but in Iowa, Nebraska, Kansas, and the Dakotas. "Manufactured" homes were purchased by many Catholic settlers in areas such as Greeley County, Nebraska, which, in 1980, was 67.6 percent Catholic. Such Catholic settlements would have been even more numerous had it not been for the stern opposition to western settlement by Archbishop John Hughes of New York (J. P. Shannon, 1957). His hostility underscores the importance of statistics. Misled by the false numbers we reviewed at the beginning of this chapter, Hughes mistakenly believed that millions of Catholics had already defected from the faith. Hughes could see no signs of such defections in New York and other eastern cities, and therefore he concluded that the scene of most defection was along the western frontier. It seemed to him that to encourage more Catholics to go west was simply to worsen the defection problem.

In addition to the western migration of Catholics, the Louisiana Purchase (1803), the annexation of Texas (1845), and the Treaty of Guadalupe Hidalgo (1848), which yielded California and the rest of the American Southwest, brought the nation vast areas that were overwhelmingly Catholic. Thus as the first American settlers—and the first Methodist and Baptist preachers—moved west toward the Mississippi, they encountered Catholics and their churches. Although the upstart Protestant sects did very well in these frontier areas, Catholic influence

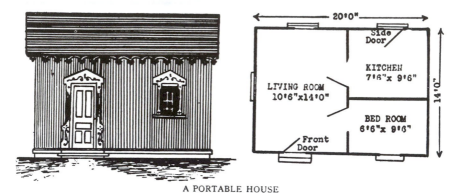

A PORTABLE HOUSE

"Admirable frame houses, 14 x 20, 'rain, wind and waterproof,' having three rooms, can be bought in the colony for about $200. These houses are made in Chicago, without nail or screw, are portable, and do not require a skilled workman to put them together, or take them apart. They do not need plastering inside, a hurricane can make no impression on them, and, if painted regularly, will last for a century."
—*Catholic Colony, Greeley County, Nebraska.*

Prefabricated housing, Catholic Colony, Greeley County, Nebraska. (From J. P. Shannon, 1957, p. 198.)

remained very strong as well. For example, Catholics were sufficiently established in Dubuque, Iowa, by 1837—long before substantial Catholic immigration had begun—that a bishop was appointed. He was Mathias Loras, originally from France, who had already served for seven years in Mobile, Alabama. Catholics still make up nearly 70 percent of the population of Dubuque in the 1990s. Similarly, Catholics further west never ceased their efforts to further church growth. Just as Bishop Francis Asbury almost lived on horseback while building Methodism westward from the Atlantic states, Bishop Juan Bautista Lamy ranged far and wide from his cathedral in Santa Fe, New Mexico, building up the church within his diocese. His territory included New Mexico, Arizona, Colorado, and southern Utah. While serving as bishop, Lamy rode as far east as Kansas City, roamed south to Mexico City, and west to Los Angeles (Horgan, 1975). He did not limit his attentions to his Hispanic flock, but sustained vigorous missionary efforts among the miners and ranchers who were drawn to the region.

On the West Coast, it was much the same. Stout missionary efforts helped the Catholic Church hold its own as the gold rush brought a horde of newcomers. Archbishop Alemany may have had to depend on priests imported from Ireland to minister to San Francisco, but he seems to have little trouble raising $100,000 to construct St. Mary's Cathedral.

Father O'Connell had to admit in his letter to All Hallows College in 1853 that on Sunday the San Francisco Catholic churches were "full to overflowing." The same is true in the 1990s; Catholics make up more than 80 percent of the church members in San Francisco, but only about a third of the population.

In the final analysis, the Catholic Church succeeded in America because it too was an upstart sect. It offered an intense faith with a vivid sense of otherworldliness—Catholic evangelists could depict the fires of hell as graphically as any Baptist or Methodist. Like the Protestant upstart sects, moreover, the Catholic Church made serious emotional, material, and social demands on its adherents—to be a Catholic was a far more serious undertaking than to be a Congregationalist or an Episcopalian. And the American Catholic Church was served by ardent clergy and nuns, recruited from the common people and prepared to make great sacrifices to serve their faith. The Catholics too could staff the frontiers and wilderness areas because they were prepared for hardship and for little or no pay.

The "sectlike" nature of the Catholic Church in nineteenth-century America is also demonstrated by the reaction of the prominent members of the old colonial mainline denominations. They were even more contemptuous of "papists" and "Romanism" than they were of Baptists, Methodists, and "muscular" religious responses. Here again the example of Lyman Beecher is instructive. On Sunday, August 10, 1834, this stalwart of the Congregationalist establishment gave three thunderous sermons in Boston during which he repeated the theme of his *Plea for the West* ([1835] 1977), a tract that warned against a plot by the Pope to seize control of the Mississippi Valley: "American travelers at Rome and Vienna, assure us, that in the upper circles the enterprise of reducing our western states to spiritual subserviency to the see of Rome is a subject of avowed expectation, and high hope, and sanguine confidence . . . the correspondence of Catholic bishops and priests in this country . . . are full of the same predictions and high hopes" (1835, p. 110). As a result of these sermons, Beecher received donations of $4,000 to help fight "popery." The next night a mob did its bit against "popery" by burning down Boston's Ursuline Convent while local fire companies refused to respond, a result that even Beecher had not desired.

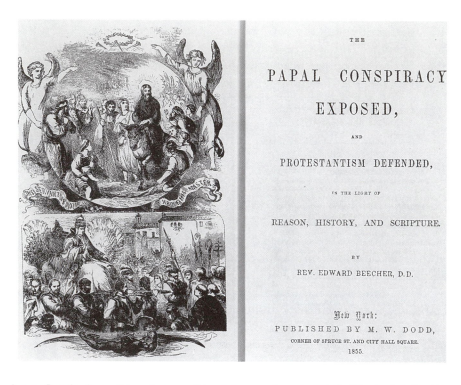

THE

# PAPAL CONSPIRACY

## EXPOSED,

AND

PROTESTANTISM DEFENDED,

IN THE LIGHT OF

REASON, HISTORY, AND SCRIPTURE.

BY

REV. EDWARD BEECHER, D.D.

New York:
PUBLISHED BY M. W. DODD,
CORNER OF SPRUCE ST. AND CITY HALL SQUARE.
1855.

Lyman Beecher's son Edward was well known as an educator and abolitionist, but like his father he warned of a "papal conspiracy." Lyman's daughter Catherine was a champion of higher education for women and his daughter Harriet was renowned for *Uncle Tom's Cabin*.

This helps us recognize a final aspect of Catholic strength and, indeed, of the strength of all sects. Sect movements can be strengthened not only by their opposition to the world but by the pressures the world imposes on them. Protestant prejudice did much to cement solidarity among American Catholics of diverse ethnic backgrounds and to spur them to high levels of commitment.

# Chapter 5

# Methodists Transformed, Baptists Triumphant

When we left them in 1850, the Methodists had just achieved a virtual miracle of growth, rising from less than 3 percent of the nation's church members in 1776 to more than 34 percent by 1850, making them far and away the largest religious body in the nation. But by 1890 they had been overtaken by the Roman Catholics.

Histories of American religion attribute this shift to the rising tide of Catholic immigrants in the latter half of the nineteenth century. But that's not the whole story. It was not simply a rising tide of Catholics that cut the Methodist market share after 1850; it was an actual decline in the relative capacity of the Methodists to attract and retain members. How can we tell? Because the Baptist market share did not decline in this era, but instead rose sharply even as the total Protestant segment of the market declined.

Consider the growth curves for Methodists and Baptists from 1776 through 1980 (see Figure 5.1). The Methodist "miracle" of 1776–1850 stands out. Holding a far smaller market share than the Baptists in 1776, the Methodists towered over them by 1850—even though the Baptists had displayed an outstanding growth rate. Notice, however, that while the Methodist market share began to decline prior to 1890 (117 to 114) and showed a sharp decline between 1890 and 1926 (114 to 101), the Baptists kept right on growing (70 to 106).[1] By 1906 the Baptists had overtaken the Methodists, and since World War II they have become much more numerous than the Methodists. If the Baptists managed to

FIGURE 5.1  Adherents per 1,000 Population for Methodist and Baptist Denominational Families, 1776–1980

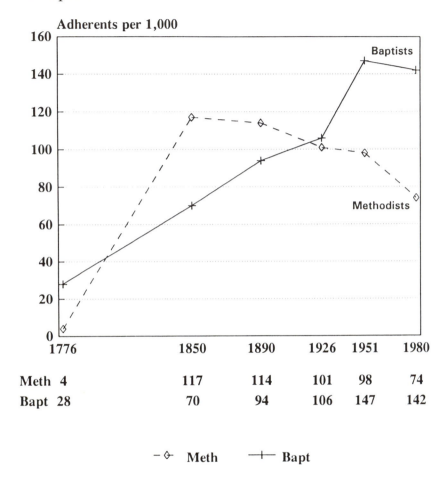

| | 1776 | 1850 | 1890 | 1926 | 1951 | 1980 |
|---|---|---|---|---|---|---|
| Meth | 4 | 117 | 114 | 101 | 98 | 74 |
| Bapt | 28 | 70 | 94 | 106 | 147 | 142 |

–◇– Meth      —+— Bapt

grow despite the waves of Catholic immigration, then Catholic growth does not account for Methodist decline.

Moreover, the Methodist decline was evident even in areas without Catholic immigration. Because the South had little immigration, and was dominated by the Methodists and Baptists in 1850, it serves as an ideal location to watch the changing fortunes of these two denominations. The pattern in the South is one of Methodist concession and Baptist growth: as the Methodists declined from 42 to 28 percent of all adherents, the Baptists grew from 30 to 43 percent (see Figure 5.2). The

FIGURE 5.2 Methodists and Baptists in the South as
Percentage of Total Adherents, 1850–1926

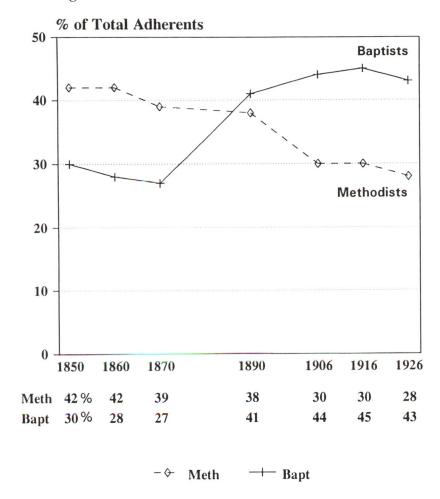

| | 1850 | 1860 | 1870 | 1890 | 1906 | 1916 | 1926 |
|---|---|---|---|---|---|---|---|
| Meth | 42% | 42 | 39 | 38 | 30 | 30 | 28 |
| Bapt | 30% | 28 | 27 | 41 | 44 | 45 | 43 |

-◇- Meth        —+— Bapt

Methodists' share of the market declined consistently from 1850 to 1906, with their sharpest decline occurring between 1890 to 1906. It is during this time period, we will argue, that the Methodists made strong efforts to abandon their sectarian origins. Methodist losses, however, were Baptist gains. Despite declines during the Civil War era, the Baptists made rapid gains from 1870 to 1890 and continued to increase their share of all southern adherents on into the twentieth century.[2]

This same pattern of Baptist growth and Methodist decline is evident if we look at specific denominations rather than denominational families. Figures 5.1 and 5.2 are based on all denominations that claim to be Baptists, on the one hand, and Methodists, on the other, in order to keep the modern data comparable with those from earlier times. It is possible, however, that the total adherence rates are made up of a welter of contradictory shifts in membership among the many bodies included in each group. In Figure 5.3, therefore, we compare only two specific groups—the largest Baptist and the largest Methodist denomination. The pattern is the same. In 1890 the Methodist Episcopal Church (including the Methodist Episcopal Church, South) had 84 members per 1,000 Americans, compared with 33 for the Southern Baptist Convention. The Methodist Episcopal Church later merged with the Methodist Protestant Church, in 1939, and the Evangelical United Brethren Church, in 1968. Yet, despite these mergers, the rate for the Methodist Episcopal Church (now the United Methodist Church) has been sliding downward while the Southern Baptists have been growing rapidly.

Thus when the time series is extended only a few years forward from 1850, we see that the Methodist "miracle" became the Methodist roller coaster. What went wrong? How could the confident, even boisterous, church of Francis Asbury and Peter Cartwright have suddenly fallen on such evil times? The same underlying processes that transformed the Puritan sect into the Congregational Church subsequently transformed the upstart Methodists into the Methodist Episcopal Church. When successful sects are transformed into churches, that is, when their tension with the surrounding culture is greatly reduced, they soon cease to grow and eventually begin to decline.

Tracing the forces that rapidly secularized Methodism in the latter half of the nineteenth century offers an opportunity to test our arguments about why the Methodists were initially so successful. That is, if we have correctly identified the sources of the Methodist "miracle," then shifts in these same factors ought to be associated with the Methodists' downward slide. If, for example, the Methodists were strengthened by relying on untrained lay preachers in the local congregations, then (other things being equal) when they changed their policies and began to rely on seminary-trained ministers, they ought to have become less successful. If we are correct about why the upstarts won, then the continued success of the Baptists ought to be associated with retaining these characteristics or finding effective substitutes.

FIGURE 5.3 Adherents per 1,000 Population for Methodist Episcopal Church and Southern Baptist Convention, 1890–1986

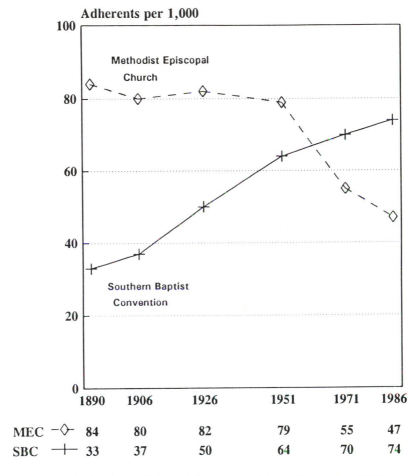

|       |     | 1890 | 1906 | 1926 | 1951 | 1971 | 1986 |
|-------|-----|------|------|------|------|------|------|
| MEC   | ◇   | 84   | 80   | 82   | 79   | 55   | 47   |
| SBC   | +   | 33   | 37   | 50   | 64   | 70   | 74   |

(The rates for the Methodist Episcopal Church are slightly inflated, after 1926, owing to mergers. The rates for 1890, 1906, and 1926 include only the Methodist Episcopal Church and the Methodist Episcopal Church, South. Later rates include the Methodist Protestant Church, added in 1939, and the Evangelical United Brethren, added in 1968.)

# From Sect to Church:
# The Methodists Transformed

In Chapter 2 we outlined the elements of sect-church theory. Successful sect movements develop strong internal pressures to lower their tension with the surrounding culture. These pressures come from having an increasingly affluent membership and from an increasingly "professionalized" clergy. Together, the privileged laity and the "well-trained" clergy begin to lift restrictions on behavior and to soften doctrines that had served to set the sect apart from its social environment—a process known as sect transformation or secularization.

## Early Signs of Methodist Secularization

In 1850 a number of Methodist ministers in the Genesee Conference, located in the Burned-Over District of western New York, began to issue complaints about the way in which the church was drifting away from its historic teachings and practices. Led by the Reverend Benjamin Titus Roberts, the dissidents were highly critical of trends in Methodist doctrines that they characterized as "liberal to the point of Unitarianism" and of a departure from "nonconformity to the world; simplicity, spirituality, and freedom in worship." They were especially critical of the introduction of "pew rentals" as abandoning the poor and of the growing centralization of "executive power and ecclesiastical machinery" and its use to oppress local congregations and clergy (Bureau of the Census, 1910, vol. 2, p. 487).

By 1857 the complaints of this outspoken minority of Genesee Conference pastors, supported by a substantial lay faction, were given widespread public expression in an article Roberts published that year in the *Northern Independent,* entitled "New School Methodism." In it he charged that Methodism had been split into "New School" and "Old School" factions, and he documented how recent changes in the church introduced by the New School Methodists departed from Wesleyan teachings and practices.

Roberts began by noting that, given the New School's abandonment of "creed," it was appropriate, though symptomatic, that its supporters had changed the name of *The Buffalo Christian Advocate* to *The Advocate*— "We commend the editor for this instance of honesty." But the majority of Robert's article is made up of quotes from articles in *The Advocate* that attacked the doctrines of the Old School as narrow, illogical, and superstitious.

> In an article on "Creeds," published in *The Advocate* of April 16th . . . a prominent New School minister lays it onto "the sects whose watchword is a creed," in a manner not unworthy of Alexander Campbell himself. He says, "No matter how holy and blameless a man's life may be, if he has the temerity to question any tenet of 'orthodoxy,' he is at once, in due ecclesiastical form, consigned to the Devil—as a heretic and infidel. Thus are the fetters of spiritual despotism thrown around human reason. . . . And so it has come to pass that in the estimation of the multitudes . . . the writings of John Wesley are held in higher veneration than the inspired words of St. John." . . .
>
> But their theory of religion is more fully set forth in the leading editorial of *The Advocate* for May 14th, under the title—"Christianity a Religion of Beneficence Rather than Devotion." . . . it was written by a leading New School member of the Genesee Conference. . . . It says, "Christianity is not, characteristically, a system of devotion. It has none of those features which must distinguish a religion grounded on the idea that to adore the Divine character is the most imperative obligation resting upon human beings. . . ."
>
> The following sneer is not unworthy of Thomas Paine himself. It falls below the dignity of Voltaire. "Christianity in nowise gives countenance to the supposition that the Great Jehovah is so affected with the infirmity of vanity, as to receive with peculiarly grateful emotions, the attentions and offerings which poor, human creatures may pay directly to Him in worship."
>
> The above may be sufficient to show what Christianity is not, in the opinion of these New School divines. Let us now see what it is. "The characteristic idea of this system is benevolence; and its practical realization is achieved in beneficence. It consecrates the principle of charity, and instructs its votaries to regard good works as the holiest sacrifice, and the most acceptable which they can bring to the Almighty. . . .
>
> "Whatever graces be necessary to constitute the inner Christian life, the chief and principal one of these is love to man." (in Norwood, 1982, pp. 375–376)

But it was not only a preference for a much more worldly theology that separated the Old and New School Methodists. Roberts was equally incensed at the affluent worldliness of the New School congregations, where even the wives and daughters of the clergy had begun to wear "gold and costly apparel," and he brought this fully into public view in his article. He noted that the New School built fancy churches and employed "organs, melodeons, violins, and professional singers, to execute difficult pieces of music for a fashionable audience." Worse yet, when they:

> desire to raise money for the benefit of the church, they have recourse to selling pews to the highest bidder; to parties of pleasure, oyster suppers, fairs, grab-bags, festivals and lotteries. . . . The New School Methodists appear to depend upon the patronage of the worldly, the favor of the proud and aspiring; and the various artifices of worldly policy.
>
> . . . unmistakable indications show that prosperity is producing upon us, as a denomination, the same intoxicating effect that it too often does upon individuals and societies. The change, by the General Conference of 1852, in the rule of Discipline, requiring that all our houses of worship should be built plain, and with free seats; and that of the last General Conference in the section respecting dress, show that there are already too many among us who would take down the barriers that have hitherto separated us from the world. The fact that the removal is gradual, so as not to excite too much attention and commotion, renders it none the less alarming. (in Norwood, 1982, p. 379)

Should the New School prevail, Roberts wrote, "it needs no prophet's vision to foresee that Methodism will become a dead and corrupting body" (p. 379). But it was already too late. The transformation of the upstart Methodist sect into the Methodist Episcopal Church was far along. Roberts was correct to see that the glory of the Methodist "miracle" was not based on appealing to the "proud and fashionable," but he was wrong to suppose that he could generate a return to higher tension Methodism.

Roberts's article provoked a vindictive reaction from the New School faction, for indeed they were in control of "executive power." Roberts was hailed before the conference, declared guilty of unchristian and immoral conduct, and sentenced to be reprimanded by the bishop. Shortly thereafter, the article was republished by a layman, which led to the formal expulsion of Roberts from the conference and from the church. The expulsion of all other clergy associated with Roberts soon followed. When a large gathering of laymen was convened to protest these expulsions, they were officially "read out" of the church on charges that by gathering they had withdrawn from the Methodist Episcopal Church. When their appeals for readmission were rejected, Roberts and his followers formed the Free Methodist Church during a convention in Pekin, New York, in 1860.

The most certain sign that a religious group has secularized to a significant degree is, of course, sect formation. And the truth is that Roberts and his Free Methodists were entirely correct that the Methodists in 1850 were no longer the church of the Wesleys or of Bishop Asbury. Leaders of the Genesee Conference did not deny that some congregations had begun to charge rent for pews, for example. Rather, they labeled Roberts unchristian for criticizing this and the many other signs of worldliness, and for publicizing the drift away from traditional standards of "simplicity and spirituality."

The departure of the Free Methodists had no statistical impact on the Methodists (nearly a half century later in 1906 they still numbered only 32,838 members), but it was a valid portent of troubles to come. As the century waned, a much larger and more influential movement emerged in response to increasing Methodist secularity. In the end, many more sects erupted and abandoned the Methodist Episcopal Church. Before we examine this development, however, it will be well to see specifically what was going on within the Methodist Church. What exactly was changing and why did it matter so much?

## The Circuit Riders Dismount and Democracy Wanes

By the middle of the nineteenth century the Methodist church was no longer staffed by local amateurs supervised by professional circuit riders—most of the circuit riders had dismounted and were now "settled" pastors. It is no surprise that clergy would prefer this arrangement. The life of a circuit rider was one of extreme hardship. Of the first 700 Methodist circuit riders, nearly half died before age thirty, 199 of them within their first five years of service (Clark, 1952).

But if dismounting was good for the clergy, it had many harmful organizational consequences. The mobility, low cost, and flexibility of the church's organization were all threatened by a stationed clergy (Nickerson, 1983). In addition, the local congregations were now under the full authority of the centralized clerical hierarchy. When the circuit rider served ten to twenty stations on his frontier circuit, and was moved from one circuit to another every year, the laity (especially the lay preachers) provided leadership and continuity for the local church. By the latter half of the nineteenth century, however, the stationing of clergy resulted in more full-time clergy and fewer lay preachers—commonly referred to as local preachers in the *Methodist Minutes*. Between

1843 and 1882 the number of full-time clergy went from approximately one third to one half of all clergy (41 percent in the South) and the number of clergy per 1,000 members increased from 3.6 to 7.0 (4.6 in the South). Not only were there more full-time clergy, but the clergy could now remain in one location for a longer period of time. The 1804 General Conference had ruled that a bishop should *not* allow full-time clergy to "remain in the same station more than two years successively," but the limit was raised to three years in 1864, to five years in 1888, and was completely removed by 1900 (Cameron, 1961). Rather than serving as a visiting "bishop" who helped to guide the local leadership, the itinerant was now the local "pastor." The esteemed itinerant, Peter Cartwright, offered this blunt evaluation in 1856: "As sure as a leaden ball tends to the earth in obedience to the laws of gravity . . . if this course is pursued a little longer, the Methodist Church will bid a long farewell to her beloved intineracy, to which we, under God, owe almost every thing that is intrinsically valuable in Methodism" (p. 82).

Recall from Chapter 3 that as long as the Methodists relied on a local amateur clergy, they enjoyed nearly as much local autonomy and democracy as did the Baptists. But with a settled clergy, the "Episcopal" structure of the Methodists became the reality—it was a church ruled by bishops who appointed and removed local pastors as they wished. What Roberts and his "reformers" were objecting to when they complained of being oppressed by "ecclesiastical machinery" was reality—a reality that got them booted out for thinking that a return to local democracy was possible and desirable.

Did it matter that the clergy gained control of the Methodist Church? We believe that a number of critical changes were the direct result of this takeover.

## Seminaries and Colleges

When Francis Asbury died in 1816 there was not a single Methodist college or seminary in America. It was not until 1847 that the Methodists opened a seminary. But then the rush for Methodist higher education was on. By 1880 there were, under official control of the Methodist Episcopal Church, 11 theological seminaries, 44 colleges and universities, and 130 women's seminaries and schools (W. W. Sweet, 1933, p. 333).

For the clergy, the educational standards were completely transformed. Not only were seminaries increasing in number and enrollment, but the educational requirements for all ministers were coming under closer scrutiny. As early as 1816, itinerants were given a recommended "course of study" by their conference, and a more experienced preacher in their local circuit would serve as a tutor; but by the mid- to late nineteenth century the apprentice program became a victim of the declining circuit system and there was increasing pressure from within the hierarchy to increase educational standards. As a result, the General Conference of 1844 authorized the development of a uniform course of study for all conferences; the local (lay) clergy were given a course of study in 1876; by the 1890s the General Conference passed legislation to ensure uniform examination procedures; and by 1900 a seminary education exempted the candidate from the course of study (Miyakawa, 1964; Rowe, 1971; Patterson, 1985). The training of clergy had gradually shifted from an informal apprenticeship program in the local circuits to a formal education at the national seminaries.

Why had this occurred? In part because of the expansion of higher education in the nation as a whole. But, in our judgment, in greater part because the larger, more affluent Methodist congregations desired educated clergy on a social par with Congregationalists, Episcopalians, and Presbyterians, and the clergy themselves desired the social status and increased pay that a well-educated clergy could obtain. As the itinerants were stationed, like the clergy of the old colonial mainline denominations, the argument soon followed that higher educational standards were needed. In 1872 Alfred Brunson (a Methodist itinerant) argued that with the "old circuit system . . . we could repeat the discourse till we had perfected it; but now [with the station system], preaching to the same congregation every time, we must have a new subject, which requires a stock of knowledge to be laid in beforehand or extraordinary genius" (in Norwood, 1982, p. 402).

Where once it had been very easy to become a local Methodist minister and they were, therefore, in abundant supply, now it became difficult to do so, and clergy soon had the advantage in bargaining for wages and locations. By 1906 Methodist salaries were above the national average, and, if they had not yet caught up with those of the old mainline, they far surpassed the Baptists' remuneration (see Table 5.1).

Perhaps an even more drastic result of clergy control and the turn toward educated ministers was the toning down of doctrine and turning away from such vigorous marketing methods as revivals and camp meetings. At the dawn of the nineteenth century, Asbury described the Methodist camp meetings as "fishing with a large net" ([1852] 1958, vol. 3, p. 250). By the end of the century they too had been transformed.

TABLE 5.1

Average Ministerial Salary, 1906

| Denomination | Aver. salary |
|---|---|
| Southern Baptist Convention and Northern Baptist Convention | $536 |
| Methodist Episcopal Church and Methodist Episcopal Church, South | $784 |
| Congregationalists | $1,042 |
| Presbyterian Church in the United States | $1,177 |
| Episcopalians | $1,242 |
| Unitarians | $1,653 |
| Roman Catholics | $703 |
| All | $663 |

SOURCE: Bureau of the Census (1910, vol. 1, pp. 94–97).

Sweet (1933, p. 333) reported, with obvious approval, that by 1880: "Many of the old camp-meeting grounds . . . were still in use, but rows of tents were rapidly giving place to streets of frame cottages, and instead of the old-time camp-meeting revival, the religious services were now interspersed with lectures on semi-religious subjects. If there was less evidence of the old-time religious fervor, fewer shouts and hallelujahs, there also was less rowdyism. In fact, many of the old-time camp-meeting grounds were rapidly being transformed into respectable middle-class summer resorts with only a tinge of religion."

Peters (1985, p. 178) illustrates how quickly this transformation took place at the famous Ocean Grove Camp Meeting. "In 1872 the report from Ocean Grove to the *Guide to Holiness* had been, 'Multitudes were sanctified wholly and many sinners were born into the Kingdom;' and in 1878, 'Nearly six hundred . . . in converting, sanctifying and reclaiming grace.' In 1894, however, the report said, 'Several persons were at the altar and some were converted.' The difference cannot be wholly a matter of reportorial accuracy.

Elsewhere Sweet (1944, p. 164) stressed how an educated clergy

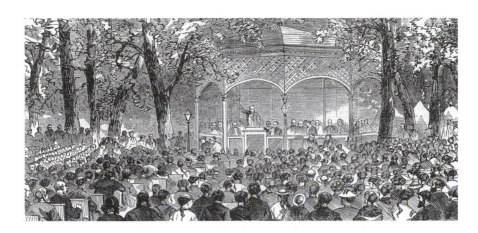

SPECIMEN OF COTTAGES.

Martha's Vineyard near Bedford, Mass., was one of the many Methodist camp-meeting sites being transformed into "respectable middle-class summer resorts" (W. W. Sweet, 1933, p. 333). In addition to the well-crafted pews and preacher's stand, the resort had two hundred cottages by 1868—one fourth of them built in the summer of 1868—and a wide range of social entertainment, including croquet, swimming, fishing, sailing, and tea-making. On September 12, 1868, *Harper's Weekly* reported: "the thousands of people who frequent Martha's Vineyard at this season have more and fresher pleasures than those who summer at Newport or Long Branch. Here you see the latest fashions, and innocent flirtation is not unknown among the lads and lassies." (Courtesy of the Billy Graham Center Museum, Wheaton, Ill.)

served as a "cool-headed leadership" exercising "a restraining influence on an overemotionalized company of people." He asserted that when there is "an educated minister in the pulpit, there is small chance that an extreme emotional revivalism will arise."

In Chapter 2 we suggested that religious doctrine often seems to become accommodated and secularized whenever it is delivered into the control of intellectuals. This may not always be the case, but it was surely true for the Methodists. When the intellectually promising students of American Methodism returned from their graduate training in the universities of Germany, they used their seats in the seminaries to challenge American Methodism's traditional notions of sin, conversion, and perfectionism (Peters, 1985). These challenges were quickly passed on to students of the seminaries, and the "course of study" underwent numerous revisions to accommodate the new insights (Norwood, 1982). The traditions of Methodism were being challenged not by the laity but by the ordained intellectuals.

In 1904, when Bishop Willard Mallalieu wrote the introduction to G. W. Wilson's book *Methodist Theology vs. Methodist Theologians*, he lamented that just as moral standards had been lowered to accommodate more worldly behavior, "theological standards of Christian experience [have been] adjusted to harmonize with a lukewarm, cold, or backslidden experience." American Methodism, according to the bishop, was rapidly becoming "unevangelical, un-Wesleyan, and un-Scriptural" (pp. 10–12). More than three decades later the president of the Iliff School of Theology, Charles Schofield (1939), reflected on the changes that had occurred with the Methodist clergy and their plans for evangelism. He noted that for the early Methodist preachers the problem of preaching was "vastly simplified," because "every sermon was an evangelistic sermon." The clergy's church planning had been consumed by evangelistic efforts: "By the time a man [the circuit rider] laid out and carried through a plan for from six to ten weeks of evangelistic preaching on each point of his circuit and made provision for camp meetings in the summer months, the year's program was pretty well filled out" (pp. 71–72). But all of this contrasted sharply with Schofield's view of evangelism and the role clergy should play in the newly formed Methodist Church:

> There has been, however, quite generally over the Church a sharp subsidence of enthusiasm for, and faith in, the evangelistic methods and objectives to which our fathers gave themselves. . . . Perhaps this in part grows

out of the fact that we have come to hold a more adequate conception of
what is involved in real evangelism. . . . Today it is not anywhere nearly
so easy to define what we mean by becoming a Christian. . . . We do not
cherish the naive confidence in the complete adequacy of one momentary
experience. (1939, pp. 73–74)

The intent of Schofield's essay was to argue in favor of increased evangelism, but his comments highlight why it is difficult for the secularized
faiths to evangelize. Evangelism is no longer *the* mission of the church,
the "adequacy" of sanctification is questioned, and the clear boundaries
between Christian and non-Christian have faded. Compared with his
ancestors, President Schofield lacked any clear message or sense of his
mission. His confusion becomes poignant in the last sentence of the
passage: "If we are to continue to be Christians at all, we must evangelize" (p. 83). But he no longer could tell his seminarians whom to evangelize, or how.

Although these changes in the style and content of Methodism were
not initiated by the people, many rank-and-file Methodists out in the
pews (some now paying rent for the privilege) welcomed a more
worldly Methodism and preferred pastors of the New School.

## Affluent Methodists

John Wesley anticipated the day when most Methodists would not be
lacking in worldly goods: "Religion must necessarily produce both industry and frugality, and these cannot but produce riches. But as riches
increase so will pride, anger, and love of the world in all its branches."
Nor would it be possible to prevent the latter by preventing the former:
"We ought not to prevent people from being diligent and frugal; we
must exhort all Christians to gain all they can, and save all they can—
this is, in effect, to grow rich. What way, then, can we take, that our
money may not sink us into the nethermost hell? There is one way, and
there is no other way under heaven. If those who gain all they can, save
all they can, will likewise give all they can, then the more they gain, the
more they grow in grace, and the more treasure they lay up in heaven"
(in W. W. Sweet, 1933, p. 336).

But though some may well have heeded Wesley's advice about giving
and about waiting to enjoy their treasure in the world to come, many
Methodists didn't want to wait. Charles A. and Mary R. Beard sneered
at Methodists who, in the 1890s, "fired by the ostentatious display of
the plutocracy, crowded the hotels at Saratoga Springs and Long

Branch, attended the opera, and made 'the grand tour' of Europe" (in W. W. Sweet, 1933, p. 337).

William Warren Sweet (1933), the dean of Methodist historians, agreed (without the sneer) that by the 1880s there were many rich Methodists determined to enjoy their wealth. He pointed to the rapidly rising scale of Methodist ministers' salaries, the building of costly churches, and the proliferation of pipe organs and paid choirs as the most obvious signs of affluence. In 1850 the Episcopalians had 7.2 times more church property per member than the Methodists, but by 1906 this ratio dropped to 3.5 (see Table 5.2). The ratio between Methodists and Congregationalists similarly fell from 4.1 to 2.3. In contrast, the Baptists' church property per member in comparison with that of the Episcopalians and the Congregationalists showed little change.

In 1884 the trustees of Indiana Asbury University, Methodists all, agreed to rename the school De Pauw University in return for a large contribution by Washington C. De Pauw, a wealthy glass manufacturer and prominent Methodist layman. Given the theology that likely prevailed there at this time, the old bishop would probably have welcomed the name change.

Sweet (1944, pp. 163–164) also pointed with pride to the closing of the cultural and respectability gap between the Methodists and the old

## TABLE 5.2
## Value of Church Properties per Member, 1850 and 1906 (reported in denominational ratios)

| Ratios | 1850 | 1906 |
| --- | --- | --- |
| Episcopal/Methodist | 7.2 | 3.5 |
| Congregational/Methodist | 4.1 | 2.3 |
| Episcopal/Baptist | 6.3 | 5.7 |
| Congregational/Baptist | 3.6 | 3.7 |

SOURCE: Calculated from denominational totals reported by the Bureau of the Census (1854, 1910)

NOTE: Each ratio represents the number of dollars of church property per member in one denomination divided by the number of dollars of church property per member in another denomination. The first row, for example, indicates that the Episcopalians had 7.2 times more dollars of church property per member than the Methodists in 1850.

colonial mainline: "Clerical culture and learning were no longer a monopoly of the Congregationalists, the Presbyterians, and the Episcopalians. Education, refinement, and dignity now characterized the ministry and services of many Methodists . . . equally with those of the formerly elite churches. Indeed, the Methodists in the towns and cities by the end of the century began to get out the robes and prayer books which had been carefully put aside in the early years of the Church's independent existence, and many of them in form and ritual went far beyond Presbyterianism and Congregationalism."

Sweet knew about upscale Methodism firsthand. During his many years on the faculty of the University of Chicago Divinity School he often visited the famous First Methodist Church in nearby Evanston. The church served Northwestern University and Garrett Seminary, both Methodist institutions. From late in the nineteenth century until the 1960s the ushers at First Methodist wore swallowtail coats and its pews were rented on an annual basis by some of the most prominent Chicago families. A pew rental chart for 1911 shows that the best seats went for $200; seats in the last two rows sold for $25 (Wind, 1990, p. 49).

Although the Sunday morning services of early Methodists were orderly and generally exempt from the emotional freedoms reserved for the camp meetings, they were still informal gatherings that allowed spontaneous responses of "Amen" or "Praise the Lord." According to Gerald McCulloh (1964, p. 636), as late as "1881 'formality' had been classed with 'worldliness' and 'improper amusements' as a peril to Methodism." But with an increasingly educated clergy and a more affluent membership, Sunday services began to display the formal liturgy and established ritual once reserved for the Episcopalians and Presbyterians. The 1905 *Hymnal* bears witness to this change: the "shouting Methodists" were now reciting responsive readings.

As the Methodists changed from a lower-class sect into a middle-class church or, as Teddy Roosevelt put it, the "most representative church in America," the clear barriers between Methodists and the outside world began to fall. In addition to losing their distinctive style of worship and their uneducated clergy, they grew increasingly lax about enforcing the strict behavioral standards that once had been their hallmark (McCulloh, 1964). As the class meetings died out, there was no means to "administer the discipline" and little attempt to find a new avenue for enforcement. An article in the *Methodist Review* in 1898 illustrates the shift from strict standards of membership to more inclusive criteria: "We do not believe anything is gained by holding up the

extreme penalty of excommunication for acts of doubtful character, or, at the worst, vanities or follies. . . . The church is not a punitive institution. It succeeds, not by casting out men, but by getting them in and developing all their capabilities for good" (Carroll, 1898, p. 183). The actual written standards for behavior changed only slowly. But by the turn of the century many Methodists could safely ignore the rules against such activities as playing cards, dancing, or attending the theater, horse races, and circuses. When, in 1924, the Methodists formally suspended their rules against these amusements, making them a matter of individual conscience, the announcement earned headlines in the *New York Times*.

Thus we see the Methodists as they were transformed from sect to church. Their clergy were increasingly willing to condone the pleasures of this world and to deemphasize sin, hellfire, and damnation; this lenience struck highly responsive chords in an increasingly affluent, influential, and privileged membership. This is, of course, the fundamental dynamic by which sects are transformed into churches, thereby losing the vigor and the high octane faith that caused them to succeed in the first place.

But not all of the people drawn to Methodism had become rich, nor did all of them desire a more worldly and accommodated faith. And, as had Reverend Roberts and his Free Methodists at mid-century, they began to complain and to seek a return to old-time Methodist enthusiasm.

## The Holiness Movement

Ironically, historians credit John Wesley as the founder of the Holiness Movement in reaction to what he perceived to be the worldliness and secularity of the Church of England. Eventually his commitment to such principles as "Christian Perfection" drove him from Anglicanism.

But the great American social movement that came to be known as the Holiness Movement arose within Methodism during the latter half

The increasing affluence and size of the Methodist Episcopal Church is illustrated by its choice of buildings for the General Conference. Bishop Asbury held the 1790 meeting in a log cabin in Kentucky (*top*). But in 1888 the Methodists met in the Metropolitan Opera House in New York City. The *Frank Leslie Illustrated Newspaper* reported that the "cost of securing the building ($5,500)" was covered "by the sale of over fifty of the boxes at $100 each for the month, and the remainder at prices varying from $50 to $90, according to location." (Courtesy of the Billy Graham Center Museum, Wheaton, Ill.)

of the nineteenth century and was, in large part, a call for return to Wesleyan principles. Linked closely to revivalism and camp meetings, the movement generally called for a reaffirmation of traditional Methodist theology and methods, placing special emphasis on the Wesleyan commitment to sanctification through baptism of the Holy Spirit. Just as the Methodist Episcopal Church began to deemphasize and to secularize their camp meetings, the Holiness Movement formed the National Camp Meeting Association for the Promotion of Holiness in 1867. The Holiness Movement was met with widespread enthusiasm and support by the Methodist laity and, at first, received cooperation from key bishops and clergy.

The result was rapid growth throughout the nation. By 1887 the national association reported holding sixty-seven national camp meetings as well as eleven Tabernacle meetings; and by 1892 the state and local holiness associations reported hosting 354 meetings for the promotion of holiness each week and maintained a list of 304 holiness evangelists. With the support of forty-one periodicals, and four publishing houses devoted exclusively to the publication of holiness materials, the growing strength of the movement became apparent to all—including the Methodist hierarchy (Peters, 1985).

The success of the movement soon brought increased criticism from the Methodist divines. As new bishops were appointed and segments of the Holiness Movement became more "radical," the movement was regarded by the Methodist hierarchy as a "sectarian" challenge like that of Roberts and his Free Methodists. Greatly concerned by the proliferation of holiness publications not under their control and by the immense number of camp meeting associations that were now independent of Methodist authority, the bishops began to express their criticism publicly. By the 1890s the Methodist hierarchy launched a serious counterattack on prominent Methodist clergy participating in the Holiness Movement.

The hierarchy's greatest fear, however, and the area over which they had the least control, was the proliferation of holiness evangelists who attracted the attention of the membership. Like the Methodist circuit rider of the early nineteenth century, these evangelists would preach whenever and wherever they were given the liberty to do so. Because many of these evangelists were not ordained or even licensed by the Methodist Church, and some were members of other denominations, the hierarchy had no means to control or regulate their behavior. They could discipline and reprimand their own clergy, but the holiness evangelists operated outside the formal structure of the church. The General Conference of 1894 described the situation: "We are confronted with a new condition. Evangelists are numbered by scores and hundreds, and multiply fast. . . . all act without appointment or supervision in this special work" (in Peters, 1985, p. 146). To address this "condition" the *Discipline* of 1894 gave the Methodist clergy full authority and responsibility to "control the appointment of all services to be held in the Churches in his charge." The professional clergy could now determine when the evangelists should be given the liberty to preach; and in most areas, this liberty was denied.

In response, holiness spokesmen began to call "all true holiness Christians to come out of Methodism's church of mammon" (Melton, 1989, p. 204). And out they came. Sect after sect. And among them was the Church of the Nazarene, known initially as the Pentecostal Church of the Nazarene. The Nazarenes are typical of the holiness sects that erupted from Methodism in the 1890s and early 1900s. The vigorous growth of the Nazarenes demonstrates once again the relatively greater competitive capacity of less secularized faiths (see Table 5.3). As will be

TABLE 5.3
Church of the Nazarene Membership, 1906–1986

| Year | Members | Members per 1,000 population |
|------|---------|------------------------------|
| 1906 | 6,657 | 0.08 |
| 1916 | 32,359 | 0.32 |
| 1926 | 63,558 | 0.54 |
| 1936 | 136,227 | 1.06 |
| 1945 | 201,487 | 1.44 |
| 1955 | 270,576 | 1.64 |
| 1965 | 343,380 | 1.77 |
| 1975 | 441,093 | 2.04 |
| 1986 | 530,912 | 2.20 |

SOURCES: Bureau of the Census (1941) and *Yearbook of American and Canadian Churches* (1988).

seen in Chapter 7, scores of new upstart Protestant sects have emerged in America since the 1890s and many of them have had spectacular growth curves.

A remarkable, if little-known, study of the Holiness Movement within the Methodist churches of Illinois offers solid evidence of the impact of clergy education and member affluence on the "secularization" of the Methodists. Carl Oblinger (1973) identified the most prominent leaders of the regular Methodist and holiness factions within the Central and Illinois Conferences in 1880. Of the thirty-eight holiness leaders, 6 percent had been educated beyond high school, and 55 percent had received little or no schooling at all. Of the one hundred leaders of the regular faction, 59 percent had attended college and most of these had gone to seminary as well.

By examining the manuscript census forms for 1880, Oblinger was able to determine the size of the farms owned by a sample of farmers who joined each faction. Only 3 percent of the holiness farmers, as opposed to 36 percent of those who supported the regular faction, had farms larger than 250 acres. Forty-four percent of the holiness farmers had less than 50 acres, but only 17 percent of the regular faction farmers had farms this small. In the nineteenth century the census asked people their net worth. Oblinger found that for this same set of farmers, only 14 percent of the regulars were worth less than $2,500 while 47 percent of the holiness farmers had this little. Thirty-five percent of the regulars were worth more than $10,000, in contrast with 17 percent of the holiness farmers. These findings are in agreement with data on the Hicksite separation of the Philadelphia Quakers, discussed in Chapter 2.

## The Design of Defeat

As the twentieth century dawned, the realization by many leaders of the Methodist Episcopal Church that they were not matching Baptist growth prompted a variety of responses. Some chose to emphasize that receipts from member contributions continued to rise quite rapidly. Others emphasized that a far more adequate and sophisticated theology now held sway and noted the immense progress toward more refined and respectable services (recall Sweet's evident relief that religious emotionalism had been brought under control). Some suggested that the whole past emphasis on conversion had been misplaced and that the church's emphasis should shift to social service, informed by the new science of sociology. There were also many comments that the slow-down was caused only by recent efforts to clean up local membership rolls—implying that growth by the Baptists and other evangelical groups was nothing more than sloppy bookkeeping.

But not everyone found these suggestions satisfactory. Speaking for those committed to old-fashioned Methodism with its emphasis on conversion, George W. Wilson bluntly rejected the prevailing views in *Methodist Theology vs. Methodist Theologians* (1904, pp. 329, 331): "a spiritual dearth has come over us [Methodists] which can not be removed by liberal giving, nor explained away by the theory that this is 'a transitional age,' or that we are 'cleaning up the Church records,' or that 'the trend of the times is towards ethics and sociology.' . . . Though the whole amount of our gifts increases yearly, it is in no reasonable proportion to the increase in our wealth."

Eight decades later, the Methodist bishop Richard B. Wilke chided his colleagues for fostering many of the same myths and deceptions. In *And Are We Yet Alive?* Wilke (1986, p. 17) reviewed the dismal declines in Methodist membership totals that had ensued in the 1960s and wrote: "What does this discouraging study of statistics mean? Some people say the situation isn't so bad as it seems. They argue that many congregations are vital and alive; millions of people are in worship; money keeps coming in . . . many church rolls have been 'cleaned.'" The bishop went on to note: "We've been cleaning the rolls for twenty years," but this simply means that "we are losing people all the time," and as long as this continues, "we will have to clean our rolls year after year" (p. 19). For those of his colleagues who responded that they didn't "believe in the numbers game" and who claimed to be more interested in the "quality, not the quantity of members," the bishop suggested they recall John Wesley's remarks in his *Journal* that any membership decline is a "sore evil," for growth is a sign of God's grace, "where the real power of God is, it naturally spreads wider and wider" (p. 15). The bishop wondered who could find anything resembling a "game" in such dismal numbers: in 1985 a third of the nation's Methodist churches had performed no baptisms, infant or adult; nearly two thirds had no membership training or confirmation classes; and nearly half had no list of potential new members.

But *why* this state of affairs? Bishop Wilke's answers are much like our own and were rather fully anticipated by Wilson in 1904—that the church had become too worldly to preach the messages and support the methods by which the Methodist miracle had occurred in the first place. Wilson (1904, pp. 333, 330) charged that "empty speculative babblings are uttered from pulpit, rostrum, and professor's chair, where positive truth should be uttered with power of the Holy Spirit resting on the speaker, convicting and not creating doubt. . . . Revivals are scarce. . . . [and] sermons are preached without a single appeal to the sinner to accept Christ Jesus now." Throughout his book Wilson argued that theologians and clergy were attempting to replace Christian experience and "spiritual impulses" with a respectable and consistent theology. For Wilson the result was: "Faith is circumscribed by finite, fallible, illogical reason (p. 329). And the blame for all this, in Wilson's view, should be placed on the clergy and especially upon the theologians in the seminaries. The church had fallen into the hands of a "self-seeking, hireling ministry, refusing to preach the whole Gospel." He rumbled on about "Christless leaders" and "looseness in examining the spiritual life of candidates for our ministry" (p. 342).

What was the alternative? Consider the more recent proposals Bishop Wilke (1986) made to reinvigorate Methodism:

> The overriding opinion held by laypeople and pastors alike is that the local church will thrive when the minister is enthusiastic, and it will founder when the minister is dry and lifeless.

> How can we energize our preachers for the challenge of the century before us?

> First, we focus on Jesus. . . . Preachers should burn, not burn out. They should shout, "I live; yet not I, but Christ lives within me!" (pp. 96–97)

> The churches that are drawing people to them believe in sin, hell, and death. Jesus, who knew what he was talking about, explained them, experienced them, and conquered them. If there is no sin, we do not need a Savior. If we do not need a Savior, we do not need preachers. (p. 98)

> Seminaries must fuel the faith of our new ministers. If they are only graduate schools, their graduates will be able to write term papers, but not to save souls. . . . Some wag has said that students enter seminary inspired to be evangelists and graduate aspiring to be seminary professors. (p. 99)

> If we are to tackle the world for Christ, the seminaries must be fiery furnaces. The task is not to grant degrees, but to inflame the minds and hearts of a generation of preachers (p. 100).

Wilson would have liked these lines. If Peter Cartwright could have read them, he might easily have taken them to be his own.

## The Baptist Triumph

Are all successful sect movements fated to "forget their errand into the wilderness," as Cotton Mather so aptly described the transformation of sects into churches? Did the Baptists simply postpone the inevitable as they retained their tension with society during the nineteenth century while the Methodists succumbed to the temptations of the world?

This question raises what is perhaps the most basic issue of social science—do humans have significant control of their destinies or are they essentially puppets dancing to the beat of the social forces that surround them? An either/or answer does not suffice. William Sims Bainbridge (1985) summed up our own position when he wrote: "Do we make our history, or does it make us? Clearly, the answer is yes!" (p. 523).

Social science has made little headway with theories postulating that humans often act in irrational ways. To predict human behavior with a high degree of accuracy, we ask what choices a given situation presents and assume that people will select what they perceive to be the most rational option—the one that provides the highest ratio of rewards to costs. What is one person's reward, of course, may be of little or no value to someone else, which is what makes human culture so rich and varied. And admittedly, the sociocultural environment greatly influences our taste. Moreover, people may have relatively little control over the options from which they may select, and in that sense it can be said that our history makes us. But the fact remains that in normal circumstances people often have a substantial range of options.

Applied to the question raised at the beginning of this section, the rational choice premise lets us see that Methodist clergy and seminary professors always had (and have) the option of embracing the otherworldly faith of the Wesleys and Francis Asbury. But they had other options as well. The underlying dynamic of sect-church theory is that social forces tend to influence the preferences of people vis-à-vis religion: that as the general affluence and social standing of a group rises, otherworldliness—as expressed through tension with the environment—becomes perceived as increasingly costly. For the clergy, the costs of remaining a high-tension sect are especially high. They often receive less pay and community respect than their counterparts in "mainline" denominations, even though they face more stringent demands on their belief and behavior. The result: the well-educated clergy and affluent membership are often the first to support a lowering of the tension with the surrounding culture.

Thus when seminary-trained clergy, often with advanced degrees, are in charge of denominational machinery, the transition from sect to church tends to occur rapidly—as in the case of the Methodists. But when less qualified local clergy and the less affluent membership have substantial power, the drift toward accommodation is delayed. In the case of the Southern Baptist Convention, at least two major periods of drift toward accommodation were halted and reversed.

The Southern Baptists have thus far managed to fend off secularization, and have not been transformed from sect to church. Some Baptists, however, followed the Methodists into decline. Like the Methodists, the Baptists split along sectional boundaries during the controversies leading to the Civil War. But unlike the Methodists, whose regional bodies remained sufficiently alike that they were eventually able to reunite (in 1939), the Northern and Southern Baptist branches became very different. The former was transformed from sect to church; the latter went on to become the largest Protestant denomination in the United States.

## The Secularization of Northern Baptists

Perhaps the most obvious difference between the Northern and Southern Baptists is that of membership growth. The Baptists' share of the religious market in the North showed a pattern of decline similar to that of the Methodists (see Figure 5.4). Although part of this decline can be explained by the rising numbers of Catholic and Lutheran immigrants, immigration does not explain the inability of the Northern Baptists to compete with other Protestants. Whereas the Baptists of the South made huge inroads on the Methodist share of the religious market between 1850 and 1926 (as we saw in Figure 5.2), the Baptists of the North fell into a decline that paralleled that of the Methodists.

The Baptists of the North and South soon differed on more than membership growth, however. At the turn of the twentieth century the Southern Baptists were still served by many untutored, unpaid farmer-preachers, who preached the "old-time" gospel to a relatively impov-

FIGURE 5.4 Methodists and Baptists in the North as Percentage of Total Adherents, 1850–1926

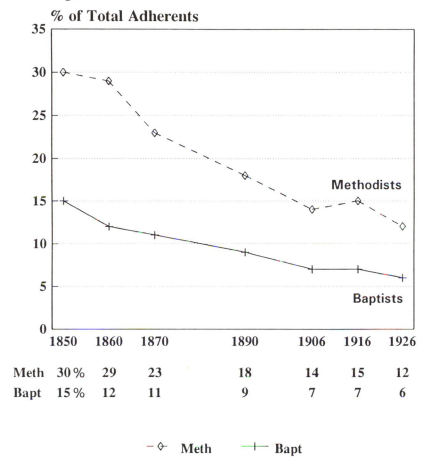

| | 1850 | 1860 | 1870 | 1890 | 1906 | 1916 | 1926 |
|---|---|---|---|---|---|---|---|
| Meth | 30% | 29 | 23 | 18 | 14 | 15 | 12 |
| Bapt | 15% | 12 | 11 | 9 | 7 | 7 | 6 |

– ◇   Meth        ┼─ Bapt

(The "North" includes all states in the Northeast and North Central census areas.)

erished membership. In contrast, the overwhelming majority of Northern Baptist clergy were comparatively well paid graduates of seminaries where liberal theology held sway. The Northern Baptist membership was also increasingly more affluent.

In 1906 the average salary was $536 per year for all Baptist clergy and $784 for all Methodist clergy (see Table 5.1). But, broken down by specific denominations, the average annual salary for clergy from the

Southern Baptist Convention was only $367, while the average salary for the Northern Baptist clergy was more than twice as high ($833)—higher even than that of Methodists in the North. These differences cannot be viewed as merely a product of the region, because the Methodists show relatively minor regional differences: $812 for the Methodist Episcopal Church and $714 for the Methodist Episcopal Church, South (Bureau of the Census, 1910).

In addition to their relatively high level of pay, the Baptist clergy of the North also could boast of their fine theological training. Even prior to the formation of the Southern Baptist Convention in 1845, Baptist seminaries were predominantly located in the North. Hayward (1836, p. 154) reports that in 1834–35 Baptist seminaries in the North enrolled 68 percent of all students attending Baptist seminaries, but only 36 percent of Baptist membership was located in the North. Even as late as 1916, when the membership of the Northern Convention was less than half that of the Southern Convention, the enrollments of the Northern Convention seminaries exceeded those of the Southern Baptist Convention by 40 percent (Bureau of the Census, 1919).[3] And just as had happened at the Methodist seminaries, the Northern Baptist seminaries gradually toned down their theology (Torbet, 1976). Hudson (1981, p. 280) judged that "all the northern Baptist seminaries were firmly in the liberal camp by the end of the [nineteenth] century." In 1915 Albert Henry Newman noted that "all of the older theological seminaries of the North have on their faculties scholars of the modern type who are outspoken in their acceptance of modernistic views of the Bible and of the evolutionistic philosophy, and no one of them . . . [has] a stalwart and aggressive advocate of the older conservatism" (p. 518).

Because most Baptist seminaries in the North were independently organized and thereby free of denominational control, they easily became a haven for the expression and development of liberal theology (Hudson, 1981). These developments did not go unnoticed by Baptists in the South. James J. Thompson (1982, pp. 71–72) reports that by the 1920s Southern Baptists had become very concerned about the lack of orthodoxy in the North, especially in seminaries such as the University of Chicago: "Southerners reserved their fiercest denunciations for the University of Chicago, charging that the once-orthodox Baptist school had become a 'satanic institution' harboring 'infidelity, atheism, rationalism, and materialism.' "

Another dramatic difference between the Northern and Southern Baptists was in the affluence of their churches. In 1906 the value of all church property owned by the Northern Baptist Convention was more than double that of the Southern Baptist Convention, despite the Northern Baptists' having only half as many members. Part of this contrast can be explained by regional differences in affluence as well as in real estate values and for this reason comparisons with other denominations are instructive. The Northern Baptist Convention's average of $70.92 of church property per member placed them above the Methodist Episcopal Church ($54.70 per member) and remarkably close to the Presbyterians ($82.07) and the Congregationalists (90.34) (Bureau of the Census, 1910).

Like the Methodists, and the old colonial mainline denominations before them, the Northern Baptists had been transformed from sect to church. As they entered the twentieth century their clergy were well-trained and well-paid professionals, their theology was becoming compatible with "modern" thought, and their members tended to be affluent. But their market share was in decline.

## Secularization and the Southern Baptists

Why weren't the Southern Baptists transformed from sect to church as their Northern co-religionists were? The answer is that they almost were—at least twice. However, certain structural features of the Southern Baptists have enabled them to offer strong resistance to secularization and, indeed, to reverse trends in that direction.

Our argument turns on three basic points. First, Southern Baptist congregations are extremely autonomous and democratic. The local laity hire and fire their preachers as they please and need not submit to any directives, theological or otherwise, from above. Local congregations retain the right to ordain ministers as they choose. This means that the interests of the clergy cannot be imposed upon the laity and that the will of the laity can, to a very considerable extent, be imposed on the clergy.

A second very significant fact of Southern Baptist life grows out of the independence of local congregations. It is difficult, if not impossible, for the Southern Baptists to root out factions—including potential sect movements. Even substantial majorities in the Southern Baptist Convention can't expel their opponents in the way that the Methodists expelled Benjamin Roberts and his Free Methodists or, later, the holiness supporters. Dissidents are thus free to stay and fight for support from

Ball Camp Baptist Church near Knoxville, Tennessee. (Courtesy of the Southern Baptist Historical Library and Archives, Nashville, Tenn.)

among rank-and-file Baptists. When the more sectlike dissidents are forced to leave a denomination, they leave behind a group in which the average member is less otherworldly than before the split. But such liberalization by expulsion and defection has not taken place among the Southern Baptists.

The third factor is that the Southern Baptists, urged on by dissident factions, never permitted their seminaries to emerge as independent organizations as did Northern Baptist seminaries. Although Southern Baptist seminaries have also been prone to "modernism," this trend has been held somewhat in check by the periodic dismissal of an outspoken seminary professor. As a result, religious intellectuals gathered in the seminary faculties have faced strong opposition when they have attempted to re-create the denomination in their own image.

For many years, however, these factors were not needed to prevent the transformation of the Southern Baptists. The Civil War left the Southern Baptists representing an impoverished and shattered South. The Baptists seized this as an opportunity to become the primary organizational vehicle for sustaining a recusant southern culture that clung to "traditional" views in political, racial, and social as well as religious spheres. As J. Wayne Flynt (1982, p. 23) put it, Southern Baptists attributed the military defeat of the South to "their own moral inadequacies," and therefore "they redoubled their efforts to purge the sins of their land and thereby create an evangelical Zion. Struggling as only those can who have stood before God's judgment, they damned every form of personal excess and wickedness, plunged into a moral crusade for prohibition, and established an evangelical hegemony unknown to the antebellum South. They created a version of American civil religion, baptizing the 'lost cause' in the blood of the Lamb." Thus through the decades when the South remained an economically depressed internal colony and southerners were the object of Yankee scorn, the sectlike qualities of the Southern Baptists were reinforced.

Other factors that propelled the transformation of the Methodists and Northern Baptists were greatly muffled among the Southern Baptists as well. Generally speaking throughout the South the Baptist clergy received low salaries, when they received any at all. Consider this example offered by Victor Masters (1916, p.98) of a Baptist farmer-preacher in Virginia who served two churches. Every Sunday he walked six miles to preach at one church and then walked five miles to the other. He also held three weeks of revivals yearly, while receiving an annual salary of $13.20. In order to live, this man farmed thirty acres of rented land, but was so poor he had to work part time for a neighbor in exchange for the use of a horse to till his field.

Among the Methodists a settled, professional clergy had largely replaced the local lay clergy by the 1880s, but even early in the twentieth century the Southern Baptists still had an abundance of farmer-preachers. Of all the active Southern Baptist pastors reporting their salaries to the 1916 census, 36 percent pursued full-time secular occupations. Of these, 71 percent were farmers.[4] By comparison fewer than 2 percent of the active clergy in the Methodist Episcopal Church, South, did not earn their entire living from the church. This helps to explain why the Southern Baptists had a ratio of one minister for every 1.5 churches and for every 151 members, whereas the Methodist Episcopal Church, South, could supply only 1 minister for every 3 churches and for every 282 members.

Like the upstart sects of the early nineteenth century, the Southern Baptists were not lacking for eager clergy, held back by the inability of small rural churches to support a full-time minister, or hobbled by the

Because Southern Baptists did not rely on a full-time professional clergy, they could support numerous small churches scattered across the countryside. Shown here is the Brier Creek Baptist Church in Wilkes County, North Carolina. (Courtesy of the Southern Baptist Historical Library and Archives, Nashville, Tenn.)

decisions of a central hierarchy. They could operate wherever a few could gather to worship—and they did.

## Secularization and Reaction: Round One

Despite being shielded from many of the forces that were transforming the Methodists and the Northern Baptists, as the nineteenth century passed the Southern Baptists began to experience internal dissent. Movements began to arise aimed at preserving the faith against accommodation with the world. Internal factions demanding a return to a more sectlike faith are always a first sign of the secularization of a religious body. Typically these movements eventually are expelled from or withdraw from a larger body, thus founding a new sect movement. In the case of the Southern Baptists, however, these movements succeeded in reversing the trend toward accommodation and thus qualify as revival or renewal movements.

### The Landmark Movement

Beginning in 1848, James R. Graves, editor of the *Tennessee Baptist*, promulgated the argument that Baptist churches were the only true churches, for only they could claim true "apostolic succession" despite the many centuries of misrepresentation on behalf of "Romish and Episcopal doctrine." Graves claimed that Baptist churches originated when Jesus Christ was baptized by bodily immersion and have existed ever since as the only true congregations of Christ, although in some eras they had to hide from public view. Graves thought it obvious that only Baptist ministers could be the true successors of the apostles, for only they had been immersed. He summed up his views:

> my position is that Christ, in the very days of John the Baptist did establish a visible kingdom on earth, and this *kingdom* has never yet been "broken in pieces" . . . or ceased from the earth, and never will until Christ returns personally to reign over it; that the organization he first set up . . . and which Christ called his church, constituted that visible kingdom, and today all his *true* churches on earth constitute it; and, therefore, if his *kingdom* has stood unchanged, and will to the end, he must always have had true and uncorrupted churches, since his kingdom can not exist without true churches. (in Baker, 1974, p. 211)

Two important emphases followed from Graves's argument. First was an emphasis on the primacy of the local congregation, a degree of emphasis that was radical even for a Baptist. As Robert A. Baker (1974, pp. 209–210) put it, the first major emphasis of the Landmarkians[5] was that, given "the authoritative nature of the local and visible New Testament congregation. . . . General bodies were suspect. . . . they should draw their authority from the local body." The absolute authority of the local church was the topic of heated debates at both state and national conventions throughout the late nineteenth and early twentieth centuries—whether the issue of the moment involved representation at conventions, the authority to examine and direct foreign missionaries, or who held responsibility for the doctrinal orthodoxy of seminary faculties. The balance of power tended to shift back and forth, but the local congregations always managed to retain significant independent power and often proved responsive to appeals by dissident factions.

A second, equally important, emphasis of the Landmarkian movement was that if the Baptists were the only authentic Christian churches constituting the kingdom, then there could be no relationships with any but other Baptists, no sharing of pulpits even with Methodists.

This position helped sustain effective opposition to "modern thought" and liberal theology. At a time when Methodist and Northern Baptist theologians were emphasizing *inclusive* membership and ecumenical activity, the Landmark supporters were advocating clear boundaries between the saved and unsaved, and between true churches and unscriptural churches.

It is not clear that Landmarkians were ever the majority in the Southern Baptist Convention, but their grass-roots support was sufficient to fend off any limitations of local authority. They were sufficiently powerful, moreover, to withstand the first doctrinal challenge from the faculty of the Southern Baptist Seminary in Louisville.

## The "Whitsitt Controversy"

The firing of William H. Whitsitt from the presidency of Southern Seminary is routinely reported by historians of American religion as the "Whitsitt Controversy." As will be evident, however, the name is as misleading as the typical discussion of it is superficial and biased. What was involved was not the martyrdom of a church historian because of his disagreement with rank-and-file Baptists over the historical validity of Landmarkian claims. What was involved, rather, was the takeover of the Southern Baptists' only seminary by a faculty who unanimously rejected *many* basic, traditional Christian tenets and who aggressively taught these unorthodox views to their students. A group of religious intellectuals had consciously attempted to "modernize" Southern Baptist theology, whether the membership liked it or not.

The first Southern Baptist Seminary was founded in Greenville, South Carolina, in 1859, with four faculty members: John A. Broadus, Basil Manley, Jr., William Williams, and the school's first president,[6] James P. Boyce. The Civil War soon caused the school to close, however, and several faculty members, including Broadus, served as chaplains in the Confederate Army. In the aftermath of the war the seminary struggled back to life and in 1869 appointed a fifth faculty member, Crawford H. Toy. In 1877, after President Boyce had spent five years in Louisville, Kentucky, raising an endowment, the seminary relocated to that city. Broadus later recalled: "It was physically no great task to remove the Seminary from Greenville to Louisville. There was nothing to move, except the library of a few thousand volumes, and three professors—Broadus, Toy, and Whitsitt—only one of whom had a family" (in Baker, 1974, p. 302). Let us examine the views of the three men who, for a number of years (along with Boyce) did all of the teaching at the only seminary training Southern Baptist clergy.[7]

*John A. Broadus* often lectured at Northern Baptist seminaries, both before and after the Civil War, and in 1889 he was invited to give a lecture at Yale Divinity School—"the only Southern Baptist ever to achieve that distinction" (Brackney, 1988, p. 134). Broadus was extremely impressed with the application of critical methods to biblical studies that was going on in European universities, especially in Germany. One of Broadus's most distinguished students, Albert Henry Newman (1915, p. 518), reported: "He encouraged his ablest students to master the German language so as to have full access to the treasures of German learning and when practicable to pursue graduate courses at German universities. While he warned his students against accepting the more radical results of the so-called higher criticism, he did not, so far as this writer is informed, denounce Biblical criticism as a wicked impertinence."

Although Broadus himself had not had the opportunity to study in Germany, his other two colleagues had done so, each receiving his doctorate. Perhaps for that reason, each was an even more ardent opponent than Broadus of orthodoxy.

*Crawford H. Toy* was hired in 1869, upon his return from Germany.

William Heth Whitsitt (1841–1911). (Courtesy of the Southern Baptist Historical Library and Archives, Nashville, Tenn.)

John Albert Broadus (1827–1895). (Courtesy of the Southern Baptist Historical Library and Archives, Nashville, Tenn.)

During his first semester at Southern he revealed to his students that he rejected the Genesis account of creation and instead fully accepted Darwin's theory of evolution, which had been published only ten years earlier. He also outlined the latest revisionist theories concerning the authorship of the Old Testament. William Henry Brackney (1988, pp. 272–273) noted: "Some complaints were forthcoming from Toy's stu-

Crawford Howell Toy (1836–1919). (Courtesy of the Southern Baptist Theological Seminary, Louisville, Ky.)

dents, and word of his heterodoxy reached many local churches." Nevertheless, it was not until ten years later that Toy got into serious trouble. Newman (1915, p. 518) explained: "For several years after Dr. Crawford Toy was known to have accepted many of the supposed results of the Old Testament criticism of the German and Dutch schools he was retained in the faculty, and only when he published an interpretation of the fifty-third chapter of Isaiah, in which he denied the direct Messianic reference and was on this account bitterly assailed by the denominational press and by influential denominational leaders, was he compelled to resign."

Toy may have forced the trustees to act. Angry at criticisms aimed at him, Toy attended the 1879 annual meeting of the Convention. There he waved a letter of resignation at the Board of Trustees and demanded their support. To his surprise the board chose to accept the resignation.

Within a year Toy was appointed Hancock Professor of Hebrew at the Harvard Divinity School, where he spent the last thirty years of his life. Harvard Divinity was at that time a bastion of Unitarianism, and it would seem odd for them to have hired a Southern Baptist, even if he were a Darwinian and held heterodox views about the authorship of the Bible. But there was nothing odd about it, because Toy had not the slightest sympathy with Baptist thought, Northern or Southern. Soon after his arrival at Harvard he announced that he wished "to be known as a Theist rather than a Christian" (in Newman, 1915, p. 519).

*William H. Whitsitt* also earned a doctorate in church history in Germany. Whitsitt's historical research, conducted in Germany and later, convinced him that the claim that there had been an unbroken succession of immersionist churches from the time of Christ was incorrect. He could find no evidence of congregations, anywhere in the world, that baptized by immersion before 1641. Whitsitt's position was in direct conflict with that of the Landmarkians. This did not prevent him from accepting an appointment as Professor of Church History at Southern Seminary in 1872. He seems to have been a bit more circumspect than Toy, however, at least when it came to publishing. Whitsitt initially took a very careful (some would say devious) approach. In 1880 he published his anti-Landmarkian views as two anonymous editorials in *The Independent*, a Congregationalist weekly published in New York. Then, in 1896, having just been appointed President of Southern Seminary, Whitsitt was bold enough to go public, laying out his views in a volume called *A Question in Baptist History.*

Predictably, a storm of protest arose. Angry delegates poured into local, state, and national convention meetings demanding that something be done, and their demands were supported by most Baptist newspapers published in various states. In 1897 the Kentucky Baptist State Convention voted the following: "Resolved, that the Trustees of the Seminary from Kentucky be requested, and they are hereby requested, to urge, insist upon and vote for the retirement of Dr. Whitsitt from the presidency of the institution and from the Chair of Church History" (in Shurden, 1972, p. 28). The Mississippi, Louisiana, Arkansas, and Texas conventions soon endorsed this resolution.

Meanwhile the other six members of the Southern faculty issued a unanimous statement of support for their president and his views. Had Whitsitt presided over a Methodist seminary he probably would have won—the bishops would simply have closed ranks and, if necessary, would have expelled Graves and his Landmarkians. Indeed, there is good reason to believe that even among Southern Baptists, many of the most prominent preachers at that time—most of them graduates of Southern—agreed with Whitsitt as they had with Broadus, if not with Toy (Newman, 1915). But only in private. Southern Baptist clergy had no hierarchy to shield them from their own local congregations. Each could be fired by a simple majority of votes cast by people who were in no mood to have professors tinkering with their cherished beliefs.

When the Virginia convention gathered in 1898, a prominent leader from Texas announced that at the 1899 gathering of the entire Southern Baptist Convention he would move to dissolve all relations (including funding) between the Convention and Southern Seminary. Faced with this ultimatum, Whitsitt gave in. On July 13, 1898, he sent a one-sentence telegram to the president of the seminary's board of trustees: "I hereby resign my office as President of Southern Baptist Theological seminary and Professor of Church History to take effect at the close of the session of 1898–99" (in Shurden, 1972, p. 29).[8]

This episode has drawn contempt and ridicule upon the Southern Baptists from religious historians ever since. Walter B. Shurden (1972, p. 22) described Whitsitt as "one of the charter members of that exclusive Southern Baptist group known as 'The Friendless Fraternity of Exiled Professors.'" R. M. Weaver (1943, p. 248) took this incident as proof that "the Southerner has always been hostile to the spirit of inquiry." David Edwin Harrell, Jr. (1985, p. 71) saw the incident as "signalling a growing resentment and insecurity among rural and lower-class Baptists . . . suspicious of the professors in Louisville." Marty (1984, p. 306) failed to mention the issues involved, reporting only that Whitsitt "ran afoul of defenders of the faith," but he quoted with apparent approval one of Whitsitt's supporters to the effect that it would be better to have "no Seminary than a Seminary in which truth cannot find a home." Ahlstrom (1975, pp. 179–180) remarked: "Rigorous historical scholarship was virtually excluded from Southern Baptist seminaries during the next half-century or more."

We agree that "rigorous scholarship" is required of those who would claim to be scholars. We do not agree that standards appropriate for evaluating secular academic institutions are necessarily appropriate for judging institutions organized around a confession of faith. The overwhelming majority of Southern Baptists—whose contributions funded Southern Seminary—had not the slightest intention of creating a "think tank" devoted to *seeking* truth. Rather they sought to create an institution devoted to *spreading* the truth.

Perhaps we can clarify the membership's reaction by posing a series of rhetorical questions. Who says that the only proper mission of seminaries is to function as research centers? Is it wrong for seminaries to regard it as their entire mission to help young clergy learn how to spread and sustain the faith? Moreover, who hired Broadus, Toy, and Whitsitt to lead the Baptists out of the darkness into the light of a more refined theology? Do those who accepted seminary appointments from a denomination, many of whose most central beliefs they held in contempt, deserve sympathy? Why was it wrong for the trustees to fire these men when their deceptions became a public scandal?

Even if one denies denominations the right to impose doctrinal requirements on those employed in their seminaries, it seems evident that the secularization of religion finds its fullest expression in seminaries whenever they define themselves as centers of scholarship. When the Landmarkians forced Whitsitt out of Southern Seminary, they were trying to reverse a real trend toward secularization and thereby to evade the fate that overtook the Methodists and the Northern Baptists.

Nevertheless, the victory of the Landmarkians was in large measure an illusion. There was no purge of Southern Seminary, and Whitsitt's firing did little more than teach Southern Baptist liberals, in and out of the seminaries, to lower their profiles a bit. Not only were the trustees very slow and reluctant to act against Toy or Whitsitt, but no one else was fired. When Whitsitt left, the other six faculty members remained, and through them the influence of Broadus and Whitsitt lived on. It soon spread to Southwestern Baptist Theological Seminary, the denomination's second seminary, which emerged from the Baylor University theology department in 1908. Albert Henry Newman, Professor of Church History at Baylor and dean of the new seminary, was candid about the power of liberals in both seminaries in his widely read college textbook, *A History of the Baptist Churches in the United States*, which first appeared in 1894. Writing in the sixth edition of the book, Newman (1915, pp. 519–521) reported:

> The members of the present faculty, most of whom were trained by Broadus, are conducting the institution in his spirit. From the books and editorial utterances of the professors, and of the ministers of the South that have sat at their feet, it is easy to see that the Southeast is becoming gradually assimilated in thought and attitude to the Northeast, though . . . a very large proportion of the laity of the Southeast and of ministers who have not enjoyed university and seminary training are still relatively conservative. . . . [In the South] several types of Baptist thought and life may be discriminated: (1) The type represented by the Southern Baptist Theological Seminary, moderately conservative but not aggressively hostile to modern modes of thought . . . alive to the obligations of Christians actively to labor for social reform . . . freely exchanging pulpits with ministers of other denominations. . . . (2)[This type of Baptist is] uncompromisingly hostile to any Biblical criticism that does not recognize the . . . inerrancy of Scriptures, to evolutionistic teaching in every form. . . .
>
> They believe in, encourage, and practice evangelism (protracted meetings) as the chief means of making converts, and do not hesitate to appeal in the most realistic way to fear of eternal torment as a motive to lay hold upon Christ by faith as the only means of escape.

Thus Newman drew a most invidious comparison between himself and his enlightened colleagues, on the one hand, and all those old-fashioned Bible thumpers out searching for souls on the other. Fortunately for the continued growth of the denomination, there was no shortage of Bible thumpers—except in the seminaries. And somehow, although they always seemed to win their battles against seminary liberals, traditional Southern Baptists could not finally win the war.

During the 1920s these tensions were the focus of attacks by J. Frank Norris, an outspoken fundamentalist. Norris was an outsider vis-à-vis the seminary-trained Southern Baptist leadership, but his theological concerns about evolution and the "liberal" interpretation of the Bible reflected the views of the majority in the pews.[9] Norris sought to have the Convention adopt a formal confession of faith affirming opposition to "modernist" doctrines. As Robert Torbet (1963, p. 427) pointed out, "most Baptists accepted the theological positions set forth by the Fundamentalists," but they were hesitant to support any creedal statements that might compromise the authority of the Bible or the independence of the local church (see also J. J. Thompson, 1982). Nonetheless, the Convention finally adopted a confession of faith in 1925 that confirmed many of the traditional teachings of the Southern Baptists. Then at the 1926 Convention the following statement was adopted as the "sentiment of the Convention" on evolution: "This Convention accepts Genesis as teaching that man was the special creation of God, and rejects every theory, evolution or other, which teaches that man originated in, or came by way of, a lower animal ancestry" (in Shurden, 1972, p. 99). Before the Convention ended, a resolution was adopted calling for all employees of Southern Baptist agencies and institutions to subscribe to this statement. For J. Frank Norris and the fundamentalists, this was victory. The headline in Norris's paper read: "SOUTHERN BAPTIST CONVENTION HEROICALLY AND TRIUMPHANTLY DELIVERS KNOCKOUT BLOW AGAINST EVOLUTION AND EVOLUTIONISTS" (in Shurden, 1972, p. 99).

The issue seemed resolved. But the fact is that no knockout blow landed, and the fundamentalists won little more than a battle of rhetoric. Bill Leonard (1990, p. 72) reported that "it is doubtful many convention employees signed the statement as required, and no employee was removed for failing to affirm the resolution." Denominational leaders, themselves products of the seminaries, chose to spare the seminary faculties the choice of resignation or conformity to the Convention. And, as we shall see, there is every reason to believe that relatively liberal teaching, in open conflict with the confession, continued. This would have been far less obvious among the Southern Baptists than among the Methodists, of course, because the clergy coming from the seminaries still had to conform to the doctrinal expectations of their congregations.

## Secularization and Reaction: Round Two

In 1961 the conflict between the seminaries and the Convention erupted again, and the terms of the conflict were the same as those involving Toy a century earlier. Broadman Press, the official imprint of the Southern Baptists' Sunday School Board, published a book by Ralph H. Elliott, a professor of Old Testament at Midwestern Baptist Theological

Seminary in Kansas City. Elliott's book, *The Message of Genesis*, was a work of biblical interpretation using the historical-critical method. Although Elliott did not advocate Darwinism, like Toy he rejected Genesis as a literal account of creation and suggested that it tells us more about early Middle East cultures than about how creation took place.

Nancy T. Ammerman (1990, p. 64) noted that: "Such claims were so common in the scholarly community as to be unremarkable—similar ideas had even been appearing in earlier Southern Baptist sources. But books by seminary professors, published by the denominational press, have an air of doctrinal authority; and this was doctrine some Southern Baptists were unwilling to accept."

Ammerman's claim that *some* Southern Baptists rejected this position on Genesis is an understatement. As recently as 1990 nearly two thirds of self-identified Southern Baptists, interviewed as part of the General Social Survey, expressed firm agreement with the statement "The Bible is the actual word of God and is to be taken literally, word for word" and rejected the alternative, "The Bible is the inspired word of God but not everything in it should be taken literally, word for word."

When the Convention gathered in San Francisco in 1962, traditionalists called for Elliott's dismissal. As had Whitsitt, Elliott retained the support of his seminary (the Board of Trustees at Midwestern Seminary confirmed their confidence in him), even though the great majority of delegates were clearly offended by his book (Shurden, 1972).

Unlike the Whitsitt episode, however, this time the traditionalist delegates wasted far less time. By huge majorities they passed three resolutions related to the Elliott controversy. The first reaffirmed faith in "the entire Bible as the authoritative, authentic, infallible Word of God." The second "opposed views which would undermine the historical accuracy and doctrinal integrity of the Bible," and the third called for a committee to prepare a new confessional statement (in Baker, 1974, p. 416). Within a year the 1925 confessional statement was revised. Furthermore, responding to traditionalist pressures, the Sunday School Board decided not to reprint Elliott's book. Elliott responded by seeking an outside publisher. At this point the seminary trustees balked and demanded that Elliott assure them that he would not seek another publisher. Elliott refused, saying that this would give the false impression that he was retracting what he had written. As a result, on October 25, 1962, he was dismissed for insubordination, as the board chose to finesse questions of doctrinal orthodoxy. Once again the issue seemed resolved and the traditionalists appeared to be the victors. Yet many felt cheated because the board had ducked questions of improper doctrine.

Less than a decade later the familiar scenario was played out once more. Again Genesis was the center of the dispute. This time the author was G. Henton Davies, an English Baptist, and the book was the first volume of *The Broadman Bible Commentary*—once again the Sunday School Board was the publisher. The volume appeared in October 1969, and by the time the Convention was held in early June 1970 the battle lines were drawn. By a vote of 5,394 to 2,170 the Convention asked the Sunday School Board to withdraw the volume and have it rewritten. But when the Sunday School Board asked the original author to rewrite the material "with due consideration of the conservative viewpoint," many Baptists felt this violated the intent of the resolution (in Baker, 1974, p. 46). The next year the 1971 Convention voted by a slim majority "that the Sunday School Board be advised that the vote of the 1970 Convention regarding the rewriting of Volume 1 of *The Broadman Bible Commentary* has not been followed and that the Sunday School Board obtain another writer and proceed with the Commentary according to the vote of the 1970 Convention in Denver" (in Baker, 1974, p. 417). Following this action the Sunday School Board secured another writer for the Genesis section of the commentary. The traditionalists had won yet another battle over biblical interpretation.

But after decades of winning the convention battles, the traditionalists finally began to realize they had been losing the war. Again and again since 1869 they had driven out a seminary professor who rejected central tenets of Baptist doctrine, only to discover that the historical-critical method of biblical interpretation continued to dominate seminary teaching and scholarship. No matter how many resolutions the traditionalists passed, the denomination seemed firmly under the control of leaders determined to ignore them and to cooperate with their opponents. Traditionalists soon learned that in response to their demands concerning the controversy over *The Broadman Bible Commentary*, the Sunday School Board chose to sell off existing stock of the original volume through a British publisher. And the new writer appointed to redo Davies's work, though more conservative than Davies, was as much influenced by the hated historical-critical method and did not reject the work of the earlier volume (Ammerman, 1990; Leonard, 1990).

During the 1960s and 1970s it thus became increasingly clear to traditionalists that they had lost control of Southern Baptist seminaries and agencies. In public, denominational authorities denied these charges, but in private they continued to make sure that the seminaries remained secure from traditionalist calls for change. And control of the seminaries gained in importance as they became the primary source of pastors. Supporting only one seminary at the end of the nineteenth century, the Convention was supporting three by the 1930s, six by the late 1950s, and now lays claim to the world's largest seminary. It took nearly a century for the Southern Baptist convention seminaries to furnish their first 10,000 graduates (1859–1950; see Table 5.4). But the next 10,000 arrived in less than a decade (1951–1960), and the following three decades produced nearly 50,000 more graduates (1961–1989). By the 1980s about half of all Southern Baptist pastors had seminary degrees (Wingo, 1984). Meanwhile there was a rapid decline in part-time pastors who earned their living through a secular pursuit—by 1987 only a quarter of Southern Baptist clergy held outside employment (Lowry, 1989).

By the 1970s, as these shifts took place, the growing awareness that "modernists" controlled the seminaries had two important consequences. First, many young Southern Baptists wishing to become min-

TABLE 5.4

Enrollment and Number of Graduates from Southern Baptist Convention Seminaries, 1930–1990

| Year | Total enrollment | Previous year's graduates | Graduates since founding |
|---|---|---|---|
| 1930–31 | 1,010 | | |
| 1939–40 | 1,345 | | |
| 1950–51 | 4,234 | 640 | 9,946 |
| 1960–61 | 6,038 | 1,277 | 21,573 |
| 1970–71* | 5,555 | 1,139 | 32,988 |
| 1980–81* | 11,957 | 2,264 | 48,527 |
| 1989–90* | 14,798 | 2,226 | 70,084 |

SOURCES: *Annual of the Southern Baptist Convention* and *The Quarterly Review.*
*Excludes seminary extension programs.

isters no longer enrolled in the Convention's seminaries, but went to independent evangelical schools such as Fuller Theological Seminary (McClellan, 1985). Many congregations began to hire only clergy who had attended these independent seminaries. The second consequence was a chronic and increasingly strident public controversy over seminary education. The modernists argued that seminaries should prepare students for the pluralism of the modern society by exposing students to a variety of viewpoints and allowing them to evaluate critically various theological positions. In sharp contrast, the traditionalists viewed this type of exposure as providing little help for ministry in the local church and opening the door for ambivalence, doubt, and heresy. In 1976 Harold Lindsell, a Southern Baptist and former editor of *Christianity Today*, charged that "in almost every case, unorthodoxy has its beginnings in the theological seminaries" (in Barnhart, 1986, p. 74).

All available evidence supports this charge. A survey of seminary students at Southwestern Baptist Theological Seminary, conducted in the early 1970s, found that students in the Master of Divinity program were less orthodox than those pursuing a two-year diploma, and those seeking a doctorate were far less orthodox than either group. Although every student in the diploma program (100%) scored high on an orthodoxy index, 82.7 percent of the Master of Divinity students and only 42.7 percent of the doctoral students scored high on the index (R. C. Thompson, 1974).

More recent data collected by Ammerman (Table 5.5) show that few ministers fell into the modernist camp unless they had a Master of Divinity degree or a doctorate. Even college graduates with no postgraduate degree fell mainly into the traditional and conservative categories. Ministers who had attended seminary were less traditional than those who hadn't, and the longer they attended the less traditional they became.

When reviewing her data on seminaries and colleges, Ammerman (1990, p. 163) concludes: "Colleges and seminaries had created both the ideology and the social networks, both the sources of meaning and belonging, out of which the old establishment was constructed. They were largely responsible for the changes in belief fundamentalists sought to oppose. Our statistical testing of responses from survey respondents confirmed what fundamentalists already knew—their foremost enemy was the denomination's educational system."[10] Moreover, *which* seminary one attended made a great deal of difference. Table 5.6 is based on

TABLE 5.5
Theological Faction by Clergy Educational Level (in percent)

| | High school or less (N = 70) | Some college (N = 48) | College graduate (N = 66) | Master of Divinity (N = 175) | Doctorate (N = 32) | Total (N = 391) |
|---|---|---|---|---|---|---|
| Modernist | 0 | 6 | 8 | 34 | 44 | 21 |
| Conservative | 26 | 38 | 45 | 42 | 31 | 38 |
| Traditional | 74 | 56 | 47 | 24 | 25 | 41 |

SOURCE: Recalculated from Ammerman (1990).

TABLE 5.6
Theological Faction by Seminary Background (in percent)

| | Elite Southern Baptist seminaries* (N = 93) | Other Southern Baptist seminaries† (N = 109) | Independent seminaries (N = 37) | Total (N = 289) |
|---|---|---|---|---|
| Modernist | 53 | 21 | 5 | 30 |
| Conservative | 31 | 47 | 35 | 39 |
| Traditional | 16 | 32 | 60 | 31 |

SOURCE: Recalculated from Ammerman (1990).
NOTE: Calculated for seminary graduates only.
*Southern, Southeastern, and Midwestern seminaries.
†Southwestern, New Orleans, and Golden Gate seminaries.

a national sample of Southern Baptist clergy surveyed by Ammerman (1990). Graduates of the three denominational seminaries that Ammerman rated as "elite" scored as "Modernists" as opposed to "Traditionalists" by more than a three to one margin. Graduates of the three less elite denominational seminaries were substantially less likely to qualify as Modernists, but only a third lined up with the Traditionalists. Only among graduates of independent, nondenominational seminaries did the Traditionalist label predominate.

The Southern Baptist traditionalists did not need these survey data to see what was going on. Each year when they attended conventions they found themselves to be an "outsider majority." They could mobilize the votes to pass strong resolutions, but they could only look on while the denominational bureaucracy pursued actions and sanctioned attitudes that they absolutely rejected. In an effort to heighten awareness to the threat of modernism in the Convention, traditionalists formed the Baptist Faith and Message Fellowship in 1973 to monitor SBC agencies. By 1977 the Pastors' Conference at the annual convention had become a forum for attacking the rising tide of "liberalism" (Leonard, 1990). But though these gatherings allowed traditionalists to vent their feelings, they were useless for reining in the denominational bureaucracy. Without the formal authority of agency administrators or trustees, the traditionalists had no avenue for implementing the changes they deemed necessary.

In 1977 Paul Pressler, a deacon and Sunday school teacher at Houston's Second Baptist Church, received a call from five of his former Sunday school students who were attending Baylor University. They complained that they were "hopelessly confused by their religion course." When Pressler met with his former students and read the text being used in the course, he was appalled that such teaching was prevalent at a Southern Baptist university and decided "to do something" (Hefley, 1983, p. 39). A fellow deacon advised Pressler to meet with a student at New Orleans Seminary, Paige Patterson, "who thinks like you do." Thus began the Pressler-Patterson partnership that was to rock the Convention to its foundations.

This partnership proved successful for at least two reasons. First, it could openly attack denominational institutions or representatives without fear of sanction. As Ammerman (1990, p. 173) points out, "since Pressler was a lay person, and Patterson was in an independent institution, the usual sanctions could not be applied to them." Sympathetic pastors could quietly organize support for the traditionalists' position, and let Pressler and Patterson take the heat.

The second and more important reason was the plan the partnership put together. Pressler, a Texas Appeals Court judge, quickly recognized that it is the Southern Baptist Convention's president who indirectly controls the appointment of trustees for denominational agencies.[11] Because the trustees make policies and control hiring, they provide an avenue for implementing changes throughout the denomination. Pressler later explained: "Conservatives had been fighting battles without knowing what the war was about. The lifeblood of the institutions are trustees. We need to go for the jugular and get to the root of the problem" (Hefley, 1983, p. 40).

Thus the plan: elect a traditionalist to the presidency so that traditionalist control could be restored through the appointment of suitable trustees. In 1979, only two years after the Patterson and Pressler partnership was formed, the traditionalists won the presidency of the Southern Baptist Convention. At first modernists viewed this victory as a fluke, a brief turn to conservatism (Leonard, 1990), but they soon realized that the traditionalists had popular support they simply couldn't match. Ammerman (1990, p. 178) explains that many modernist leaders were "relatively remote from the majority of Baptists." Moreover, even though they were preachers "with polished literary and rhetorical flair," their oratory skills couldn't compare with the popular traditionalists who "were preachers of remarkable ability, able to stir crowds with their words, able to evoke response in their hearers . . . [they] were broadly admired as the leading pulpiteers of the day, even by people who later joined the moderate cause against them" (Ammerman, 1990, p. 178). This appeal has helped traditionalists win the presidency every year since 1979. Modernists have cried foul, but past president Jimmy Draper argues that this is merely a "midcourse correction, with our leadership being responsive to the constituency. A turning back to where we were" (Hefley, 1982, p. 41).

But can they go back to where they were? And is the Patterson-Pressler plan actually working? Theirs was, from the start, a long-term plan. New trustees can be appointed only as serving trustees complete the terms of their appointments, which are often relatively long, or as vacancies occur because of death or resignation. Initially, therefore, the trustees appointed by traditionalist presidents found themselves in the minority, with little opportunity to implement change. It was not until about 1986 that the traditionalists began to be a majority on most of the SBC boards, and thus there has not been much time for the Patterson-Pressler plan to produce results. But a close examination of the impact of traditionalist trustees on the seminaries is revealing.

From the start, the seminaries have been the primary "take-over target" of the traditionalists. Unlike the theology schools of many mainline denominations, the Southern Baptist seminaries rely heavily on the financial support of the Convention. Even today the seminaries receive approximately half of their operating budgets from the Southern Baptist Convention—only 15 percent is raised from student fees (*The Quarterly Review*, 1990). Each of the seminaries depends on the resources of the Convention and is forced to acknowledge the authority of the trustees appointed by the Convention's president.

Thus as the seminary boards came to be dominated by trustees appointed by traditionalist Convention presidents, the seminaries waited for the showdown. But the wholesale changes, anticipated by both sides, have not occurred. Ammerman (1990, p. 245) quotes one traditionalist as saying that there were "no more than three or four real conservatives on the entire faculty at either Southern or Southeastern." Yet not a single faculty member has been fired or forced to resign at Southern. The most significant changes have occurred at Southeastern, where the president, ten administrators, and a third of the faculty resigned between 1987 and 1989 (Ammerman, 1990). But at the remaining four seminaries no one has been forced to resign and few have faced a formal review by the trustees. Moreover, although seminary presidents have agreed to present the conservative point of view to their students, there have been no wholesale changes in the curriculum or in how the courses are taught.

The most significant changes in the seminaries, as well as in other Southern Baptist bureaucracies, have come in the area of hiring. The new trustees have taken an active role in reviewing faculty selections and have held the presidents accountable for the choices made. Even at Southern Baptist Seminary in Louisville, President Roy Honeycutt instructed a faculty search committee to find an inerrantist for an opening in New Testament. But despite some traditionalist success in this area, implementing change through new faculty appointments is even slower than changing the outlook of the boards of trustees. For traditionalists to outnumber moderates among seminary faculties, it will take nearly a generation if traditionalists limit themselves to replacing moderates who retire or resign voluntarily. And despite all the bad publicity directed toward the traditionalists supposedly set to purge seminaries, they have shown no signs thus far of adopting more rapid methods of change.

In the aftermath of the moderate "theft" of Baylor University on September 21, 1990, however, many traditionalists have become impatient. After secret meetings with lawyers and taking elaborate precautions to prevent any hint of his plans from leaking to the traditionalist minority among Baylor regents, President Herbert Reynolds introduced a surprise motion (on the agenda as "miscellaneous business") to amend the school's charter so that only a small minority of regents would henceforth be chosen by the Texas Southern Baptist Convention. President Reynolds had even arranged to have an ally stationed at the State Capitol in Austin to file the amended charter immediately, thus frustrating any potential efforts by traditionalists to seek legal injunctions. President Reynolds defended his actions as necessary to prevent a "power grab" by traditionalists, but of course that was not the way they saw it. The incident stirred up concern that the moderates still hoped to frustrate the will of the Convention and to maintain their hold over the seminaries. The Reverend Jerry Johnson, a twenty-seven-year-old rising star among traditionalists, called for more rapid action to end what he calls the "coverup at Southern." "We given them our money to teach what we do not believe in," he said (Goode, 1991, p. 22).

Once again, the traditionalists have won nearly every major public battle. They have elected presidents, appointed trustees, and passed resolutions that are sympathetic to their position, but control of the seminaries still eludes them. In many ways this is reminiscent of what happened in the late nineteenth century with Toy and Whitsitt. Yet there is an important difference between the seminary battles of that period and those of today. When Toy and Whitsitt were removed, only a small proportion of the clergy were products of Southern Seminary, then the only Southern Baptist seminary. The denomination was still dominated by farmer-preachers who had little use for a seminary education and no contact with the seminary. Today, however, the proportion of bivocational pastors is dropping and the proportion with seminary training continues to rise. Thus the influence of the seminaries is far greater than before.

That this influence is widely resented by rank-and-file Southern Baptists is evident in data on dismissals of local pastors. Clifford J. Tharp (1985) reported that during an eighteen-month period between late 1982 and early 1984 approximately 1,600 Southern Baptist pastors were fired.

Of these, 71 percent were seminary graduates—far higher than the proportion of all Southern Baptists pastors, only 45 percent of whom held seminary degrees in 1982 (Wingo, 1984). It is estimated that the rate at which local congregations fire their pastor has risen by 32 percent since 1984. In 1988 at least 1,390 were fired (Goode, 1991).

Although the immense autonomy of local congregations made it impossible for moderates to evict their traditionalist opponents during their many years of control of the Convention and ultimately gave traditionalists the chance to build up popular support, local autonomy has more recently given the moderates sufficient freedom to build alternative institutions without withdrawing. The Southern Baptist Alliance was formed in 1987 and now issues "alternative" publications, supports "alternative" missions, and recently approved plans for an "alternative" seminary. This freedom of minorities to operate within the Convention inevitably leads to conflict, of course, and it remains to be seen whether an increasingly modernist subculture can sustain itself within a hostile sea of those committed to biblical inerrancy.

Have the Southern Baptists shown that a large and successful religious body can resist the forces that typically transform sects into churches? Maybe.

*Chapter 6*

# *Why Unification Efforts Fail*

In 1959, Eugene Carson Blake, a leader of the United Presbyterian Church who had just completed his term as president of the National Council of Churches, noted that the latest *Yearbook of American Churches* listed 258 separate denominations. Of course, he pointed out, the twenty-four largest of these bodies accounted for more than 80 percent of America's church members. Still, "even twenty-four churches . . . is entirely too many" (1959, p. 76).

Blake's solution was religious unity, to be achieved through what he referred to as the "ecumenical mission" of the churches—a mission to bring about mergers among the Protestant denominations. Blake's call for merger was not restricted to the liberal bodies, which he designated as the "old-line Churches." He wanted a real union. But he recognized that major resistance to ecumenism came from those "who style themselves as 'Bible-believing' Christians" and who embrace many "cultural crudities" (pp. 82, 77). Nonetheless, he suggested to his colleagues that they begin to cultivate leaders of "the conservative churches. . . . to bring these sincere men out of theological isolation and personal provincialism" (p. 83). He acknowledged "the cleavage between unscholarly literal Biblical interpretation and scholarly higher criticism" (p. 83). But he warned that not all the "weaknesses of Biblical interpretation" were to be found among conservatives and concluded that through sincere study of the Bible the theological impediments to union could be overcome.

Blake's aims and observations, which appeared in an edited volume with the confident title *The Ecumenical Era in Church and Society,* were hardly novel. From the beginning, American pluralism has vexed many observers. How are people to be saved if they confront dozens of Christianities, each claiming it has the real truth? To William Warren Sweet ([1930] 1950, p. 424), "Our divisions are indeed the scandal of Christendom." And the solution has always been sought in unification. In 1827 Beecher warned that Finney's "new" form of revivalism must be stopped or "it will prevent the great evangelical assimilation, which is forming in the United States" (Beecher and Nettleton, 1828, p. 98). A decade later a number of religious leaders involved in the antislavery movement gathered in Syracuse "for the purpose of . . . adopting the most feasible methods, to annihilate the existing denominational distinctions." Their concern was that real unity could not be gained on the issue of slavery until the churches "abandon their exclusive creeds, and incorporate nothing in their articles that will shut off their fellowship with any true child of God" (in W. R. Cross, 1950, p. 280). Without a definition of a "true child of God," we cannot determine what Christian doctrines can be retained without excluding some from fellowship. But because in practical terms proposals of this sort reduce to a call to Unitarianism, it is not surprising that nothing came of this ecumenical effort.

Nor a century later, in the 1930s, was any progress toward unification actually in the offing, despite Sweet's ([1930] 1950, p. 424) pronouncement that "there is hope for a better day." True, Sweet was able to list an impressive number of mergers of American Protestant bodies since 1900. But these mergers had all taken place within narrowly defined denominational "families." Baptists had merged with Baptists, Presbyterians with Presbyterians, Lutherans with Lutherans, and Reformed with Reformed. All of this merging was capped by what Sweet called the "largest unification movement to take place in the United States" (p. 425), which, in 1939, joined three denominations: the Methodist Protestant Church, the Methodist Episcopal Church, South, and the Methodist Episcopal Church. The ecumenical aspect of such unions is hard to discover.

By the 1950s, nevertheless, despite the repeated failure of any real progress toward unity, it was so widely believed that massive mergers were at hand that a book was even published to explain ahead of time why it had happened: *The Social Sources of Church Unity,* by Robert Lee

(1960). Among the many reasons cited by Lee, one of the most compelling was simple economics. All else being equal, it is incredibly inefficient to operate so many congregations. Surely even "Bible-believing Christians" could grasp this obvious fact.

In addition to more mundane justifications, proponents of religious unions have always condemned pluralism as sinful and unbiblical.[1] For example, during his stay in Boston, George Whitefield ([1756] 1969, p. 459)—a committed pluralist—severely antagonized local clergy when he claimed: "It was best to preach up the new birth, and the power of godliness, and not to insist so much upon the form: for people would never be brought to one mind as to that; nor did Jesus Christ ever intend it."

Dr. Timothy Cutler immediately challenged Whitefield, "Yes, but He did." Cutler's proof: "Christ prayed, That all might be one, even as Thou Father and I are One" (p. 459). Incredibly, two centuries later this same claim was advanced in the pages of *The Annals of the American Academy of Political and Social Science* by Roswell P. Barnes (1960, pp. 136–137), a well-known Protestant who served as an executive both in the National and the World Council of Churches: "Basically, Christian unity is a given fact derived from a common belief in Jesus Christ as God and Savior. It is, therefore, not created by men, but gratefully acknowledged and manifested. It is furthered and developed by men as they progressively respond in obedience to what they believe to be God's will. Christ prayed for his followers of all time 'that they all may be one.' The ecumenical movement is essentially an expression of conviction, a matter of faith derived from biblical and theological authority."

That same year similar views were affirmed by the popular Jesuit theologian John Courtney Murray. Although Murray admitted that pluralism was inevitable in democratic societies, he felt that there was no theological alternative but to conclude that "religious pluralism is against the will of God" (1960, p. 32). And European theologians, of course, have always known that American religious life is a tower of Babel. Hence Dietrich Bonhoeffer's (1965, p. 94) condescending jibe: "It has been granted to the Americans less than any other nation of the earth to realise on the earth the visible unity of the Church of God."

Sinful and inefficient it may be, but denominationalism continues to prosper in American life, while ecumenical movements have inevitably failed to achieve anything more than peripheral cartels such as the one currently vested in the National Council of Churches. Why is this the case? In reviewing the two major efforts at ecumenism in America during the twentieth century as well as several episodes of cartel formation, we test the proposition offered in Chapter 1: that pluralism is, as Father Murray recognized, the natural condition of any unregulated religious economy and that therefore voluntary ecumenical movements must fail. We also suggest that mergers involving major religious bodies will be limited to denominations already undergoing decline (with the possible exception of mergers within a denominational family).

## Ecumenism and Country Life

In 1860 only one American in five lived in an urban community—that is, a community of more than 2,500 people. By the turn of the century two of five were urbanites and by 1920 more than half of all Americans lived in towns and cities. Although some portion of urban growth was caused by immigration, the bulk occurred because people deserted the countryside for the city.

In the wake of rapid urbanization a great deal of concern was expressed about the potential loss of many virtues and values associated with rural life. These concerns culminated in the appointment of a Commission on Country Life by President Theodore Roosevelt in 1908. The commission held thirty hearings throughout the country and distributed more than a half million questionnaires, of which slightly more than a hundred thousand were returned and partially tabulated. In 1909 the commission issued a report that was soon regarded as having "more influence on rural life in this country than any other document" (Sanderson, 1942, p. 712). Among its many recommendations, the commission proposed the creation of the agricultural extension service, initiation of massive agricultural research and training programs at the nation's land grant colleges and universities, and the inclusion of agricultural and home economics courses in the nation's high schools. Each of these proposals was soon put into effect, but these were only means to an end: the commission called for an all-out effort to "unite the interests of education, organization and religion into one forward movement for rebuilding of rural life" (in Sanderson, 1942, p. 712).

The mention of religion was not incidental. Rather, the importance of the rural church and the special relationship between religion and rural life were central to the commission's whole conception and soon emerged as dominant themes in the "Country Life Movement" that took over the work started by the commission. Kenyon L. Butterfield, president of the Massachusetts Agricultural College and a leading member of the commission, went on to conduct and publish many studies of rural religion and, in 1921, was a founder of the Institute of Social and Religious Research in New York City. We shall have more to report about Butterfield and his associates at the institute in a moment. But first it is useful to consider the fundamental thesis that religion fares better among rural folk than it does among urbanites.

## The Myth of Urban Irreligion

Since the dawn of recorded history, the city has been depicted as a precinct of sin and impiety. Whether the cities were Sodom and Gomorrah, Corinth and Rome, or New York and Chicago, observers have taken it for granted that city life not only encourages vice but also fosters skepticism and doubt—and that the pious life is easier in the hinterlands. John Lancaster Spalding wrote in 1880: "In the city neither the rich nor the poor can realize the infinite charm of the Christian ideal. The heart is troubled there, and God is not in the whirlwind of human passion" ([1880] 1967, p. 8).

Not only prophets and preachers regard the city as wicked and secular. Social scientists also assert that city life is corrosive of the moral order and that urban life is inevitably more permissive than life in the country. As Gideon Sjoberg (1960, p. 340) explained, urban religion sustains norms that "are generally permissive" because the "divergent, and often contradictory, roles, and the new technology ensures a continuous cycle of change, all of which requires flexibility of norms." Moreover, from Durkheim on, sociologists have been certain that the unavoidable tendency toward religious pluralism in cities weakens faith.[2] Indeed, Harvey Cox (1965, p. 1) flatly asserted that secularization has occurred because the "cosmopolitan confrontations of city living exposed the relativity of the myths and traditions men once thought were unquestionable." Similar views inspired Peter Berger's *The Sacred Canopy* (1967), an influential work in the sociology of religion.

Historians of religion have also affirmed the secular atmosphere of the city. American historians have taken it for granted that the city is especially inhospitable to Protestantism. Ahlstrom (1975, p. 194) claimed that one of the "particularly devastating consequences" of urbanization was that "large elements of the new urban population had no contact with any Protestant churches." Similarly, Robert Handy (1969, p. 90) noted: "There is wide agreement that Protestant churches have historically tended to be more at home in rural and town America than in the America of great cities."

But it just isn't so. The growth of cities increased religious participation, and even Protestant churches did better in the cities than in the hinterlands. Suppose the members of the commission (or any historian of American religion since then) had consulted the 1906 report on religious bodies published by the Bureau of the Census (1910). What they would have found are the figures for 1890 and 1906, shown in Table 6.1. In both years the percentage of the population reported to be church members was substantially higher in the principal cities (those of 25,000 residents and larger) than in less urban areas. Moreover, the gap between city and country was increasing. The difference was not an artifact of denomination; when the 1906 figures are transformed into adherence rates, the rate for cities remains higher.

In fact, the gap between the countryside and the city is probably larger than indicated in Table 6.1. Because the rural totals included many small towns, where rates are also higher, the rates for rural areas are inflated. Indeed, when rural reformers sponsored by the Institute of Social and Religious Research conducted a national survey of 140 small towns (250–2,500 residents) in the early 1920s, they found a vast differ-

TABLE 6.1
Rural/Urban Comparisons in Church Membership
(in percent)

|  | Church membership rate | | Adherence rate* |
|---|---|---|---|
|  | *1890* | *1906* | *1906* |
| Principal cities | 37.9 | 46.9 | 56 |
| Outside principal cities | 31.2 | 36.3 | 50 |
| Nationwide | 32.7 | 39.1 | 51 |

SOURCE: Church membership rate from Bureau of the Census (1910, vol. 1, p. 70).
*The adherence rate includes children in the membership totals.

ence between the small town and the countryside. The percentage of the population affiliated with a church was far lower for those living in the country than it was for the villagers, regardless of region (see Table 6.2).

Why is religious mobilization higher in cities and towns? For one thing, it is easier for people to get to church—many farmers live a considerable distance from the nearest church. But the more important reason is that people in cities, and even in small towns, are more likely to have access to a church that is right for them. That is, the primary impact of religious pluralism is to provide a broad spectrum of specialized religious firms competing to attract and hold a segment of the market. When we analyzed data for the 150 largest American cities in 1906, we found that cities with a greater degree of religious pluralism[3] had higher rates of religious adherence (Finke and Stark, 1988). Rather than being a source of secularization and religious decline, pluralism strengthens religion.[4]

The question remains, however, which religious groups were best suited to the urban environment. Is it true that Protestantism is inherently rural? An obvious way to settle that issue is to calculate the proportion of members resident in urban areas for the larger denominations (see Table 6.3). In 1926, Protestant bodies were about as urban as Catholics and most were far more urban than the nation as a whole

## TABLE 6.2
## Village/Countryside Comparisons in Church Membership for 140 Villages, 1923

| Region | Percentage of the population belonging to a church | |
| --- | --- | --- |
| | *Village* | *Countryside* |
| Middle Atlantic | 41 | 25 |
| South | 45 | 28 |
| Middle West | 33 | 26 |
| Far West | 21 | 14 |

SOURCE: Adapted from Brunner, Hughes, and Patten (1927, p. 183).

TABLE 6.3
Percentage of Church Membership in Urban Areas, 1926

| Denomination | Percentage membership urban |
|---|---|
| Protestant Episcopal | 83.5 |
| Roman Catholic | 79.6 |
| Presbyterian Church in the United States of America (Northern) | 71.0 |
| Congregational | 69.3 |
| Northern Baptist Convention | 68.6 |
| United Lutheran Church in America | 67.3 |
| Presbyterian Church in the United States (Southern) | 59.9 |
| Disciples of Christ | 54.6 |
| Methodist Episcopal Church | 54.2 |
| Evangelical Lutheran Synod Conference of America | 53.6 |
| Methodist Episcopal, South | 35.6 |
| Southern Baptist Convention | 28.0 |
| All church members | 64.4 |
| All Americans | 53.2 |

SOURCE: Calculated from Bureau of the Census (1930, vol. 1, pp. 82–90).

(reflecting superior urban membership rates). Episcopalians were more urban than Catholics, and even the Lutherans and the Methodists outside the South were as urban as the nation as a whole. Keep in mind, too, that the apparent ruralism of Southern Methodists and Baptists reflected the fact that in 1926 two thirds of Southerners lived in rural areas, rather than any special affinity of these denominations for rural residents.

The Commission on Country Life was thus wrong to suppose that the health of religion, and especially of Protestantism, required the renewal of rural America. Even had the commission's members read these census data (and some of them probably did), however, they would not have changed course. Their agenda was not simply the renewal of rural religion or, indeed, of rural life. They had very firm notions about what *kind* of religion as well as what *kind* of social and economic philosophy they wanted rural Americans to embrace. In addition, many of their plans for rural America were based on misguided, and sometimes arrogant, assumptions.

## The Myth of the Country Church Crisis

Two years after the Commission on Country Life offered its report, Warren H. Wilson (1911b, p. 677) informed readers of the *American Journal of Sociology* that "the growth of the cities has been in part at the expense of the country" and that "the community life in the country has generally been destroyed." But Wilson's main concern was the "decay of the country church," which he attributed to two causes. The first was the wasteful rural economy. Wilson claimed that progress toward renewing rural America could occur only if farmers ceased taking an individualistic approach and began to farm in more cooperative fashion. He also charged that the individualistic economic orientation of American farmers was reflected in their preference for competitive churches. This resulted in the second cause of the decline of rural churches, a "wasteful ecclesiastical economy." He explained: "The country church has been a mere means for distributing the hope of personal salvation. . . . Any small group of believers has been at liberty to build a meeting-house and maintain an organization. National denominations have been all too willing to support these competing congregations in the country community. We have, therefore, in almost all the older states too many country churches" (p. 681). Wilson warned that a "divided religious ministry . . . is fatal to the interests of religion" and proclaimed that "church unity . . . is forced upon the churches as a means of arresting the decay of religious institutions" (p. 688). Two years later, after a survey of churches in Indiana, Wilson (1913, p. 23) complained of widespread competition for members and new buildings and groused that "churches feel they are doing well if they can leave each other alone."

Wilson's conclusions on the necessity of church unity were based on two commonly held assumptions: first, that the growth of the cities led to the decline of the rural population, and second, that owing to the oversupply of rural churches, all denominations were being forced to close congregations and to subsidize others. These were simply the facts—"so well known" as to need hardly any discussion, according to Wilson (1911b). Nevertheless, both claims are false.

It is true that at the turn of the century urban areas were growing rapidly and that the *proportion* of the population living in rural areas was declining. In terms of absolute numbers, however, the population of rural America was *growing*, not declining, in this era. Consider that in 1890, 41 million people lived in rural America. In 1920 they numbered 51 million and by 1940 this total had risen to 57 million. Many young men and women were abandoning rural life in this period, of course, but the rate of natural increase in rural areas could sustain growth despite high rates of migration. Consequently, the closure of rural churches could not have been the result of a decline in the potential church population.

How could the reformers have been mistaken about the "fact" that rural churches were closing left and right? It depends on what kind of churches one counts. If we confine our attention to the mainline churches, Wilson's comments are not only accurate but prophetic. Between 1916 and 1926 the Presbyterian Church in the U.S.A. lost 826 churches ( − 8.5 percent), the Congregationalists dropped 872 ( − 14.8 percent), the Disciples lost 748 ( − 8.9 percent), and the Methodist Episcopal Church lost 3,185 ( − 10.9 percent). Many, if not most, of these losses were country and village churches.

But if we broaden our view to take in the entire landscape of rural American religion, the picture looks very different. Between 1916 and 1926 there was a *net increase* of 4,667 in the total number of American churches. The number of Lutheran and Catholic churches increased by 2,746, but this can account for only a modest part of the gain in churches. Given that the mainline churches mentioned above had lost 5,631 congregations, more than ten thousand new churches were needed to reach the new total. If the mainline was declining, someone else must have been quickly gaining. In addition to the Southern Baptists, who gained 1,178 churches, the "someones" included the Assemblies of God ( + 553 percent), Church of God (Cleveland, Tenn.) ( + 442 percent), Christian and Missionary Alliance ( + 169 percent), Church of the Nazarene ( + 577 percent), Churches of Christ ( + 656 percent), Free Will Baptists ( + 274 percent), the Pentecostal Holiness Church ( + 60 percent), and the Salvation Army ( + 310 percent). Only the last was an urban movement. The other growing denominations tended to be even more rural than those that were declining. The Southern Baptists, for example, increased their total number of churches by 5 percent, despite having more than 90 percent of their churches in rural areas.[5] Of the 553 new churches added by the Assemblies of God in this decade, approximately half were in rural areas. The "decay" of the country church was limited to the mainline: the evangelical Protestant sects still flourished.

If the rural population was increasing and new rural churches were opening, why did Wilson (1911b, p. 688) conclude that church unity is "forced upon the churches as a means of arresting the decay of religious institutions"? The answer: because the "respectable" churches were struggling for survival in the rural areas. As we saw in Chapters 3 and 5, churches relying on well-paid professionals are unable to survive in rural areas where only small congregations can be gathered. And in the early twentieth century the rural churches were small. Surveys conducted in 1920 showed that the average congregation in towns had 144 members, the average village church had 84 members, and the average country church only 46 (Morse and Brunner, 1923). According to Butterfield and his colleagues, an oversupply of rural churches had reduced the size of congregations so that most were made up of a tiny band of worshipers who could not even afford to pay the salary needed to secure an educated and qualified minister. Many congregations were forced to make do with uneducated locals or to share a pastor with several other congregations. Worse yet, many of these rural churches were subsidized by their denominations and therefore drained valuable home mission funds from more worthwhile causes. For mainline denominations, unity was a way of reducing subsidies, paying for full-time clergy, and uniting against the growing threat of sectarianism.

Thus an unacknowledged source of concern about the "wasteful ecclesiastical economy" was that the "respectable" denominations were not faring well in competition with the "emotional sects" (Brunner, 1927), who did not have to subsidize salaries in order to staff their rural churches. The actual country church crisis thus consisted of two factors: the decline of mainline churches and the growth of sectarian groups. For the rural reformers of the early twentieth century the sectarian churches were part of the problem, not the solution. Like the American Home Missionary Society of the early nineteenth century, not just any church counted—it had to be the right kind of church and served by the right kind of clergy.

But for all of the concern about the minister's training and salary, it is doubtful that rural congregations were much better off if they were served by a seminary-educated pastor—local farmer-preachers had long seemed adequate to the tasks at hand. Such an objection would have been dismissed as fatuous or heretical by the activists in the Country Life Movement, however. They knew what was wrong. Moreover, they knew how to fix it.

## God's Sociology and Rural Ecumenism

In 1912, during the second quadrennial convention of the Federal Council of Churches—the forerunner of today's National Council of Churches—a dozen men committed to solving the problem of the rural churches met in Kenyon Butterfield's Chicago hotel room to form a rural section of the American Sociological Society (Madison, 1986). This section sought to encourage the denominations to create research departments with a primary emphasis on conducting massive surveys of rural churches and to formulate plans for renewal based on their results. This wedding of sociology and religious renewal had by then become commonplace—in 1900 the highly respected Charles E. Hayward had written: "The sociological movement is born of God, and is destined to be the mightiest power behind the Gospel the world has ever known" (in Madison, 1986, p. 647). And in 1911 Warren H. Wilson explained that though the home missions program of the churches had long been directed to the geographical frontier, now home missions "are based upon the discovery of a frontier no longer geographical, but sociological" (1911b, p. 682).

Butterfield, Hayward, Wilson, and a host of others, including Charles Otis Gill, Edmund deS. Brunner, Paul L. Vogt, and H. Paul Douglass, men with formal training in both theology and sociology, were soon conducting rural church studies across the country. Everywhere they made the same diagnosis: "cut-throat competition" (Burr, 1924) was destroying the rural church. In Wilson's (1911a, p. 35) words, "communities cannot be built out of competition: they must be dominated by union." He went on to condemn the belief commonly held by the "household farmer" that "country churches are maintained by competition." A highly influential report by Charles Otis Gill and Gifford Pinchot, published by the Federal Council of Churches, claimed in 1913: "With the whole world turning to combined or cooperative action as the basis of efficiency, the program of the country church continues to deal wholly with individuals, and hence remains defective and one-sided" (in Madison, 1986, p. 652).

Charles J. Galpin (1923, p. 287), a major figure in early rural sociology, thought even church architecture contributed to the cooperative spirit: "It is the small, weak, pastorless church, poorly located, which tends to surrender agriculture to destructive individualism. It is the strong church, with noble permanent architecture, properly located, with a capable resident pastor, which unifies agriculture: a unified agriculture, in time, matures the church." According to Benson Y. Landis (1922, p. 70), who served as editor of the *Yearbook of American Churches* for twenty-five years: "This weeding out process cannot begin too soon. Many churches deserve extinction. They are sectarian in spirit, lack community vision, and exist for the worship of a mere handful of individuals."

These authors seldom failed to remind readers that their conclusions were based on "scientific investigations" that were done not out of preconceptions or commitments "but simply to ascertain exact facts" (Madison, 1986). The cure for the rural churches was also justified in the name of science and efficiency. Landis (1922, p. 70) proposed that the solution to the "over-churching" of rural America was to "eliminate the large numbers of extra churches which are not worth what they cost." And the way to eliminate extra churches was to merge them into nondenominational Protestant community churches.

The campaign for rural ecumenism was given impetus by the Interchurch World Movement (IWM), founded in 1919. Under its auspices, sociologists intent on merging rural churches soon produced detailed plans and justifications for their cause. Under the direction of Edmund Brunner (and heavily funded by John D. Rockefeller, Jr.), the IWM published two volumes from its 1920 World Survey Conference that laid out specific guidelines for a minimum standard of efficiency: "There should not be . . . more than one church for one thousand . . . population. [At a minimum, each church must have] a resident pastor, adequate equipment for worship, religious education and community service; regular worship and preaching; purposeful pastoral visitation; adequate financial program; organized graded church school; enlistment and training of local leaders . . . adequate provision for recreation and social life; and definite, cordial cooperation with other churches of the community" (in Madison, 1986, p. 658).

Soon after this report was released, Landis expanded greatly on what he called the "Par Standard for Country Churches." Under his proposal a full-time pastor was to receive no less than $1,200 a year and a rent-free modern parsonage. In addition, all churches must have an organ (or at least a piano), toilets, a well-equipped kitchen, and a moving picture projector (or at least a stereopticon).

It seemed clear that the only way such standards could be met by rural churches required that small churches merge to create a larger "community church." The reformers suggested that mergers might be achieved in several ways. A denomination could withdraw from a community and merge its congregation with that of another denomination, which could return the favor by withdrawing from some other community. Or local churches could merge and maintain an affiliation with the denomination having the greater local support. A third option was to create a federated church within which individual members retained ties to various denominations.

But however it was to be done, rural church reformers were confident that church unity was the wave of the future and the salvation of rural churches and communities. Just as Robert Lee was to do nearly fifty years later, sociologists hurried to explain how it all would come to pass. John Hargreaves (1914, pp. 258–259) wrote in the *American Journal of Sociology* that the rural churches would soon follow a trend of consolidation similar to that of rural schools. He predicted that: "The community churches of today are very few in number, but before ten years have passed they will be all over the land, and the countryside will have come to its own." A decade later, however, the 1926 religious census reported only 301 federated churches out of a total of 167,864 churches in rural areas. Country churches might be small, but they weren't merging.

## Barriers to Unification

Why didn't the rural churches obey the logic of efficiency and merge? The most important reason was that rural people did not think that they had too many churches or that a church lacking an organ was inadequate. When reformers noted with disdain that most rural clergy thought their primary job was to "preach and conduct weddings and funerals" rather than to pursue the liberal agenda of the social gospel, the great majority of rural Christians said "Amen" (Madison, 1986). The reformers demanded that "the old efficiency which was reckoned in new converts and new congregations must be replaced by a new efficiency reckoned in social service" (Madison, 1986, p. 650). But they found that people went to church in search of salvation, not social service. Indeed, the reformers seemed to have nearly forgotten about religion altogether. Questions about the doctrinal basis for unification went virtually unasked, let alone answered, in the voluminous publications

# SCORE CARD
## (*Concluded*)

| | 1 | 2 | 3 |
|---|---|---|---|
| **V. RELIGIOUS SCHOOL ROOMS** . . . . . | | | 200 |
|   A. Location and connection . . . . . . . . . . | 15 | 15 | |
|   B. Assembly room . . . . . . . . . . . . . . . . . | | 60 | |
|     1. Size and shape . . . . . . . . . . . . . . . | 10 | | |
|     2. Seating . . . . . . . . . . . . . . . . . . . . | 8 | | |
|     3. Illumination . . . . . . . . . . . . . . . . . | 10 | | |
|     4. Walls, ceiling and floor . . . . . . . . | 10 | | |
|     5. Stage . . . . . . . . . . . . . . . . . . . . . | 10 | | |
|     6. Musical equipment . . . . . . . . . . . | 5 | | |
|     7. Visualization equipment . . . . . . . | 5 | | |
|     8. Auxiliaries . . . . . . . . . . . . . . . . . | 2 | | |
|   C. Class rooms . . . . . . . . . . . . . . . . . . | | 90 | |
|     1. Adequacy of number . . . . . . . . . | 30 | | |
|     2. Size and shape . . . . . . . . . . . . . . | 15 | | |
|     3. Seats and desks . . . . . . . . . . . . . | 10 | | |
|     4. Illumination . . . . . . . . . . . . . . . . | 10 | | |
|     5. Walls and ceilings . . . . . . . . . . . | 5 | | |
|     6. Floors . . . . . . . . . . . . . . . . . . . . | 5 | | |
|     7. Blackboards and bulletins . . . . . . | 5 | | |
|     8. Doors and closets . . . . . . . . . . . . | 5 | | |
|     9. Instructional equipment . . . . . . . | 5 | | |
|   D. Cloak rooms and wardrobes . . . . . . . | 15 | 15 | |
|   E. Superintendent's office . . . . . . . . . . . | 10 | 10 | |
|   F. Supply rooms . . . . . . . . . . . . . . . . . . | 10 | 10 | |
| **VI. COMMUNITY SERVICE ROOMS** . . . | | | 190 |
|   A. Rooms for general use . . . . . . . . . . . . | | 60 | |
|     1. Recreation and dining . . . . . . . . . | 30 | | |
|     2. Kitchen . . . . . . . . . . . . . . . . . . . | 15 | | |
|     3. Library and reading room . . . . . . . | 15 | | |
|   B. Rooms for social service . . . . . . . . . . | | 70 | |
|     1. Women and mothers' room . . . . . . | 15 | | |
|     2. Girls' club rooms . . . . . . . . . . . . . | 10 | | |
|     3. Men's club room . . . . . . . . . . . . . | 15 | | |
|     4. Boys' club rooms . . . . . . . . . . . . | 10 | | |
|     5. Nurses' and rest room . . . . . . . . . | 8 | | |
|     6. Day nursery room . . . . . . . . . . . . | 5 | | |
|     7. Civic center . . . . . . . . . . . . . . . . | 5 | | |
|     8. Social workers' office . . . . . . . . . | 2 | | |
|   C. Recreation and athletic rooms . . . . . | | 60 | |
|     1. Gymnasium . . . . . . . . . . . . . . . . | 20 | | |
|     2. Locker rooms . . . . . . . . . . . . . . . | 10 | | |
|     3. Showers . . . . . . . . . . . . . . . . . . | 10 | | |
|     4. Swimming pool . . . . . . . . . . . . . | 5 | | |
|     5. Hand-ball court . . . . . . . . . . . . . | 5 | | |
|     6. Game and amusement rooms . . . . | 5 | | |
|     7. Bowling alley . . . . . . . . . . . . . . . | 5 | | |
|       Total possible score . . . . . . . . . . . | 1,000 | 1,000 | 1,000 |

The *Standards for City Church Plants* of the Interchurch World Movement included a ten-page introduction, a three-page "Score Card" (of which the final page is shown here), forty pages of detailed instructions on scoring, a six-page appendix offering sample specifications for pipe organs, and another fifteen-page appendix outlining the data to be collected before the actual scoring could begin. The organization also published a *Standards for Rural Church Plants*. These publications were offered "for use in measuring the adequacy of church and religious educational plants" (Interchurch World Movement, 1920). (Courtesy of the Billy Graham Center Museum, Wheaton, Ill.)

of the movement. To the extent that matters of doctrine were discussed at all they were dismissed as trivial—the "minutiae of creed"—or were condemned as "dogma" (Madison, 1986). Yet the reformers' own research studies found time and again that people cared a great deal about doctrine and about their differences over what Whitefield had identified as "the form" of belief and worship.

No matter what sociological theologians no longer believed, most rural Americans saw an important difference between adult and infant baptism and recognized that matters of great significance were involved in disputes over whether salvation was by faith alone or by a combination of faith and works. Never mind that scientific sociologists condemned those who clung to such outmoded ideas or castigated those who abandoned community churches for the "emotional sects"; rural America simply didn't care about such criticism (Brunner, 1927; Brunner, Hughes, and Patten, 1927; Madison, 1986).

Indeed, when reformers traveled forth to instruct rural congregations in these matters, it was they who were regarded as out of touch. An informant in Michigan told an investigator that "countryfolk would go to hell before they would leave their church" (in Madison, 1986, p. 666). And a farmer commented that she was "very weary of rural uplifters and country-life specialists who live in New York City. . . . If the city folks would only let us alone, there would be no rural problem" (in Jent, 1924, p. 126).

In the end, rural Americans were right. Perhaps the most amazing aspect about this whole interlude is that the essential good health of rural churches was staring the sociological reformers right in the face. Table 6.4 is adapted from one of the most influential works of the period, Brunner's *Village Communities* (1927). Where the IWM ideal of only one church per 1,000 population was met, only 27 percent of the population belonged to a church. In contrast, in the "lamentably overchurched" communities where four or more congregations competed for members, 43 percent of the population belonged. Similarly, the percentage enrolled in Sunday schools was more than twice as high in the "overchurched" communities as in those that conformed to the ideal.

We hasten to note that Brunner was a competent statistician who was entirely aware that far higher rates of participation obtained in the "overchurched" communities. And although he didn't put it very generously, he did report this relationship: "Judged by these superficial tests of their total impact on the community, competitive denominational churches would seem to succeed in proportion to their relative

## TABLE 6.4
## Pluralism and Participation in Rural Areas, 1923–1925

| | Number of churches per 1,000 population | | | |
| --- | --- | --- | --- | --- |
| | *One* | *Two* | *Three* | *Four or more* |
| Percentage who belong to a church | 27.4 | 36.0 | 34.8 | 43.4 |
| Percentage enrolled in Sunday schools | 15.8 | 22.3 | 25.2 | 37.4 |
| Percentage with a resident minister | 55.7 | 46.3 | 38.7 | 30.1 |

SOURCE: Adapted from Brunner (1927, p. 74).

number. An organized church of each small sectarian group enlists more people (1927, p. 73).

Brunner's own view, however, was that things were not really as they seemed. He was quick to note that much of the "competition was not so much among the established denominations" as it was between such bodies and the "newer emotional sects." Thus he reasoned that church unions could proceed among the respectable churches, and it mattered little if the emotional sects held back. These he characterized as "on the fringes" of the community and reduced to meeting "in tents, vacant stores, halls, or homes." When such groups did have their own church buildings, these were "largely inexpensive structures." As to their clergy, they usually were "untrained and poorly paid, if paid at all. Many are laymen." As to their membership, Brunner characterized them as a pathetic lot, including one group he described as "a poor class of mixed blood and of moronic intelligence" (1927, pp. 75–76).

High rates of church membership that included such riffraff were apparently not a significant trade-off for the elimination of overchurching. In the paragraph immediately following his admission that more churches meant more participation, Brunner returned to the theme that competition prevented the "concentration of forces" needed to provide the "minimum program of conventional church activities." He also noted that although his study was not able "to measure the spiritual effects of overchurching" these were known to be dire. Finally, Brunner kept returning to the issue of minister's pay and education, something he and his fellow reformers seemed to prize above all else: "[unified churches] were able to pay an unusually high salary to their ministers, thereby securing a higher than ordinary proportion of full-time resident ministers with a liberal education" (1927, p. 80).

Table 6.4 bears him out. Communities with few churches per 1,000 were more likely to have a resident, professional clergyman. But unless we are willing to assume that religion is somehow healthier where fewer people take part in it, then it is not at all obvious that professional clergy were a plus in rural America.

In any event, not even a God-given sociology was able to produce any significant ecumenical movement among rural American Protestants. The people who mattered, those who sat in the pews and paid the bills, didn't think anything was wrong with denominationalism—and they still don't.

## The Mainline Cartel

The Federal Council of Churches was organized in Philadelphia by delegates from thirty-three Protestant denominations in 1908. The aims of the council were ecumenical and political. In its first public pronouncement, the council committed itself to a lengthy statement of political faith in which it called for enactment of a list of social reforms that included a minimum wage, pensions, disability payments, a reduced workweek, and the "most equitable division of the products of industry that can ultimately be devised"—all of which prompted Ahlstrom (1975, vol. 2, p. 72) to characterize the delegates as the "praying wing of Progressivism." On matters of religious faith the council was far less explicit, avoiding all mention of doctrine except for this reference in the preamble to its constitution: "the essential oneness of the Christian Churches of America, in Jesus Christ as their Lord and Saviour" (Ahlstrom, vol. 2, p. 271).

On the ecumenical agenda, the aims of the council included the replacement of the many "redundancies" resulting from denominational competition with coordinated and consolidated activities conducted by interdenominational commissions and boards. Although the long-term

Built in 1914, this small church in rural Colorado would have received a poor rating by Interchurch World Movement standards. The Churches of Christ denomination did not condone the use of instrumental music in the worship service, were opposed to the "modern pastor," and discouraged anything that fostered pride and worldliness—including immodest church facilities. Yet the Churches of Christ had a net increase of 656 churches (+12%) between 1916 and 1926, with 86 percent of all their churches located in rural areas. (From Adams, 1970.)

goal was unification, in the meantime the council would allow Protestantism to speak with one authoritative voice.

Because many Protestant bodies, including the huge Southern Baptist Convention, did not belong to the council, it was never an "authentic voice of Protestantism," as Ahlstrom (1975, vol. 2, p. 272) pointed out. Nor were the council's efforts to eliminate "needless" competition and duplications of effort among Protestant bodies really inclusive efforts at rationalization and unification. Instead, the council resorted to illusions based on cartel arrangements among its members. These were presented to the public as interdenominational and ecumenical in precisely the same way that, a century earlier, the American Home Missionary Society claimed to be serving unchurched areas that actually abounded in Baptist and Methodist congregations.

In the long run these cartels not only proved ineffective but probably harmed those denominations that entered into them. In the short run, however, some of these efforts were quite successful. Perhaps the most significant of these involved the way in which the council used a powerful cartel arrangement to restrict access to radio and television time so that, authentic or not, the public voice of American Protestantism tended to speak only the language of liberalism and ecumenism.

## The Media Cartel

In 1960 a former executive of the National Council of Churches noted that having brought order to "the allocation of time *among themselves* on radio and television" was a major accomplishment of NCC members (Barnes, 1960, p. 137, emphasis added). He pointed out that "if it were not for the broadly representative National Council of Churches, there would be competition among the churches in radio and television broadcasting of religious programs."

But that same year the competition for media time that the council had worked so hard to prevent began to appear. The Federal Communications Commission, reversing its long-standing policy that only free air time counted toward radio and television stations' public service contribution, ruled that henceforth paid programming could be given public service credit. This decision, which received little attention when it was made, broke the cartel through which members of the National Council (and the Federal Council before it) had monopolized air time.

Ever since it began regulating radio stations in the 1920s, the Federal Communications Commission has classified religious programming as public service broadcasting. Because all stations are required to devote a minimum percentage of air time to public service and because the production costs of much religious broadcasting amount to little or nothing, stations have for decades found it attractive to offer free time to religious groups. Faced with dozens of groups seeking their free time, however, the stations sought guidance about whom to choose (Whitehead, 1982). Only one visible body claimed to represent a broad spectrum of the most "respectable" faiths—the Federal Council of Churches and its local chapters. Somehow these groups never suggested that free time go to evangelicals or other outsiders, preferring instead to keep it all for council members.

The council's monopoly on air time was further strengthened as it succeeded in persuading the national networks not to sell time for religious broadcasts. NBC never sold time to religious broadcasters, nor did ABC (which in its early days was a second NBC network, known as the Blue Network). CBS, which began in 1927, did sell time to religious broadcasters for its first several years, but ceased doing so in 1931. Only the Mutual Broadcasting System continued to sell commercial time to religious broadcasters and thus allowed evangelical Protestants their only national access to radio. But even with limited access the evangelicals produced the most popular religious shows on radio: Charles E. Fuller's "Old-Fashioned Revival Hour"; "The Lutheran Hour," sponsored by the Missouri Synod Lutherans; and the "Voice of Prophecy," which was produced by the Seventh-day Adventists. These shows attracted millions of listeners. Elsewhere on the network dial, however, American Protestantism was whatever the Department of Religious Radio of the Federal Council of Churches said it was. The council signed up many local stations to receive free religious programming in exchange for an agreement to refuse to sell air time to noncouncil denominations.

Noting that broadcasts by evangelical Protestants, "and others of the same stripe, have long been distasteful to liberal church leaders" (Crowe, 1944, p. 973), a campaign was mounted in 1944 through the auspices of the Federal Council to persuade the Mutual network to observe the cartel arrangement. The central claim was that only by discontinuing the sale of radio time to religious groups could the nation be spared the din of fundamentalism on the air waves (Whitehead and Conlan, 1978). The arrogant tones of this campaign can be seen in the accompanying excerpts from the *Christian Century*. In addition to the campaign against the Mutual radio "loophole," local committees of clergy were formed in many communities to seek similar policies at local stations. Miron A. Morrill (1945, p. 461) proposed that such committees should solve "this radio problem" by bringing sufficient pressure to bear so as to "claim our fair share of time over local radio stations, leaving national broadcasting to the Federal Council, which can do it better."

Charles Fuller *(right)*, with his chorus director, Leland Green. Despite being banned from every major radio network, Charles Fuller's "Old-Fashioned Revival Hour" remained one of the most popular religious radio programs. (Courtesy of the Billy Graham Center Museum, Wheaton, Ill.)

The campaign appeared to achieve rapid success when Mutual adopted new rules for paid religious programming, effective September 14, 1944. First, such programs could not run longer than thirty minutes. Second, no air time could be used to solicit funds to pay for the broadcasts. Third, paid religious programming would be aired only on Sunday mornings (when most of the regular listeners to Mutual's popular religious shows would be in church).

Thus by the end of 1944 the council media cartel seemed in complete control of network religious broadcasting. But the loss of access to the Mutual network prompted evangelical Protestants to respond. Their first, and most dramatic, response was to buy time on scores of local stations across the nation, thus inventing syndication. That is, rather than offer a live feed to a hook-up of local stations as the networks did, transcriptions were sent to local stations to fill the time slot purchased from each. There were too many struggling local stations with too much

# The Christian Century Campaign
# for "Good" Religious Broadcasting

### February 4, 1942: "Religion on the Air"

... Dr. Fred Eastman ... has been studying religious programs on Chicago radio. Seventeen stations submitted their religious programs to the analysis on which Professor Eastman reports.... Seventy-seven programs, filling 46 hours of broadcasting, were studied. Of these, 54 were Sunday programs. Of the Protestant programs, 61 per cent were found to be fundamentalist in character and this did not include the approximately 100 programs which are broadcast every week by the station owned by the Moody Bible Institute.... the report ... emphasizes the fact that religious broadcasting is overloaded with talk, that much of it is on a low level of taste and artistic performance.

### February 16, 1944: "Religious Radio Programs Need Much Improvement"

In most religious broadcasts there is too much talk—that is, preaching and exhortation—and too little use of other radio techniques of proved effectiveness, such as dramatization, forums, round table discussions and great music. The talk is not only excessive in quantity but, on average, not very good in quality. The religious program too often impresses the critical listener as being a cheap show, with too much sentimentality, too little artistry, and a too crude appeal for contributions. Some of the most blatant appeals for money seem to be most successful in getting it, to the point of making a few of these enterprises very profitable—which, it would seem, is a fact about the listening public quite as a much as a fact about the broadcasting evangelists.... A religious broadcast without a sermon might offer attractive and edifying possibilities.

### March 22, 1944: "Mutual to End Radio Religious Begging"

... the Mutual Broadcasting System ruled that after next September 14 all religious programs over its network shall be forbidden to solicit funds. Just how much of a sacrifice Mutual was making is shown by its report for last year, which revealed that out of a total of $12,527,000 paid for time on the air, $3,367,000 came from seven religious broadcasters, most of whom have specialized in raising money by appeals

*(continued)*

during their programs ... *Old-Fashioned Revival Hour* led by Charles E. Fuller, spent $1,566,130 last year ... *The Lutheran Hour* (about $500,000 last year); the *Voice of Prophecy*, a Seventh Day Adventist program ($395,420); the *Young People's Church of the Air* ($395,420); and the *Wesley Radio League* ($172,384). The other leading chains— National, Columbia and Blue—have never permitted religious organizations to buy time or to ask for money.

### August 23, 1944: "Religion on the Air," by Charles M. Crowe

Mutual's action will not remove the commercial type of program from the air—by which I mean the program whose time is paid for by the preacher or the church group. It already has been announced that *The Lutheran Hour*, the *Young People's Church of the Air* and the *Voice of Prophesy* (Seventh Day Adventist) will continue on the same network earlier in the day but without solicitation of funds. These programs evidently have a large enough clientele so that they can be supported by direct mail appeals for money to those who write in for free gifts or for copies of sermons....

The *Old Fashioned Revival Hour* and others ... will utilize a new network, the Associated Broadcasting Corporation, formed to handle such religious programs.... Solicitation of funds will be permitted.... This new network ... is composed in the main of smaller stations.

These programs and others of the same stripe, have long been distasteful to liberal church leaders, to much of the listening public and to network officials ... the new Mutual policy will serve only to intensify the problem.... The network religious radio program racket, capitalized by independent superfundamentalist revivalists, will not be eliminated until Mutual goes the whole way and bans paid religious programs altogether, as the other networks have done,

The National Association of Broadcasters, leading radio trade organization, has been powerless thus far to establish or enforce regulations covering paid religious programs. Perhaps the only way such programs can be eliminated is by a ruling from the Federal Communications Commission against the sale of time for religious broadcasting, coupled with a parallel ruling requiring each station and network to give a specified minimum allotment of suitable time each week to religious programs.

time to sell for local clergy committees to be effective in promulgating policies against purchased time for religious broadcasts. The second response of evangelical Protestants was to organize the National Religious Broadcasters, which launched a vigorous campaign to redress inequities in radio access. In the long run this move was as significant as syndication, for eventually the NRB succeeded in influencing the FCC to count paid religious broadcasts as public service time. Still, for many years the evangelicals continued to be discriminated against in terms of media access.

The advent of television initially strengthened the grip of the liberal cartel over religious broadcasting (Hadden and Shupe, 1988). To this day evangelicals remain locked out of network television and must rely on syndication over local stations (or their own cable stations). During the 1950s the Broadcasting and Film Commission of the National Council of Churches again tried to exclude the evangelicals from local access by campaigning in various states for a prohibition on paid religious broadcasting. But, as with radio, neither the council nor local clerical committees could gain substantial control over local television stations. In consequence, evangelicals bought time on local stations, and as they had pioneered on radio, they produced syndicated shows that were broadcast by hundreds of stations a week. By the 1970s evangelicals operated their own cable channels.

By being excluded from free radio and television time, the evangelicals were forced to develop the means to pay for their broadcasts. Hence, when the 1960 FCC ruling caused local stations to replace free religious time with paid broadcasts, this posed no new barrier to the evangelicals; their broadcasts had already attracted a substantial audience willing to send in contributions to keep the shows on the air. In contrast, the elimination of free time virtually silenced religious broadcasts by the council and its affiliated denominations. This is precisely what Adam Smith would have predicted. A free ride in terms of radio and television time meant that the NCC member bodies, like the established churches Smith had criticized two centuries earlier, were soon "reposing themselves upon their benefices" until they "were incapable of making vigorous exertion" ([1776] 1937, p. 740).

## Misperceiving the Mainline

Nearly every discussion of religion in the American news media distinguishes certain denominations as the "mainline" churches while applying terms indicative of extremism, such as "sects," "fundamentalists," or "the Religious Right," to the rest of the nation's religious bodies. That a set of denominations enrolling only a minority of Protestants, and whose members had been notable for their inactivity and their rapidly declining numbers, can still be identified as the mainline is a tribute both to the public relations skills of the National Council of Churches and to the biases of the media against any religious body that puts primary stress on faith and worship.

Quite aside from sustaining a false image of "mainstream" Protestantism, these misperceptions give false weight to pronouncements by the NCC. Appearances notwithstanding, the NCC represents but a minority of American Protestants. Only thirty-two of the many hundreds of Protestant denominations in the United States belong to the NCC. The total membership of NCC-affiliated denominations is estimated, somewhat optimistically, to be 42 million, or about 40 percent of all American Protestants. Nevertheless, through the years the NCC and the Federal Council before it have been represented as comprising the vast majority of the nation's Protestants. In 1948 William Warren Sweet claimed that the Federal Council "includes in its membership 75 percent of American Protestant membership" (p. 51). In 1952 Herbert Schneider, Professor of Religion at Columbia, also attributed 75 percent of American Protestants to the Federal Council, and then added that "after its extension in 1950 into the National Council of Churches it now embraces practically the whole of Protestantism" (p. 52). Little wonder that evangelical Protestants, including millions of Southern Baptists, became increasingly angry about the assumption that the NCC speaks for "everybody."

Martin Marty has written: "everybody knows that when the mainline churches take a position, it is only six people in a room on Riverside Drive" (in Reichley, 1986, p. 280).[6] But most people know nothing of the sort. Moreover, not only is it the case that the NCC member denominations are not the real American mainstream, but the NCC typically has not reflected the views of even the leaders of its member denominations, let alone the rank and file (Hadden, 1969; Billingsley, 1990).

In the fall of 1988, the NCC issued a lengthy confession of its failures—including "the erosion of constituent support" and the failure of the NCC "to embody the full ecumenical vision." These admissions were accompanied by further reductions in staff—in 1976 the NCC had 187 full-time employees, but by 1989 there were fewer than 70. Nevertheless, the NCC continued to issue the kinds of political statements and sponsor the same speakers that caused its support to erode. At a meeting of the NCC board in 1989 a World Council of Churches executive proposed that the United States be required to pay "reparations" to developing nations as atonement for the many evils it had committed in the world. None of the board members was moved to disassociate the NCC from these views, although this was not a position agreed to by its member denominations. In May 1990 the NCC adopted a resolution condemning Christopher Columbus's arrival in the New World as an "invasion." The NCC further suggested that celebrations in 1992 of the 500th anniversary of Columbus's voyage should not be held. The issue here is not whether these positions taken by the NCC are "correct," but whether they are the authentic voice of American Protestantism.

It seems significant that the rise and fall of the NCC retraces the career of the Federal Council of Churches. When that body had engendered sufficient opposition to its stress on the social gospel and to its seeming disdain for matters of faith and worship, it was disbanded and reconstituted as the National Council of Churches. Can we soon expect the debut of an American Council of Churches? Whatever the case, we can expect the ecumenical urge to remain strong among most liberal denominations, especially as their fortunes decline.

## Ecumenism and Suburban Life

If urbanization ushered in efforts to merge America's rural churches, the suburbanization of the nation in the late 1940s and 1950s ushered in the greatest wave of ecumenical hoping and planning in the nation's history. And once again, a primary justification was efficiency.

As millions of Americans moved into sprawling new suburban communities, they created an immediate need for new churches. As the denominations struggled to form the thousands of new congregations and construct the new buildings needed, many influential spokesmen began to urge that nondenominational community churches were the obvious solution. Nor surprisingly, these were many of the same experts who had been ardent promoters of unified churches for rural America. As early as 1934 H. Paul Douglass, a major figure in the rural church movement and a leader at the Institute of Social and Religious Research, had called for a shift from interdenominational "competition" to alliances that would produce consolidated community churches all across the nation. The next year Douglass joined with Brunner (1935, p. 326) in proclaiming: "The movement for church unity is backed by powerful emotional and practical attitudes widely diffused throughout the nation, in all regions, among both clergy and laity and including persons of virtually all denominations."

In the 1940s the arguments about efficiency and about higher clergy salaries were joined to a potent new ideology concerning the necessary Christian response to the horrors of World War II: faced with a relentlessly evil world, Christians must finally abandon their selfish differences and achieve the "gathering" of "the whole world into one fellowship" (Visser t' Hooft, 1959, p. 29). Or, as William Warren Sweet put it:

> The most widely used term in American Protestantism since the end of World War II is the word "ecumenical"—world wide. Never before has world Protestantism been so conscious of its world obligation; the vast destruction, both spiritual and moral, wrought by the war has brought to American Protestantism especially, a new sense of mission. Out of the realization that Protestantism faces a world demanding a united front, there is emerging a World Council of Churches, largely under American Protestant leadership and inspiration. The war and its aftermath have done much to bridge the chasm between American and European Protestantism and also between the several denominational members of the American Protestant family. Numerous church unions, which were hardly dreamed of a generation ago, have been effected, and many others are in the offing. (1948, pp. 51–52)

It was soon common wisdom among major American religious commentators that not only must the denominations unite, but they would no longer face any substantial doctrinal stumbling blocks to merger. Back in 1934 Douglass had claimed that his research showed "basic agreements as far outweighing disagreements," and he expressed confidence that "a few more years of frank discussions" among the denominations would be all that was needed to resolve the remaining difficulties (in Douglass and Brunner, 1935, p. 327). In similar terms, one of the most influential books of the post-war period, Will Herberg's *Protestant-Catholic-Jew* (1960), declared that the remaining denominational differences within Protestantism were organizational and ethnic, not doctrinal. Herberg took a very hopeful view of ecumenical relations, not simply among Protestants, but between Protestants and Catholics and even between Christians and Jews.

In full agreement with Herberg, the Protestant writer Robert Lee (1960) explained that a "common core Protestantism" had evolved in the place of the old doctrinal diversities and disagreements. Sweet (1948) attributed this development to the shift away from denominationalism by the leading American seminaries, which now recruited "increasingly interdenominational" faculties. The perceptions of doctrinal consensus were even accepted by many of those, such as Marty (1959), who deplored this state of affairs.

Sociologists were equally committed to the end of denominationalism. Richard D. Lambert (1960, p. 155) noted that "old doctrinal cleavages" had become "irrelevant in American thought today." The word "denomination" did not even appear in the index of Gerhard Lenski's (1961) widely read empirical study of religious effects, *The Religious Factor.* Lenski was content to compare Protestants with Catholic and Jews, separating Protestants only on the basis of race, thus assuming that one kind of Protestantism was pretty much like another.[7]

Peter Berger (1963, p. 89) was equally convinced that denominational differences had become nothing more than "functionally irrelevant embellishments and packaging," because American Protestant denominations had undergone a "process of intense product standardization." Berger called upon the denominations to merge and to form "cartels," which would rationalize competition among the denominations "by reducing the number of competing units by amalgamation and also by dividing up the market between the larger units that remain" (p. 87). Noting that American denominations were spending more than a billion dollars a year on the construction of new churches, Berger claimed that a "rational limitation of cutthroat competition" was an "economic necessity" (p. 84).

Within this intellectual climate, in 1960 the Consultation of Church Union was initiated by the Presbyterian Church in the U.S.A., the Protestant Episcopal Church, the Methodist Church, and the United Church of Christ (formerly the Congregationalists and the Evangelical and Reformed Church) for the purpose of planning the union of these four bodies. In 1966 the Presbyterian Church in the United States joined the group. The day of major mergers seemed at hand.

But the years passed, and somehow nothing ever seemed to come of these consultations. Moreover, the attempts at local unification efforts in order to replace denominationalism with community churches in the rapidly growing suburbs never seemed to come into their own. With the exception of nondenominational fundamentalist churches, which often did very well, people generally didn't seem to want to belong to a nondenominational church.

Meanwhile, in 1963 the first large-scale survey research studies of

American religion were launched by Charles Glock and Rodney Stark. When the data were in they dealt a devastating blow to the notion of a common core American Protestantism. Indeed, it would have been difficult to conceive of greater doctrinal diversity and division than Stark and Glock (1965) reported in an article revealing what they called the "New Denominationalism."

Table 6.5 reprints a few of the key findings from this survey. In some of the denominations to the left of the table, only a minority of members expressed faith in major doctrines of the Christian tradition: only 41 percent of members of the United Church of Christ expressed unwavering faith in the existence of God. But at the right side of the table, overwhelming majorities express unwavering faith in the divinity of Jesus, in the Virgin Birth, in the Second Coming, and in the reality of the Devil. The data "indicate that the fissures which map what might well be called the 'New Denominationalism' fragment the very core of the Christian perspective. The new cleavages are not over such matters as how to worship God properly, but whether or not there is a God of the sort it makes any sense to worship; not over whether the bread and wine of communion become the actual body and blood of Christ through transubstantiation, or are only symbolic, but over whether or not Jesus was merely a man. . . In light of these findings it is difficult to account for the hopes and activities directed towards general ecumenicalism" (Stark and Glock, 1965, p. 14).

How was it possible that the experts could have been so wrong about the state of American denominationalism? We think they were entirely correct about the existence of a common core Protestantism, but failed to realize it was limited to a small select circle. Denominational differences *had* become irrelevant on Riverside Drive, at the famous divinity schools, and in the editorial offices of the *Christian Century*. But the members of this religious elite were not representative even of their own denominations, to say nothing of how out of touch they were with the evangelical Protestant majority. In America's suburbs and cities, as in its rural areas earlier in the century, denominationalism was regarded as neither a scandal nor an irrelevant embellishment; it was the backbone of religious commitment and participation.

In the end, the planned mergers never took place. Instead, the denominations most actively involved in talks of merger soon began to experience rapid declines in their membership. It is possible that when these bodies have become sufficiently weak, they will finally merge in an effort to forestall a complete collapse.

TABLE 6.5

The New Denominationalism, 1963

|  | | | | | Percentage responding affirmatively | | | | | | | |
|---|---|---|---|---|---|---|---|---|---|---|---|---|
| Doctrinal statements | U.C.C. (151) | Meth. (415) | Episc. (416) | D. of Christ (50) | Presb. (495) | Am. Luth. (208) | Am. Bapt. (141) | Mo. Luth. (116) | S. Bapt. (79) | Sects (255) | Total Prot. (2,326) | Total Cath. (545) |
| "I know God really exists and I have no doubts about it." | 41 | 60 | 63 | 76 | 75 | 73 | 78 | 81 | 99 | 96 | 71 | 81 |
| "Jesus is the Divine Son of God and I have no doubts about it." | 40 | 54 | 59 | 74 | 72 | 74 | 76 | 93 | 99 | 97 | 69 | 86 |
| It is completely true that "Jesus was born of a virgin." | 21 | 34 | 39 | 62 | 57 | 66 | 69 | 92 | 99 | 96 | 57 | 81 |
| Definitely, "Jesus will actually return to the earth some day." | 13 | 21 | 24 | 36 | 43 | 54 | 57 | 75 | 94 | 89 | 44 | 47 |
| It is "completely true" that "the Devil actually exists." | 6 | 13 | 17 | 18 | 31 | 49 | 49 | 77 | 92 | 90 | 38 | 66 |

SOURCE: From Stark and Glock (1965).
NOTE: The Protestant churches represented are United Church of Christ (Congregationalists), Methodists, Episcopalians, Disciples of Christ, United Presbyterian Church, Lutheran Church in America and American Lutheran Church, American Baptist Church, Missouri Synod of Lutherans, and Southern Baptist Church. The numbers in parentheses represent the number of respondents.

## Shall the Weak Merge?

Bryan Wilson, Britain's leading sociologist of religion, has been a relentless advocate of the secularization thesis. Indeed, it would be very difficult to conceive of any fact or event (with the possible exception of the Second Coming) that would not strike Wilson as further proof that religion is rapidly on its way out. For example, not only does the decline in membership and attendance in Britain count in favor of secularization, but *so do the high rates* of membership and attendance in America: "the long recognized lack of depth of religious manifestations in the United States suggest that religion is in decline in both countries" (Wilson, 1966, p. 126). A few pages later he again notes "the generally accepted superficiality of much religion in American society" (p. 166).

During the 1960s Wilson drew his principal evidence for "the essential weakness of religious life" from the ecumenical movement. He argued that ecumenism could only become a "new faith" among clergy who need to have "something to believe in," having lost their ability to accept traditional Christian doctrines. The prospect of widespread denominational mergers, according to Wilson, could exist only if secularization had so eroded commitment that doctrinal differences no longer provided a reason to sustain separate organizations: "As the process of secularization has continued, so the differences between denominations have lost their social significance" (1966, p. 128). The vested interests of the clergy and the denominational bureaucracies in retaining separate organizations had faded because "the extreme weakness of religious commitment" threatened the continued survival of each religious organization. Thus Wilson advanced the proposition that "organizations amalgamate when they are weak" (p. 126).

Wilson's belief that all American denominations were on the brink of collapse was as misguided as his capacity to find religious depth only in solemn high church rituals. But, if the scope of his proposition is properly delimited, we are prepared to agree: strong organizations are seldom interested in merging—the urge to merge typically is prompted by weakness. Thus if substantial mergers do occur among Protestant denominations, these will be limited to the more secularized bodies.

Data offering strong support for this proposition were published by Douglass in 1935, based on a questionnaire study of 16,355 church members conducted in 1932 (Douglass and Brunner, 1935).[8] Among the items was one aimed at measuring support for ecumenism:

If you had to decide now what religious people of the United States should do about church union—would you

(1) Continue essentially the present system of separate denominations?
(2) Unite the various church bodies into one church?
(3) Adopt some form of permanent and binding federal union of denominations, after the analogy of the state and Federal Government in the United States? (p. 328)

Although the more liberal bodies were very overrepresented in the survey, only 31.7 percent of the respondents favored unification into one church. Moreover, among these were members of nonliberal bodies (particularly Southern Baptists and Missouri Synod Lutherans), whose idea of a unified church probably indicated not their willingness to make significant compromises, but their hope that others would see the light and embrace their creed. Another 30.3 percent selected the option of some sort of federal union (presumably a strengthened Federal Council of Churches), but with denominations retaining their autonomy. An additional 4.5 percent selected more than one answer. And 33.5 opted for the denominational status quo.

These totals, however, mask immense variation among the Protestant bodies included in the sample (see Table 6.6). For example, 89.5 percent of Missouri Synod Lutherans and 58.4 percent of Southern Baptists preferred to stay with denominationalism (that is, they chose answer 1), as compared with 21.1 percent of Congregationalists and 10.1 percent of the Evangelical Synod. Only 7.5 percent of Missouri Synod Lutherans and 19 percent of Southern Baptists supported unification into a single church (answer 2), while 51.1 percent of Disciples of Christ and 39.9 percent of Methodists did.

If it is true that willingness to merge reflects organizational weakness, then we ought to expect that members of denominations that are doing well in the marketplace would be the ones most inclined to reject unification. To test this hypothesis, we turned to census data and calculated the rate of growth (or decline) for each of these denominations between 1916 and 1926. Because the nation's population grew by 15.1 percent during this decade, we subtracted the rate of growth (or decline) for each denomination from 15.1. Thus a denomination that scored zero would have grown by the precise amount of the population, thereby neither gaining nor losing in terms of market share.

TABLE 6.6
Growth and Ecumenism, 1932 (in percent)

| Protestant denominations | Net growth 1916–1926 | % Rejecting ecumenism | Perceived differences |
|---|---|---|---|
| Missouri Synod Lutherans | 51.1 | 89.5 | 75.7 |
| Lutherans* | 45.7 | 60.0 | 22.3 |
| United Lutherans | 43.9 | 51.4 | 15.0 |
| Southern Baptists† | 15.0 | 58.4 | 14.8 |
| Presbyterian, U.S. | 11.0 | 52.9 | 12.0 |
| Episcopalians | 3.8 | 40.2 | 14.3 |
| Southern Methodists | 2.6 | 40.3 | 8.7 |
| Presbyterians, U.S.A. | 1.4 | 20.9 | 7.1 |
| Disciples of Christ | − 2.7 | 24.7 | 12.0 |
| Methodists | − 5.3 | 23.1 | 9.1 |
| Congregationalists | − 6.1 | 21.1 | 6.7 |
| United Brethren | − 6.9 | 27.9 | 7.2 |
| Reformed, America | − 9.0 | 36.0 | 9.4 |
| Reformed, U.S. | − 10.2 | 14.7 | 5.8 |
| Northern Baptists | − 11.5 | 44.9 | 13.6 |
| Methodists, Protestant | − 12.3 | 34.2 | 7.6 |
| Friends | − 16.2 | 43.2 | 19.2 |
| Evangelical Synod | − 22.6 | 10.1 | 9.3 |

SOURCE: The data on "% rejecting ecumenism" and "perceived differences" are from Douglass and Brunner (1935, pp. 328, 260).
*All Lutherans except Missouri Synod and United Lutherans.
†The American Baptist Association was included in Southern Baptist totals for 1916, but not 1926. With the ABA included in the 1926 totals, the net growth for Southern Baptists was 19.4.

Denominations with positive scores had a net gain over and above simple population growth. Those with negative scores failed to keep pace with population growth.

Eight denominations had positive scores, and the majority of their members (51.7 percent) were opposed to any form of merger. But of the thirteen denominations with negative scores, the great majority (71.4 percent) favored some form of merger (see Table 6.6). There is a strong positive correlation (.79) between growth in market share and choosing to retain denominationalism. Members of growing denominations did not want to merge; those belonging to declining denominations did.

Douglass also helps us understand why the growing denominations were not predisposed to merge: they were inclined to see very substantial differences separating themselves from other denominations. Respondents were asked how willing they would be to enter into various relationships with members of other denominations. Among these relationships were: "Sending a child to their Sunday school; . . . receiving communion from their minister; . . . Uniting in observing their Holy Days; . . . Marrying a member of that church; . . . Having a burial service conducted according to their rites; . . . Acknowledging their church as a genuine church of Christ; . . ." (Douglass and Brunner, 1935, p. 259). These are nicely designed measures of social distance (and were a highly original contribution to survey research methods).

Denominations differed immensely on these measures. The Missouri Synod Lutherans scored at the top end the scale, while the Reformed Church in the United States and the Congregationalists anchored the bottom end, seeing little to separate them from most other bodies (see Table 6.6). It is not surprising that denominations strongly committed to traditional confessions saw substantial differences between themselves and groups ready to waive doctrinal concerns. Douglass and Brunner, however, characterized all perceptions of differences as "prejudice" and claimed that "denominations which have the greatest prejudice strongly incline to vote for the existing denominational system, while those with the least prejudice are most strongly for union" (1935, p. 330). Although we do not accept these value judgments, we calculated that there was a strong positive correlation (.79) between degree of perceived religious difference and unwillingness to support unification in the data reported by Douglass and Brunner.

Our use of Douglass's data leads to the following conclusions:

1. Growing churches perceive substantial religious differences between themselves and others (which justifies their efforts to bring in new members).
2. Growing churches do not want to merge.
3. Churches that are shrinking see merit in mergers.

A question lingers: why did Douglass fail to report these relationships? It was not that they were unimportant. Given that one of the primary arguments for church unity was to increase the effectiveness and efficiency of religious organizations, membership growth and involvement were central matters. Nor could it have been that Douglass was an incompetent statistician, unfamiliar with rates or correlations. Douglass was quick to notice the strong correlation between "religious distance" and opposition to unity, and he published a scatterplot to illustrate this association. Nor could it have been that Douglass was unfamiliar with the religious census reports for 1916 and 1926 from which we took our data on membership growth or decline. He often cited these sources. Indeed, he knew very well that what he and his colleagues at the Institute of Social and Religious Research often referred to as the "respectable" denominations were losing members to what they called the "emotional sects" (Brunner, 1927). This awareness was a major element in his intense desire to end religious competition. Douglass valued church union far more than he valued the "minutiae of creed." He was supported by an institute and surrounded by colleagues dedicated to discovering how to achieve religious unification. Obviously, the sects were not about to discard their competitive ways. But it seemed equally obvious to Douglass and his friends that the reunification of Protestantism was the wave of the future. Thus Douglass wrote: "The present urban age still witnesses the backwash of sectarianism in certain quarters, especially in the less prosperous and more backward sections of the nation; but on the whole the age is distinctly dominated by integrative forces" (Douglass and Brunner, 1935, p. 257). If these characterizations were true, then it seemingly *had to be* that the "respectable" mainline bodies would soon bounce back and resume their historic role of cultural leadership.

Although we have focused on Douglass, he was by no means alone in viewing sectarianism as a temporary "backwash." Then, as now, there was considerable bias among scholars against the "emotional sects." As we noted earlier, Brunner (1927, pp. 75–76) described the emotional sects as being "organized on the fringe of the larger community" and was entirely willing to mention "mixed blood" and "moronic intelligence." If Brunner sounds like a bigot as well as an elitist, his colleagues in the Country Life Movement would not have noticed. Consider Warren H. Wilson's (1925, p. 58) assessment of these groups and of rural people in general: "among country people there are many inferior minds." He then displayed his contempt for an unregulated, that

This photograph was taken at a Pentecostal Holiness Revival in 1932 near Kennett, Missouri. The twenty-three-year-old evangelist, Russell Ridgeway, reportedly baptized 400 persons as 10,000 more watched from the banks of the Mississippi. The back of the photograph reads: " 'Ole man river' witnesses a wholesale baptism." (Courtesy of the Billy Graham Center Museum, Wheaton, Ill.)

is to say free, religious economy: "the prevalence of revivalism among country people has a justification. Until a better administration of life is possible and the weak can be sifted from the strong, until we can lift the administration of popular institutions that are governed by public opinion out of the hand of the weak brother and the silly sister, we shall do well to use a method that steadies and arouses them and forbids them to express the impulses of the imbecile and moron. We must be content with the negative result which the old methods have given" (p. 58). It has been more than sixty-five years since these words were published. The temporary "backwash" of sect growth shows no signs of slowing down, and the "weak brother and the silly sister" still enjoy a good prayer meeting as much as ever.

In the final chapter we bring together many factors governing why some religious groups prosper, while others fail. Here our interest has been not in how organizations grow, but in attempts by some denominations to create cartels and thus to prevent the growth of new firms. We have also explored why the denominations that are doing best at a given moment are not prepared to support such cartels or to merge with others. Thus are ecumenical movements doomed. The most vigorous, growing, and significant organizations will not join, and a merger of failing groups cannot fulfill the essential ecumenical hope.

# Chapter 7

# Why "Mainline" Denominations Decline

Since at least 1776 the upstart sects have grown as the mainline American denominations have declined.[1] And this trend continues unabated, as new upstarts continue to push to the fore. Consider that the Church of God in Christ (3.7 million members) is already substantially larger than the United Church of Christ (1.7 million), the Presbyterian Church, U.S.A. (2.9 million), the Episcopal Church (2.4 million), and the American Baptist Churches in the U.S.A. (1.6 million). The Assemblies of God now number 2.2 million and the Churches of Christ enroll 1.6 million. As for the Latter-day Saints, their American membership now trails only that of the Roman Catholics, Southern Baptists, United Methodists, and the newly merged Evangelical Lutheran Church in America.

These historical trends are not oddities of the American religious economy or of recent history—they are not new things under the sun. Rather, they reflect basic social forces that first cause successful religious firms to compromise their "errand into the wilderness" and then to lose their organizational vigor, eventually to be replaced by less worldly groups, whereupon the process is repeated. That is, the *sect-church process is always under way,* and the less regulated the religious economy, the more rapidly and thoroughly the process will occur.

Our view is not shared by most sociologists of religion, let alone most church historians. Most scholars interested in the subject see the religious condition of the United States, and of societies generally, as the product of unique, if periodic, cultural crises and eruptions. Thus, the preference is for *ad hoc* explanations that often amount to little more than identifying some eras as periods of religious excitement and others as periods of lethargy.

For example, writing about the growth of "emotional sects" during the 1920s, Edmund Brunner (1927, pp. 75–76) first characterized this as a sudden and temporary annoyance, a mere "backwash," and then noted that "many theories were advanced to account for the rapid growth of this type of religion. . . . it was only a natural part of the westward movement; . . . it was a stab at modernism . . . it was part of the post-bellum state of mind." A few years later H. Paul Douglass and Brunner (1935, p. 257) explained that this "backwash of sectarianism" was limited to the "less prosperous and more backward sections of the nation." Both authors were convinced that the future of American religion lay securely in the hands of the mainline Protestants.

They were wrong, of course. And, in our judgment, so are most scholars who identify sudden shifts and eruptions in American religious history. In Chapters 2 and 3 we challenged claims about the first and second "Great Awakenings," which we see as merely the routine activities of evangelists enthusiastically in pursuit of souls. We also reported that the "low ebb-tide of religion," as the end of the eighteenth century has typically been portrayed, was little more than the onset of hard times for the old colonial mainline.

To open this chapter we shall examine claims about four major eruptions in American religion during the twentieth century and show that these too are mainly in the eyes of the beholders. Then we will more fully develop the proposition that *religious organizations are stronger to the degree that they impose significant costs in terms of sacrifice and even stigma upon their members.* Herein lies the key to the trends noted throughout this book. People tend to value religion on the basis of how costly it is to belong—the more one must sacrifice in order to be in good standing, the more valuable the religion. A major reason people rate religion this way is that as religious bodies ask less of their members their ability to reward their members declines proportionately. Thus in terms of real costs and benefits, the more "mainline" the church (in the sense of being regarded as "respectable" and "reasonable"), the lower the value of belonging to it, and this eventually results in widespread defection. Finally, we shall review our basic model of why mainline churches succumb by briefly noting some recent trends in American Catholicism.

# Four Recent Religious Eruptions That Didn't Happen

The literature on cult[2] and sect formation in contemporary America is saturated with the belief that we have recently been living through strange times—through an interrelated set of cultural crises that have resulted in four major religious eruptions. The first of these is sometimes known as a "Consciousness Reformation" and refers to an "eruption" of cult formation and religious novelty during the sixties and early seventies (Wuthnow, 1976, 1978; Glock and Bellah, 1976). The second concerns an eruption within an eruption; the sudden influx of Eastern, and especially Indian, faiths, during the cult eruption of the sixties and early seventies. The third eruption involves the transformation of many of the Eastern teachings that came to the fore during the late sixties and early seventies into the New Age Movement of more recent years. Popularized by actress Shirley MacLaine and others, the movement has received a great deal of press coverage and has generated serious concern and organized opposition from evangelical Protestant groups. The fourth eruption is the "explosion" of evangelical Protestantism and the corresponding decline of mainline denominations over the past several decades. This conservative eruption is often seen as a reactionary response to the same cultural crises that produced the religious novelties of the sixties (Marty, 1979; Tipton, 1982; Berger, 1982; Marsden, 1982).

Real social crises often do have real consequences for religious culture, and the greater the degree of suffering and social disorganization, the greater the likelihood that radical changes will occur in the religious sphere (Stark and Bainbridge, 1987; Stark, 1991, 1992a). Nevertheless, such moments are very rare and play no role in the birth or death of most religious movements. Indeed, we argue that whether or not there have been cultural crises in recent times, they did not prompt significant religious reactions—because the alleged eruptions of cult and sect activity never took place. We argue instead that the recent history of cults and sects is far better characterized by stability and continuity. Although significant changes have occurred, or at least have been recently recognized, they were the result not of sudden eruptions but of gradual, long-term, linear shifts.

## The Mystical Sixties

*Everyone* knows that the latter part of the sixties turned into a "magical mystery tour" during which an explosion of cult formation and importation took place and that, for the first time, the cultural climate was right for faiths from the East, and especially from India, to make significant headway. That these perceptions are accurate seem obvious. Nevertheless, we believe that these, like many other seemingly self-evident assertions about American religion, are mainly myths. That is, we intend to show that there was nothing unusual about the number of cults that formed in this era and that the sudden surge in Indian religious influence had mundane causes having little or nothing to do with deeper cultural matters.

Let us first examine the claim that the sixties were a period when there was an unusual outburst of cult formation. Consider the number of cult movements founded per year for each of the four decades, 1950–1989 (see Table 7.1).[3] At first glance it would seem that there was a dramatic shift between the fifties and the sixties in terms of the number of foundings, but, as will be explained shortly, this is probably an illusion. In any event, the sixties did not stand out from either the seventies or the eighties in terms of cult formation. It also seems reasonable to take population growth into account (on the assumption that the larger the population, the greater the absolute number available for recruitment).

TABLE 7.1
Formation Rate of Cult Movements, 1950–1989

|  | 1950–1959 | 1960–1969 | 1970–1979 | 1980–1989* |
|---|---|---|---|---|
| Number of groups founded per year | 8.6 | 16.4 | 20.6 | 20.2 |
| Number of groups founded per million population | 0.52 | 0.84 | 0.95 | 0.85 |
| Percentage Eastern | 7.0 | 17.1 | 18.6 | 11.8 |

SOURCE: Melton, (1988). Based on the files of the Institute for the Study of American Religion, University of California at Santa Barbara.
*Projected from 1980–1985 data.

In terms of the number of cult movements founded during a decade per million population (at mid-decade), the sixties exceed only the fifties.

What these data really show is great stability over the entire period. This stability becomes even more evident when it is realized that the data for the fifties were not assembled until the late sixties and early seventies. Many obscure and short-lived groups, having failed to leave sufficient traces so that reliable data about them could be gathered a decade or two later, would necessarily have been missed. For example, about 20 percent of the groups included in the rate for the sixties are defunct today, and little if any information would be recovered about them by a data collection campaign inaugurated now. We believe that the actual cult formation rate for the fifties was probably about the same as for the other decades.[4] For those determined to remember the fifties as the quiet and conformist decade of Eisenhowerism, it may be worth pointing out that Scientology was founded in 1954, that Elizabeth Clare Prophet's Church Universal and Triumphant was founded in 1958,[5] and that the first American converts to the Unification Church were gathered in Eugene, Oregon, during 1959.

That an unusual number of new cults did not appear during the sixties does not rule out the possibility that far *more people actually participated* in such movements during this brief era. Were that the case, then the eruption thesis is salvaged. But there seems to be no support for this alternative. Rather, what is striking is how poorly contemporary cult movements have done in gaining converts when compared with movements from earlier times. With the exception of Transcendental Meditation—which represented nothing more than a brief experiment in self-improvement for all but the tiniest portion of those who encountered it (Stark and Bainbridge, 1985)—no cult movement of the sixties or early seventies seems ever to have attracted more than a few thousand American members, and most of even the well-publicized groups counted their true membership in the hundreds, not the thousands. For example, after more than thirty years of missionizing, it is estimated that there have never been more than 5,000 followers of the Unification Church (the Moonies) in the United States, some of whom are from abroad. After more than twenty years of operations, the membership of ISKCON (the Hare Krishnas) is estimated at 3,000 (Melton, 1989). In 1984 a Toronto magazine estimated that there were 10,000 Hare Krishna members in that city. But when Irving Hexham, Raymond Currie, and Joan Townsend (1985) checked on the matter, they found that the correct total was 80.

In 1990 Barry A. Kosmin (1991) and his colleagues at the City University of New York conducted the largest survey ever devoted to American religious affiliation. All told, 113,000 randomly sampled Americans were interviewed about their religious preference. Because such an immense sample yields very stable statistics, Kosmin projected his distributions back to the total adult population of the forty-eight contiguous states. Kosmin projected a nationwide total of 8,000 members of Wiccan groups and, nearly forty years after their founding, 45,000 Scientologists (or about 1 percent of the number of members claimed by the group in 1978).

In contrast, the Mormons grew from six members in 1830 to more than 30,000 a decade later, more than 60,000 by 1850, and more than 80,000 by 1860. In similar fashion, Christian Science grew from 27 members in 1880 to 8,724 in 1890, 65,717 in 1906, and 202,098 by 1926. Moreover, the Mormons and Christian Scientists achieved their rapid growth from a far smaller population base than has been available to recent movements.

These data are utterly at variance with the perception that an eruption of cults took place in the late sixties and early seventies. How is it possible for informed opinion to be so wrong? As we have already seen, misperceptions, even ones of this magnitude, are common in the histories of American religion. When quantitative claims are involved, the opinions of people who fail to count, shouldn't count. It is also possible that cult movements were more prominent on campuses during the sixties than had been the case earlier and therefore attracted more notice. Young adults are always the primary source of converts for such movements, and probably no cohort of young people was ever so overreported and overinterpreted as the baby-boomers, whose antics *were* the sixties.

## The Eastern Aspect

In their foreword to Part I of *The New Religious Consciousness*, Charles Y. Glock and Robert N. Bellah (1976, p. 1) noted: "One of the most striking characteristics of the counterculture [of the sixties] and of the movements growing out of it is the influence of Asian religions. Of course, Americans have been interested in Asian religions for over a century, but the present period seems to differ from earlier ones both quantitatively and qualitatively. . . . Most important of all was the fact that

Asian religions were attracting not only the curiosity of educated youth but also serious devotion and commitment."

That same year Harvey Cox stressed the same points in his book *Turning East: The Promise and Peril of the New Orientalism*. Cox wanted to explain this phenomenon. Why was it happening? What did it all mean? In a 1983 interview he commented that Americans embraced Eastern faiths because "they've been maddened by a consumer culture." Cox continued: "In American society, I believe we're now in the late phase, the most deteriorated, decadent phase, of consumer capitalism. When I say 'consumer capitalism,' I don't mean simply the form of our economic life; I mean our whole culture. . . . People's primal energies are fixated on commodities that are supposed to bring satisfaction of inner hungers. Through the suggestive and hypnotic power of the advertising industry, a direct connection is made from very basic and underlying needs and fears to material commodities which are touted as things which satisfy those needs; but of course they do not" (1983, p. 42). In conclusion, Cox noted a great irony, that though many critics charge that "vulnerable kids . . . are picked off the streets and brainwashed into the cults," it is only those who have not yet been brainwashed into the "existing distorted values of society" who are clear-headed enough to be "open to other life-patterns."

Underneath Cox's polemics one can detect a very common belief about the phenomenon in question: Indian religions arrived here in a sudden eruption and therefore they *must* reflect a serious cultural crisis. But such crises are, in fact, rare and have little, if anything, to do with the instance at hand.

Glock and Bellah were correct to note that there had been substantial interest in Indian and other Asian religions for more than a century. Gordon Melton (1987) has sketched the extensive involvements of Harvard professors and various proper Bostonians in Eastern religions during the latter part of the nineteenth century. The Boston Unitarian Church was responsible for the initial visits by Hindu teachers to the United States. According to Melton, the first of these was Protap Chundar Mozoomdar. In 1883 he gave his first American lecture in the Concord living room of the widow of Ralph Waldo Emerson. Other gurus soon followed.

In the wake of World War I, however, Congress passed very restrictive immigration laws that effectively excluded all Asians and thereby limited authentic Eastern religious teachers to brief visits on tourist visas. Thenceforth, Americans interested in exploring Eastern religion had to rely on books, travel abroad, or depend upon American teachers—some of whom pretended to be authentic Indians.[6]

In 1965 the exclusionary rules against Asian immigration were quietly dropped.[7] Before the year was out Swami Bhaktivedanta, founder of ISKCON, had become a resident of New York. Many other teachers of Eastern religion quickly followed, and some succeeded in attracting a following. It is their success that Cox and others were trying to explain. But it seems to us that there is much less here than meets the eye.

Given the existence of a sizable audience for books and periodicals dealing with "Eastern wisdom," it does not seem surprising that when talented gurus finally arrived and offered direct teaching they had little trouble finding at least some followers. Put another way, it was not so much that Eastern faiths suddenly struck a responsive chord in the American counterculture as that their growth had been artificially thwarted until then. With the barrier removed, normalization occurred. Given the structure of guru-based religions (Shinn, 1985), virtually each new guru who came to the United States founded a *separate* movement. Thus it took only a relatively small number of American converts to Hinduism to generate a substantial total of Hindu-based cult movements. Herein lies the explanation of the fact that an unusual number of the cult movements founded in the late sixties were of the Hindu variety. The bottom row in Table 7.1 indicates this increase. Only 7 percent of the groups founded during the fifties were based on Eastern faiths, but 17.1 percent of those founded during the sixties and 18.6 of those formed in the seventies were of the Eastern variety. Notice, too, that this has declined in the eighties—which supports the notion that the surge was simply a normalization of "frustrated" demand. The ability of a sudden influx of Eastern and Indian religious teachers to collectively round up a few thousand followers in the vast American religious economy was at most a blip, not an eruption.

## The New Age

The term "New Age" is an old one, as is the practice of "channeling." In 1881 and 1882 John Ballou Newbrough, a New York spiritualist, "channeled" a manuscript later published as *Oahspe: A New Age Bible*. The phrase "New Age" was recurrent in the Theosophical Society at the turn of the century, and was commonly used by followers of Vedanta and the Rosicrucian Fellowship. During the 1950s, when "flying saucer cults" were popular, many spoke and wrote about the New Age that would begin when the "brothers from outer space" revealed themselves to the world. It was in the 1980s, however, that the term became widely known, largely owing to the publicity given to channelers such as J. Z. Knight and Kevin Ryerson by Shirley MacLaine (Melton, 1990).

Most observers of the American religious scene regard the New Age movement as the truly important and lasting legacy of the earlier eruptions of new mysticisms (Burrows, 1987; Babbie, 1990; Robbins and Anthony, 1990). In this they have been much abetted by the news media, for both the print and the electronic media uncritically pass along New Age press releases claiming that hundreds of thousands (perhaps millions) of Americans are sleeping in homemade pyramids and attending channeling classes. And judging from the shelf space devoted to anti–New Age materials in most Christian bookstores, the New Age is *the* cult threat of the moment.

Once again, we dissent. We believe that most people who can in any way be said to have responded to the New Age movement regard it as more of an amusement than a religion. Most are no more than casual dabblers in the various pseudo-scientific activities and techniques promoted as New Age. Indeed, we suspect that for all but a handful of committed participants, the New Age movement is an audience cult (Stark and Bainbridge, 1985) and reflects interest levels on a par with reading astrology columns.

A recent report suggests how tiny the New Age movement is. Based on Barry Kosmin's (1991) survey, discussed above, it can be estimated that 20,000 Americans regard their religious preference as New Age. Admittedly, some people who reported themselves to be Baptists or Lutherans take part in the New Age *audience.* But audiences do not constitute movements. And even this audience is probably not all that large. For example, the *New Age Journal* claimed an average circulation of fewer than 150,000 copies for 1990. It seems to us that the New Age is no more potent or relatively popular today than it was in the heyday of Theosophical Society, which claimed a total membership of 6,780 in 1926.

## The Evangelical Eruption

In 1972 Dean M. Kelley, an executive of the National Council of Churches, provoked a storm of controversy, especially among religious liberals, with his book *Why Conservative Churches Are Growing.* His first sentence noted: "In the latter years of the 1960's something remarkable happened in the United States: for the first time in the nation's history most of the major church groups stopped growing and began to shrink." Kelley was among the very first to attempt to explain what Martin Marty (1979, p. 10) would later describe as a "seismic shift" in American religion: the sudden and very steep membership declines that began to hit the mainline denominations during the sixties. Summing up the evidence of a series of graphs showing membership figures for a number of major denominations, Kelley noted that in the sixties the "strong upward curve weakens, falters, and tilts downward like a spent skyrocket" (p. 2). As the title of his book revealed, however, not *all* denominations had hit the skids. The evangelical Protestant bodies were still growing—many of them quite rapidly.

What was going on? According to Marty (1976, p. 71) it was another cultural crisis: "mainline churches always have the advantage . . . [when] the official culture is secure and expansive . . . [but they] suffer in times of cultural crisis and disintegration, when they receive blame for what goes wrong in society but are bypassed when people look for new ways to achieve social identity and location. So they looked good in the 1950s as they looked bad in the 1970s." Kelley disagreed. He claimed that the mainline bodies were failing to offer credible religion, that they had become so accommodated to the secular culture that people could no longer satisfy their need for the sacred by attending services at their local Methodist, Congregationalist, Episcopalian, or Presbyterian church.

As much as we admire Kelley's book, and his courage in writing it, we think the whole discussion of the sudden decline of the liberal denominations and the sudden "resurgence" of evangelical groups is based on a distorted historical perspective. Like Marty, Kelley was still trying to explain why this "sudden change took place in the 60's." Several years later Kelley (1984, p. 89) expressed continued confidence in his explanation of why the "conservatives" grew (as the "liberals" declined), but he confessed he was "less satisfied" that he had explained "why it happened at this particular time in history [the 1960s]."

But did anything akin to an eruption take place? Kelley's skyrocket image to the contrary, what is involved here is a gradual trend that has been going on for at least two centuries. The notion of a "seismic shift" is based on the fact that it was only in the sixties that this trend was finally noticed. If we are correct, all efforts by Marty and others to link the fate of the liberal churches to the "cultural crisis of the 1960s" (Marsden, 1982, p. 156) are falsified by the inability of consequences to precede their causes in time.

The general consensus of church historians (and most sociologists) is that the decline of the liberal Protestant churches was a product of the sixties. For example, Winthrop S. Hudson (1981, p. 439) claimed that the declines which "had begun in the 1960's . . . constituted a marked reversal after a century and a half of steady growth." Likewise, Marty (1979, p. 10) noted: "From the birth of the republic until around 1965, as is well known, the churches now called mainline Protestant tended to grow with every census or survey." But in light of the two centuries of church statistics we have examined, it is obvious that a group can add members and still fail to keep pace with the growth of the population and of other religious firms.

Social scientists who mistakenly accepted that an eruption of cult activities took place in the sixties can rightly claim that appropriate numerical estimates have been very hard to come by. But those who think there has been a "recent" surge of evangelical growth lack such a defense. Consider Table 7.2. The mainline denominations do not qualify as rockets that suddenly ran out of fuel in the sixties—their market shares were falling in the forties and fifties too, and throughout the century. In contrast, the evangelical groups—some of them rapidly becoming the new upstart sects of our era—do look like rockets. So much, then, for perceptions of a "seismic shift" or a sudden response to a cultural crisis. The speed of conservative growth and liberal decline will no doubt change from time to time, but the general trend has remained consistent for more than two centuries of American history. Thus, while it is true, as Hudson and Marty claim, that the total number of members of these mainline bodies increased regularly until the 1960s, each year they represented a smaller fraction of total church membership.

Even those without the slightest awareness of market share cannot long ignore an actual decline in numbers. And by the seventies the numbers were falling fast. Attempts to dismiss these declines as purely demographic (cf. Hoge and Roozen, 1979) or as symptomatic of the general decline in religiousness produced by modernity fall apart when it is noted that *only some* religious bodies were losing out. And indeed, as Dean Kelley bravely noted, the "conservative" Protestant bodies were still growing.

There have been many attempts to explain this "unwelcome" fact away. Carl Bangs (1972) charged Kelley with using "deceptive statistics." Others suggested that Kelley had fallen into the trap of confusing

TABLE 7.2

Market Shares of Mainline, Evangelicals, and Catholics
per 1,000 Church Members, 1940–1985

| Denomination | 1940 | 1960 | 1985 | Percentage loss or gain |
|---|---|---|---|---|
| **MAINLINE** | | | | |
| United Methodists | 124.7 | 93.0 | 64.3 | −48% |
| Presbyterian, U.S.A. | 41.7 | 36.4 | 21.3 | −49% |
| Episcopal | 30.9 | 28.6 | 19.2 | −38% |
| Christian (Disciples) | 25.7 | 15.7 | 7.8 | −70% |
| United Church of Christ (Congregationalists) | 26.5 | 19.6 | 11.8 | −56% |
| **EVANGELICALS** | | | | |
| Southern Baptists | 76.7 | 85.0 | 101.3 | +32% |
| Assemblies of God | 3.1 | 4.4 | 14.6 | +371% |
| Church of the Nazarene | 2.6 | 2.7 | 3.7 | +42% |
| Church of God (Cleveland, Tenn.) | 1.0 | 1.5 | 3.6 | +260% |
| **ROMAN CATHOLICS** | 330.0 | 367.9 | 368.4 | +12% |

SOURCE: Calculated from *Yearbook of American and Canadian Churches* (1988).

quantity with quality—that though the evangelicals grow rapidly by "herding insecure and frightened masses together into a superficial conformity," it is the liberal churches who are the "faithful remnant of God's people whose prophetic courage and lifestyle will truly point the way" (Miller, 1978, p. 257). Others claimed that the growth of evangelical Protestant bodies was nothing but inflated membership roles caused by people who frequently hop from one sect to another, thus being counted again and again (Bibby and Binkerhoff, 1973, 1983). Some even suggest that it was all a function of disparities in absolute size, because it is easy for small evangelical sects to have high percentage rates of growth, but virtually impossible for large denominations to keep growing rapidly (Nelson and Bromley, 1988). This excuse not only ignored the fact that the nation's largest Protestant body, the Southern Baptist Convention, was among those growing rapidly, but also ignored the huge potential for growth that actually exists in the American religious economy.

Two cases are illustrative. Between 1960 and 1970 the Assemblies of God grew by 22.9 percent to reach a total membership of 625,027. This was one of the "small" groups, thereby able to grow fast, cited by Kelley's critics. Meanwhile, the United Church of Christ (formerly the Congregationalists) declined by 12.5 percent, to 1,960,608 members, between 1960 and 1970. In 1987 the Assemblies of God numbered 2,160,667 members and the United Church of Christ had only 1,662,568. Does anyone really think that the advantage currently rests with the U.C.C., now that it has become the smaller group? It seems clear that the decline of the Protestant mainline is a long, steady trend. It is pointless to search the 1960s for the causes of a phenomenon that was far along by the War of 1812. But the question persists: why do mainline faiths fail and why do the sects always overtake them?

## The Rewards of Costly Faith

By the time Kelley published his controversial book it was common knowledge that the mainline churches were shrinking. This realization had been dealt with in a number of ways. Some blamed it on secularization—religion is in retreat from modernism, probably never to recover. Others suggested that religion is not meaningfully reduced to membership counts; what matters is what is in people's hearts (and presumably that is beyond measure). Many proposed that the churches were badly in need of liberalization and modernization—that they must drop their unreasonable moral demands, which only drove people away.

Kelley's book stirred up so much controversy for many reasons. First, not only did he publicize the liberal losses, he accepted claims by conservative bodies of continued growth. Second, he was unwilling to brush this growth off as a momentary "backwash." Instead, he saw it as the key fact. Kelley said that the mainline churches were declining not because they asked too much of their members but because they asked too little. It was this position that antagonized so many of his critics.

Kelley argued that the flourishing conservative denominations:

not only give evidence that religion is not obsolete and churches not defunct but they contradict the contemporary notion of an acceptable religion. They are not "reasonable," they are not "tolerant," they are not ecumenical, they are not "relevant." Quite the contrary!

It is ironic that religious groups which persist in such "unreasonable" and "unsociable" behavior should be flourishing, while more "reasonable" and "sociable" bodies are not. It is not only ironic, but it suggests that our understanding of what causes a religious group to flourish is inadequate. Some dynamic seems to be at work which contradicts prevailing expectations. (1972, pp. 25–26)

Kelley outlined this dynamic in three propositions (italics omitted):

Strong organizations are strict . . . the stricter the stronger. (p. 95)

A strong organization that loses its strictness will also lost its strength. (p. 96)

Strictness tends to deteriorate into leniency, which results in social weakness in place of strength. . . . traits of strictness are harder to maintain in an organization than traits of leniency. (p. 96)

As Kelley knew they would, these propositions fueled many angry denials and attacks. Nearly a decade later he reported that his book "excited a certain amount of controversy, if not actual scandal, among those who thought such things were better off unannounced" (Kelley, 1984, p. 93). But he was unrepentant: "Despite all the howls of outrage and screams of annoyance, I am not aware that anyone has clearly disproved any of them [his major theses]."

Nor would we expect anyone to be able to do so. People tend to value religion according to how much it costs—and because "reasonable" and "sociable" religion costs little, it is not valued greatly. It seems appropriate here to explore this thesis in greater depth, invoking recent work on the micro economies of religious commitment (Iannaccone, 1989, 1990, 1992; Stark and Iannaccone, 1991, 1992).

## Traditional Models of Religious Belief and Sacrifice

How can people possibly believe in supernatural beings and forces, and whatever drives them to make such irrational sacrifices in the name of faith? Social scientific thinking about religion has been dominated by this question. When it is posed this way, social scientists have been virtually forced to frame answers that postulate personal flaws in those who believe and sacrifice. Many have offered elaborate psychopathological explanations of religious commitment. For others, the explanation of preference has been ignorance, usually defined in terms of cultural backwardness or false consciousness.

Fortunately, this whole line of thought has nearly exhausted its credibility and is rapidly being replaced by models of individual religiousness based on the assumption that people typically choose to be, and to remain, religious for entirely rational reasons.

The psychopathological theory of piety has appeared in many forms, all of them bristling with antagonism and contempt. Consider Freud, who managed to characterize religion as a "neurosis," an "illusion," a "poison," an "intoxicant," and "childishness to be overcome" all on one page of his famous book on the subject (1927, p. 88). But the evidence failed to cooperate. In a survey of all published empirical studies Allen E. Bergin (1983) found that most reported a positive, rather than a negative, relationship between religiousness and mental health, and that most of the studies that did report a positive association between religion and psychopathology were tautological, having included religious items in their measures of psychopathology.

The "false consciousness" explanation has fared just as badly. After conducting a comprehensive survey of the research literature, Robert Wuthnow (1973, p. 126) reported that religious commitment is, "contrary to expectations, either unrelated or negatively related to [political] conservatism." The recent history of Eastern Europe, in which the churches played a leading role in the democratic transformation of nation after nation, is instructive. Although religion may well have been an "opiate" of the people in some times and places (especially when monopoly religious organizations have put their fate irrevocably in the hands of the ruling elite), in other instances it would be equally apt to describe religion as the "amphetamines" of the people.

Nor can religiousness be dismissed as backwardness and ignorance. There tends to be a positive association between religious involvement and social class (Stark, 1971), and religion is no stranger on American campuses. Among American college students, those who say they have been "born again" are slightly more likely than other students to enroll in the sciences. Data on faculty members reveal that engineers and physical and natural scientists are substantially more likely to belong to a church and to express religious commitment than are social scientists or those in law or the humanities (Steinberg, 1974). And it is the sons and daughters of secular humanists who are most likely to convert to a cult or sect movement (Stark and Bainbridge, 1985).

## Rational Models of Religious Belief and Sacrifice

In the wake of these disappointments, social scientists have begun a new approach to explaining personal piety.[8] This analysis leads to the conclusion that the more individuals sacrifice on behalf of their religion, the more benefits they receive in return. Hence religious behavior may be fully justified in terms of rational choice theories of behavior.

Like all rational choice theories, this approach begins with the assumption that individuals will evaluate religion in essentially the same way that they evaluate all other objects of choice. They will evaluate the costs and benefits (including the "opportunity costs" that arise when one action can be undertaken only by forgoing others) and will "consume" those religious goods that, together with their other actions, maximize net benefits. In particular, individuals will weigh the promise of tremendous rewards (for which the supernatural is the only possible source) against both the cost of qualifying for these rewards and the risk that the rewards will not eventuate.

The second step in the rational choice theory of religious commitment is the postulate that religion is a *collectively produced* commodity. Religion is a collective good for several reasons. First, many of the emotional and psychic rewards of religion are greater to the degree that they are socially generated and experienced. One can, of course, enjoy singing hymns alone. But that experience falls far short of singing along with hundreds of others to the accompaniment of a piano or pipe organ. A second reason is a bit more subtle. Because many results promised by religion can occur only elsewhere and far in the future, religion is an inherently risky good. Individuals therefore rely on interactions with others to help them determine whether the value of religious rewards outweighs the risks—that is, to evaluate the cost of qualifying for the reward versus the risk that the reward will not be forthcoming. To the extent that others with whom an individual interacts display confidence in the value of future religious rewards, that individual will gain greater confidence in them too.

The next step in this analysis postulates that because religion involves collective action, religious groups are always potentially subject to exploitation by *free riders*.

Free rider problems are the nemesis of any form of collective action. Michael Hechter (1987, p. 27) explains: "Truly rational actors will not join a group to pursue common ends when, without participating, they can reap the benefit of other people's activity in obtaining them. If every member of the relevant group can share in the benefits . . . then the rational thing is to free ride . . . rather than to help attain the corporate interest." The consequence, of course, is that too few collective goods are created because too few contribute, and thus everyone suffers—but those who gave their fair share suffer the most.

Free riding is a problem for all collective activities, but it poses a special challenge to voluntary organizations. Churches, for example, especially mainline congregations, are plagued with "members" who draw upon the group for weddings, funerals, and holiday celebrations, but who give little or nothing in return. Even if they do contribute money, they weaken the group's ability to create collective religious goods in that their inactivity devalues both the direct and the promised religious rewards by reducing the "average" level of commitment. There can be little less inspiring than attending services in a nearly empty church.

The inevitable dilemma is clear. On the one hand, a congregational structure that relies on the collective action of numerous volunteers is needed to make the religion credible and potent. On the other hand, unless these volunteers are mobilized to a high level of participation, that same congregational structure threatens to undermine the level of commitment and contributions needed to make a religion viable.

Costly demands offer a solution to the dilemma. That is, the level of stigma and sacrifice demanded by religious groups will be positively correlated with levels of member participation.

*Religious stigmas* consist of all aspects of social deviance that attach to membership in the group. A group may prohibit some activities deemed normal in the external society (dancing, for example) and require other activities deemed abnormal by the world (speaking in tongues, for example). By meeting these expectations of the group, members deviate from the norms of surrounding society. In the extreme case, when the state attempts to sustain a religious monopoly, membership alone in a dissenting group can be an immense stigma.

*Sacrifices* consist of investments (material and human) required to gain and retain membership in the group. The requirements of some religious groups involve stigma and sacrifice simultaneously, in that stigmatized persons must often forgo rewards such as career opportunities.

On the surface it would seem that increased costs must always make a religion less attractive. And indeed the economists' law of demand predicts just that, *other things remaining equal.* But it turns out that other things *do not* remain equal when religions impose these sorts of costs on their members. To the contrary, costly demands strengthen a religious group by mitigating "free rider" problems and by increasing the production of collective religious commodities.

When high costs create a barrier to group entry, potential members can no longer reap the benefits of attendance or membership without first incurring substantial costs. To take part at all a prospective member must qualify by accepting the stigmas and sacrifices demanded for everyone. Laurence R. Iannaccone (1989, p. 9) explains: "Potential members are forced to choose: participate fully or not at all. The seductive middle-ground of free riding and low participation is eliminated." High cost serve to *screen out* potential members whose commitment and participation would otherwise be low. The costs act as nonrefundable registration fees which, as in secular markets, measure seriousness of interest in the product. As a result, the demanding sects speak of "conversions," "being born again," and "submitting their lives to the Lord." The less demanding churches refer to affiliations that are seldom life-altering events. Sectarian members are either in or out; they must follow the demands of the group or withdraw. The "seductive middle-ground" is lost.

For those who do join, high costs increase their level of involvement because it makes activities outside of the group more costly. Group members find that the temptation to free ride is weaker, not because their human nature has somehow been transformed, but because the opportunities to free ride have been reduced and the flow of rewards for displaying high levels of commitment have been substantially increased. Looked at another way, prohibiting an activity effectively increases its price, because the full cost now includes the cost of discovery and, often, the price of concealment. As the increased price of the prohibited activity reduces demand for it, the demand for substitutes rises. If we may not attend dances or movies, play cards, go to taverns, or join fraternal organizations, we will probably look forward rather eagerly to the social activities at church.

Finally, it must be noted that the higher the costs of membership, the greater the material and social, as well as religious, benefits of membership.

At first glance it seems paradoxical that when the cost of membership increases the net gains of membership increase too. This is necessarily the case, however, when the commodity involved is collectively produced and when increased costs result in increased levels of participation in collective action, for this results in a greater supply of collective goods. An individual's positive experience in a worship service increases to the degree that the church is full, members enthusiastically participate (everyone sings and recites prayers, for example), and others express their positive evaluations of what is going on. Thus, as each individual member pays the cost of high levels of commitment, each benefits from the higher average level of participation thereby generated by the group. In similar fashion, people will value the otherworldly rewards of religion more highly to the extent that those around them do so. Or, to leave the realm of the immaterial, because Mormons are asked to contribute not only 10 percent of their income but 10 percent of their time to the church, they are able to lavish social services upon one another. Thus are the rewards of Mormon membership made tangible.

Membership in strict religions is, for many people, a "good bargain" in terms of a conventional cost-benefit analysis. We should acknowledge, however, that there are limits to the amount of sacrifice or the level of stigma people are willing to endure. Requiring members to withdraw from all secular opportunities, as some communes do, will clearly limit the growth of the organization. But most churches and sects do not increase sacrifice and stigma over time. As the circuit rider Peter Cartwright complained of the Methodists in 1856, the recurring trend over the past two hundred years has been for "expensive" sects gradually to lower the costs of membership and, by doing so, to reduce the benefits of membership as well. Thus our attention must focus on why and how the reduction of tensions with the surrounding culture weakens religious organizations. Against this theoretical background, let us now examine the current situation of American Catholicism.

## Recent Currents in American Catholicism

In the early 1960s, the American Catholic Church appeared as solid as ever. During the fifteen years following World War II, the church had

## Peter Cartwright on Sacrifice and Stigma

*Writing in 1856, at the age of seventy-two and in the fifty-third year of his ministry, Peter Cartwright contrasts the Methodist Episcopal Church of the 1850s with the church of the early 1800s. The famous Methodist itinerant was well aware that the sacrifice and stigma of being Methodist was being reduced, and he notices that the class meetings no longer bar the free rider.*

### Clergy

A Methodist preacher in those days, when he felt that God had called him to preach, instead of hunting up a college or Biblical institute, hunted up a hardy pony of a horse ... he cried, "Behold the Lamb of God, that taketh away the sins of the world." ... he went through storms of wind, hail, snow, and rain; climbed hills and mountains, traversed valleys, plunged through swamps, swam swollen streams, lay out all night, wet, weary, and hungry.... Under such circumstances, who among us would now say, "Here am I, Lord, send me"? (p. 243)

### Dress

... When I joined the Church her ministers and members were a plain people; plain in dress and address. You could know a Methodist preacher by his plain dress as far as you could see him. The members were also plain, very plain in dress.... may we not well question whether we are doing right in the sight of God in adorning our bodies with all this costly and extravagant dressing? ... would not the simple fund that might be created by disposing of the ornaments of the members of the Methodist Church alone, send the Gospel to hundreds of thousands.... (p. 515–516)

undergone a new period of growth. From 1916 through the 1930s Catholic adherents had hovered between 150 and 160 per 1,000 population. But the combined effects of the baby boom and the resumption of immigration from Europe caused the Catholic market share to jump to 190 per 1,000 by 1950 and to 235.9 by 1960.

*(continued)*

### Prayer Meetings

Prayer meetings have accomplished great good, as practiced in the Methodist Episcopal Church; but are they not growing into disuse among us? . . . there have been fashionable objections to females praying in public, but I am sure I do not exaggerate when I say I have often seen our dull and stupid prayer meetings suddenly changed . . . when a sister has been called on to pray. . . . (p. 517)

### Class Meetings

Class meetings have been owned and blessed of God in the Methodist Episcopal Church, . . . For many years we kept them with closed doors, and suffered none to remain in class meeting more than twice or thrice unless they signified a desire to join the Church. . . . Here the hard heart has been tendered, the cold heart warmed with holy fire; . . . But how sadly are these class meetings neglected in the Methodist Episcopal Church! . . . is it any wonder that so many of our members grow cold and careless in religion, and finally backslide? . . . And now, before God, are not many of our preachers at fault in this matter? (pp. 519–520)

### Camp Meetings

I am sorry to say that the Methodist Episcopal Church of late years, since they have become numerous and wealthy, have almost let camp meetings die out. I am very certain that the most successful part of my ministry has been on camp-grounds. (p. 523)

Then, in 1962, Pope John XXIII convened the Second Vatican Council, gathering all of the bishops of the Church in Rome to reassess and restructure doctrine and practice. The Italian word *aggiornamento,* which means updating, was used so often by the Pope to describe his aims to open the church to new ideas and influences that for a time it entered the vocabulary of the news media.

For four years the church fathers met periodically, making decisions that resulted in many far-reaching changes. The mass was no longer to be said in Latin, but in the local language. The faithful were no longer prohibited from eating meat on Friday. Many other prohibitions on Catholic behavior were also relaxed, and many traditions were greatly deemphasized. Moreover, the council stressed a new spirit of ecumenism. If, in the end, the liberals did not achieve their every goal, the changes were far more dramatic than anyone had expected.

Although there were many within the church who did not greet these changes with open arms, the reactions from non-Catholics were almost universally enthusiastic. Martin Marty (1964, pp. 107–108) wrote:

> No feature of the Vatican Council was more reported upon than that which revealed Roman interest in non-Roman Christians; no aspects of the papal encyclicals of recent years were more enthusiastically greeted than those which carried the broadest Christian vision. . . . Think of the meaning of joint work in the areas of race relations and other ethical issues. Think of the missionary significance to the world when Christians re-evaluate their stands on issues of censorship, church-state relations, population growth, peace, with the whole of human need in view and the whole of Christian populace implied.

Noting that Pope John XXIII not only had called his bishops to a Vatican Council, but had at the same time appointed a Secretariat for Promoting Christian Unity, Marty remarked: "His action made John XXIII the most recognized ecumenical leader of his generation and made ecumenism a household word" (p. 108). Could a really successful ecumenical age be far away?

Oddly enough, Will Herberg—the Jewish spokesman who had played a major role in mounting the ecumenical movement of the 1950s—warned vehemently against too much aggiornamento. Speaking before a national convention of Catholics belonging to the Newman Apostolate, Herberg criticized the many Catholic intellectuals who urged the church to "slough off its old ways and bring itself up to date by adjusting itself to the spirit of the age. I say just the opposite: in all that is important, the Church must stand firm in its witness to the truth that is eternal and unchanging; it needs no updating. . . . If it is to remain true to its vocation, it must take its stand against the world, against the age, against the spirit of the age—because the world and the age are always, to a degree, to an important degree, in rebellion against God" (in Fox, 1966, p. 85). Herberg concluded by condemning many Catholics as "eager for a crumb of recognition from the secular culture and . . . ready to swallow practically anything to get it (p. 85). Herberg's remarks went almost unnoticed, being reported briefly in the 1966 *Catholic Almanac*. And for a little while some other things went almost unnoticed as well.

A primary symptom of the vigor of American Catholicism was its ability to generate religious vocations, to attract thousands of young Catholic men and women each year to a life of full-time dedication to the church. In 1966, as Vatican II ended, the American church was staffed as follows:

| | |
|---|---|
| Diocesan priests | 36,419 |
| Religious priests | 22,774 |
| Brothers | 12,255 |
| Sisters | 181,421 |
| Seminarians | 48,046 |

These totals were never again equaled, and sharply downward trends immediately ensued. In 1965 there were 10.6 seminarians for every 10,000 Catholics (see Table 7.3). After that the bottom fell out. By 1990 there were only 6,233 men enrolled in American Catholic seminaries, or a rate of 1.1 seminarians per 10,000 Catholics. Put another way, in the pre–Vatican II era, young Catholic males were about ten times as likely to study for the priesthood as they are now.

There was also a rapid decline in brothers and sisters (see Table 7.4). The total of 181,421 sisters and 12,255 brothers in 1966 had shrunk to 103,269 and 6,743 by 1990. The drop in rates was even more dramatic given that the total number of Catholics continued to grow.

Just as the drop in seminary enrollments has resulted in a decline in the number of priests, the decline in the number of sisters stemmed in large part from a rapid decline in the number of women entering religious communities—from a total of 4,110 in 1965 to 1,486 in 1968 (Modde, 1974). In 1971 only 506 women entered a religious community—based on reports from 274 communities representing 70 percent of the total membership. These sudden declines were even more alarming given that the large "baby boom" cohorts were coming of age in the late 1960s, which greatly expanded the pool of potential recruits.

Finally, subsequent to Vatican II there was a substantial decline in the proportion of Catholics attending mass during any given week. During the 1950s more than 70 percent of American Catholics claimed weekly attendance at mass. This continued into the early 1960s—71 percent told the Gallup Poll in 1964 that they had been to church within the past

TABLE 7.3
Number Enrolled in Catholic Seminaries
per 10,000 U.S. Catholics, 1950–1990

| Year | Total | Diocesan | Religious |
|------|-------|----------|-----------|
|      | 9.2   | 4.5      | 4.7       |
| 1955 | 10.1  | 4.9      | 5.1       |
| 1960 | 9.8   | 5.0      | 4.8       |
| 1962 | 10.5  | 5.4      | 5.1       |
| 1965 | 10.6  | 5.8      | 4.8       |
| 1968 | 8.4   | 4.7      | 3.7       |
| 1970 | 6.0   | 3.6      | 2.4       |
| 1976 | 3.5   | 2.3      | 1.2       |
| 1980 | 2.8   | 1.8      | 1.0       |
| 1986 | 2.0   | 1.3      | 0.7       |
| 1988 | 1.4   | 0.9      | 0.5       |
| 1990 | 1.1   | 0.8      | 0.3       |

SOURCE: *Official Catholic Directory.*

seven days. But the next year, attendance at mass began a decline that continued until 1978, when it stabilized at slightly more than 50 percent (D'Antonio et al. 1989). Reduced attendance, however, was not the only symptom of an apparent decline in Catholic commitment. The frequency of going to confession, participation in church activities, and even daily prayer fell sharply between 1963 and 1974 (Greeley, McCready, and McCourt, 1976). Church contributions, as a percentage of annual income, fell from 2.2 percent in 1963 to 1.1 percent in 1983 (Greeley and McManus, 1987). In general American Catholics displayed a serious drop in religious commitment, dating from the end of Vatican II.

Andrew M. Greeley and his associates (Greeley, McCready, and McCourt, 1976; Hout and Greeley, 1987; Greeley and McManus, 1987; Greeley, 1989) attribute this drop in lay commitment to the unpopular papal encyclical on birth control issued in 1968, *Humanae Vitae.* That may be true, but it can be only part of the story. As Greeley has argued,

TABLE 7.4
Number of Catholic Brothers and Sisters
per 10,000 U.S. Catholics, 1955–1990

| Year | Brothers | Sisters |
|---|---|---|
| 1955 | 2.7 | 47.5 |
| 1960 | 2.6 | 41.2 |
| 1965 | 2.7 | 39.4 |
| 1970 | 2.4 | 33.6 |
| 1975 | 1.8 | 27.8 |
| 1980 | 1.6 | 25.3 |
| 1985 | 1.4 | 22.1 |
| 1990 | 1.2 | 18.1 |

SOURCE: *Official Catholic Directory.*

the encyclical was an attempt to impose higher costs in an area in which Catholics did not agree with their pontiff and were unwilling to accept his authority. Even prior to the encyclical, national surveys found that a majority of married Catholic women were not conforming to papal teachings on birth control (Ryder and Westoff, 1971).

But we will argue that the *decreasing demands* in other areas were as important, and probably more so, for reducing the commitment of Catholics. As Iannaccone (1989, p. 15) has commented, "the Catholic church has managed to arrive at a remarkable, 'worst of both worlds' position—discarding cherished distinctiveness in the areas of liturgy, theology, and life-style, while at the same time maintaining the very demands that its members and clergy are least willing to accept."

The distinctive sacrifices and stigmas of being Catholic were abandoned (without replacement) by the reforms of Vatican II. Recent declines in the vigor of American Catholicism reflect one more cycle of the sect-church process whereby a faith becomes a mainline body and then begins to wilt.

## Social and Cultural Assimilation

In previous chapters we have often observed the link between wealth and a desire for a less otherworldly faith. The vigorous era of the

American Catholic "sect," covered in Chapter 4, was also an era during which Catholics tended to be poor. This was still true in the 1940s. Writing in the *American Journal of Sociology,* Hadley Cantril (1943, p. 575) reported that the results of national survey studies "offer evidence for certain commonly known facts: Catholics are poorer and less educated than Protestants." But not for much longer. Reanalyzing data collected by Stouffer in 1955, Seymour Martin Lipset and Reinhard Bendix (1959) found that the difference between the occupational status of Protestants and Catholics disappeared when first- and second-generation immigrants were excluded. Moreover, by the mid-1960s there was little doubt that Catholics had achieved economic and educational parity with Protestants (Greeley, 1963, 1964; Glenn and Hyland, 1967; Alston, 1969). Today, because the Catholic population is so urban and non-southern, the average Catholic earns slightly more and has a job of slightly higher status than does the average Protestant.

If Catholics are no longer poorer than Protestants, they are no longer more prolific either. When reporting on recent trends in Catholic fertility in 1955, the demographer Dudley Kirk noted that "it is a matter of common observation that Catholic families . . . have more children than their non-Catholic neighbors" (p. 93). But in 1979 Charles F. Westoff wrote of "dramatic convergence of Catholic with non-Catholic" fertility (p. 239). From 1955 to 1975 the difference had gone from one of "common observation" to one of insignificance on a national survey of fertility.

In 1979 James McCarthy reported a substantial convergence in the divorce rates of Protestants and Catholics, although Catholics were still less likely to get divorced. When we examined data for a merged sample of six years of the General Social Survey (1985–1990), we found that 25 percent of Protestants and 19 percent of Catholics had been divorced at least once. And survey data from 1987 show that nearly 60 percent of American Catholics think a good Catholic can ignore the "Church's teaching regarding divorce and remarriage" (D'Antonio et al., 1989). These changes removed major impediments to Protestant-Catholic marriages, and the church quietly removed another impediment when it ceased to require that a non-Catholic spouse agree to rear the children as Catholics. Consequently, a majority of American Catholics now agree that one can marry outside the church and still remain a "good Catholic" (D'Antonio et al., 1989). Not surprisingly, the intermarriage rate has been rising rapidly (McCutcheon, 1988; Alba, 1990; Kalmijn, 1991).

Meanwhile, another convergence took place. For generations, Roman Catholics were overwhelmingly Democrats. As recently as the early 1970s Catholics still differed greatly from Protestants in terms of party identification and in support of Democrat candidates. But this too is history. In the last three elections the majority of American Catholics have voted for the Republican presidential candidate. Similarly, Catholics are becoming ever more similar to Protestants in terms of identifying themselves as Republicans or conservatives (Bird, 1990).

As Catholics shed these distinctive cultural and social patterns, they also began to dismantle their parallel structure of institutions and organizations. In 1964 the *American Catholic Sociological Review* changed its name to *Sociological Analysis*. In 1970 the American Catholic Sociological Society changed its name to the Association for the Sociology of Religion. These changes did not go unremarked or without causing some hard feelings. Several former presidents of the organization, seeing no need for another secular sociological organization, resigned (Morris, 1989). But neither did sufficient numbers of Catholic sociologists wish any longer to encourage non-Catholic perceptions of parochialism. Similar changes took place in other Catholic professional societies. Between 1965 and 1970 the number of such associations listed in the *National Catholic Almanac* declined by 17 percent.

## Religious Assimilation

But it wasn't only in the secular sphere that Catholics were becoming highly assimilated. Suddenly the mass was in English, and it proved to sound surprisingly similar to the ritual portions of services at high church Protestant bodies such as the Episcopalians and Lutherans. Moreover, the strict prohibitions against even entering a non-Catholic church building, let alone attending a non-Catholic wedding or funeral service, simply disappeared in the midst of the new ecumenism. Many Catholics thus began to have religious contacts with Protestants. Not only did the Catholic charismatic movement mirror Protestant pentecostalism but the two were soon intertwined at the local organizational level.

An important aspect of assimilation involved the decision by the council to make meatless Fridays no longer mandatory, but to leave it to individual Catholics to discover and observe their own practices of penance. In "Catholic" nations this change may have mattered little, except to the fishing industry. But in a pluralistic setting the observance had been a clear cultural marker and social boundary. When Catholic teenagers at drive-ins on Friday nights counted down to midnight before ordering their burgers, everyone present was reminded who was Catholic and who was not. To waive this very visible rule necessarily raised serious questions about the basis of religious truth and institutional credibility. From the point of view of teenagers and even of some adults, the scrapping of meatless Fridays for Catholics appeared as radical as a decision by the Mormon Church to authorize cola and coffee drinking or one by the Southern Baptists to market beer. As William D'Antonio and his colleagues (1989, p. 17) explained:

> this new norm regarding fasting also opened the door to independent thinking for the Catholic believer. The fact that eating meat on Friday was no longer considered a mortal sin raised for many Catholics the larger question about the attribution of sinfulness to other actions. It had, for many Catholics, a kind of "hole in the dike" effect. . . .
>
> In sum, the result of the changes of Vatican II was that Catholics began to believe that sin was perhaps not an objective phenomenon out there for all time, determined by some external unchanging authority, but highly situational and subject to legitimate redefinition over time.

By the same token, when you inform your parishoners that it no longer is a sin to miss mass, you can expect fewer people in the pews on a given Sunday. Indeed, Catholics now attend church like Protestants. Before Vatican II, Catholics far surpassed Protestants in the proportion attending church *every* Sunday. But if the cutting point were dropped slightly, to the proportion attending several times a month, the Protestant and Catholic figures would be about the same (Stark and Glock, 1968). Once Catholics placed no more stress on attendance than Protestants do, their behaviors converged.

A final aspect of the religious assimilation of American Catholics is the secularization of Catholic higher education. Most Catholic colleges and universities were founded by religious orders or the local diocese, and were considered important components in the comprehensive Catholic subculture. But as Catholics became increasingly assimilated, many Catholic scholars wanted to break out of the ghetto of Catholic education. Speaking at the Catholic Commission on Intellectual and Cultural Affairs annual meeting in 1955, John Tracy Ellis, Professor of Church History at the Catholic University of America, charged American Catholics with a failure "to exercise commanding influence in intellectual circles" (in Power, 1972, p. 382). But not for much longer. With the increasing size and affluence of Catholic universities and the reforms of Vatican II, Catholic higher education became quite secularized. The laity were given partial or complete control of the boards of trustees, the number of lay administrators gradually increased, and new faculty were hired and promoted on the basis of secular standards of professional achievement (Greeley, 1969). The new style of Catholic university placed more stress on academic freedom and encouraged a greater diversity of research and scholarship (Annarelli, 1987). But the secular achievements of the new university were at the expense of the mission of the old, and many questions can be raised about how and whether these universities now differ from their secular counterparts (Gleason, 1967). They make substantial contributions to scholarship and professional training, but they are not good places for preserving the faith or for the encouragement of religious vocations. And this takes us back to the crisis in Catholic vocations.

## The Religious

The ability of the Catholic Church to compete effectively in the free market American religious economy rested upon its ability to motivate sacrifice—on the willingness of thousands of men and women to take up lives of chastity, poverty, labor, and obedience. Just as the Methodists and the Baptists could sustain churches on the frontiers, so could the Catholics. Nor did the Catholics lack for dedicated revival preachers. Moreover, Protestant sects for many years never matched the Catholics in offering religious roles to women, without whom American Catholics could never have sustained their institutional separatism.

The extraordinary decline in religious vocations therefore strikes at the very foundation of the church. Not only are far fewer young Catholics entering seminaries or joining religious orders, but many priests, monks, and sisters have been dropping out of the religious life. Prior to Vatican II the annual rate of those leaving the priesthood was about one in a thousand. But immediately after the council the rate shot upwards. During 1969 2 percent of the nation's priests dropped out, or twenty of every thousand. The rate of priestly defections has declined since then, but has been holding steady at about seven per thousand (Schoenherr and Young, 1990). Sisters followed a similar pattern of defection, peaking in 1970 (Modde, 1974).

There has been an immense amount of research aimed at explaining why Catholic seminaries have been closing for lack of students and why men and women who took sacred, lifelong vows have so frequently been asking to be released from them. The consensus among researchers is that the *personal costs* of the Catholic religious life are too great for many to bear. Among the most frequently cited costs are celibacy, loneliness, unpleasant assignments, and, among the women religious, the subordinate role of women in the church (Fichter, 1968; Greeley, 1972; Schoenherr and Greeley, 1974; Ebaugh, 1977; Seidler, 1979; Seidler and Meyer, 1989). The question must arise, however, why only recently? These have been the costs of Catholic religious life for centuries. In 1962, as the council opened its first session, the seminaries were full of young men fully aware of the costs involved in the life they sought. The thousands of young women who took their vows that year knew full well what was expected of them as "brides of Christ." Costs alone cannot provide the answer, because the costs did not rise. Indeed, liberalization of the rules governing most religious orders would appear to have substantially reduced the personal sacrifices of belonging. And yet defection rates rose.

Faiths that impose high costs offset them by providing high levels of reward. Hence, when people cease choosing to sacrifice we must suspect that they no longer are getting a good deal—or at least that they no longer perceive the exchange as favorable. Because the sacrifices asked of American Catholic religious did not rise, their terms of exchange could have turned unfavorable only if there was a decline in the rewards entailed in the religious life.

Why would anyone want to become a priest or a sister? The first answer must involve religious motivation. The sacrifices involved are far too great for anyone who is not inspired by religious convictions to accept them. When Mother Teresa corrected a reporter who referred to her fellow sisters as social workers, saying "We are not social workers, we do this for Jesus," she expressed the inner conviction that makes sense of her life's work. Research on priests has always found that the primary motives and satisfactions are of a religious nature (Fichter, 1961; Schoenherr and Greeley, 1974; Verdieck, Shields, and Hoge, 1988). It follows that if there has been a decline in the rewards of the religious life, the first place to look is in the realm of the faith.

If changes ushered in by Vatican II caused the average Catholic to become confused about the nature of sin, this applies even more seriously to the religious. Consider the confusion that soon arose concerning the religious resources available for the enforcement of conformity to church standards of behavior.

Helen Rose Ebaugh (herself a former sister) argued in her 1990 presidential address to the Association for the Sociology of Religion that Vatican II caused an extraordinary shift away from a churchly faith based on clear doctrines and rules, backed by a strong, hierarchical institution, to a highly personalized faith. Ebaugh (1991, p. 7) believes that "the autonomy of individual conscience has replaced official pronouncements of morality" and that this in turn has led to a "selective Catholicism," in which people pick and choose which doctrines to accept and in which aspect of institutional life they wish to take part. This process did not result simply from lay impulses, but has been encouraged by the sudden reluctance and perhaps doctrinal inability of priests to enforce the rules. Ebaugh (1991, p. 6) reported that "while divorce and remarriage without attaining a formal annulment automatically incurs excommunication in terms of exclusion from the sacraments, there are hundreds of thousands of such excommunicated Catholics participating in the sacraments with no recriminations whatsoever. . . . The Church, in effect, has lost any meaningful instrument of law enforcement." Much more is involved here than the unwillingness of priests to withhold sacraments—far more important is that Catholics have lost their fears concerning excommunication. Not many years ago all good Catholics, religious and lay, regarded excommunication as a guaranteed ticket to hell. It didn't matter if the church found out your mortal sins and formally rang the bell, closed the book, and put out the candle. God knew and so did Satan, and the gates of hell yawned.

If the threat of excommunication has lost its impact, that is because Catholics have become very vague on the subject of damnation. As Marty (1991, p. 23) recently asked: "whatever happened to hell, the threat of hell, the system of punishments explicit and implicit in earlier Catholicism?" A recent event reveals the difficulty this question poses for many Catholic clergy. In 1986, during one of his weekly audiences, Pope John Paul II expressed caution about attributing individual behavior to diabolical possession. The Pope noted that we must accept in principle, however, that "Satan can arrive at these extreme manifestations." He added that Satan is "only a creature with all the limits of a creature" and therefore is destined finally to be "totally defeated" (in Neuhaus, 1987, p. 103). From this it would appear that Satan and his fiery hell remain pillars of Catholic doctrine. But the Jesuit editor of *Civilta Catto-*

*lica* immediately ridiculed the Pope's statements: "The devil cannot have a proper name because he represents nothing . . . [the names applied to the devil are] only a useless sequence of names, born of tradition and popular fantasy. No serious Christian must think of monsters, of dragons, of being possessed" (in Neuhaus, 1987, p. 103).

So what is a priest to tell his flock? Do the fires of hell await sinners or not? Do angels really exist? And what about saints? Do they really do miracles? Do they hear our appeals? Are they as yet the only Christians to have entered heaven, while everyone else waits in purgatory? The Pope says yes. But many other church leaders seem to say no—or at least they never mention these matters.

Such a softening of doctrines is precisely what one expects as a religious organization moves from sect to church, becoming a "respectable" mainline body. But this creates a very special problem for the Roman Catholic Church, because intense otherworldliness is needed to motivate the religious. It is one thing to accept a life of sacrifice if one is certain that his or her actions are seen from above. It is something else again to make great sacrifices on behalf of modernized doctrines and within a church that has greatly relaxed the standards of faith and behavior expected of the laity. Put another way, to become the bride of Christ one must be utterly confident of Christ's personal awareness of you; otherwise it is a purely symbolic relationship. It is not at all clear that one can accept vows of celibacy and poverty on behalf of abstract ideas about virtue and goodness. We conclude that the crisis of vocations thus reflects a crisis of faith and the deep erosion of the power of traditional Catholic symbols and sacraments. Greeley (1982, p. 88) has expressed this point as well as anyone: "anyone save an academic or a bishop would have anticipated that, when you change that which was unchangeable for 1,500 years, you are going to create a religious crisis. Attempts to put together a new system of religious symbols were half-hearted, unplanned and, most of all, insensitive to the actual religious needs of the Christian people."

But because people take up the religious life primarily for religious reasons must not obscure that fact that they respond favorably to worldly, tangible rewards as well. Chief among these for Catholic religious have been status and power. The immense respect in which American Catholics held their priests and sisters in pre-Vatican days would be hard to exaggerate.[9] Ebaugh (1991, p. 8) has noted: "While the notion of papal infallibility strictly applied only to doctrinal pronouncements of the Pope, it carried for the laity the generalized notion that the

Pope had the god-given authority to speak the truth in all matters, spiritual and temporal. The aura of authority filtered down through the hierarchical ranks such that bishops and local priests were also considered dispensers of truth even in the slightest matters of faith and morals." The power and authority of priests was a matter of specific Catholic doctrine. In 1888 Pope Leo XIII wrote: "It is indeed certain that in the Church there are two orders . . . the leaders and the people. The first order has the duty to teach, to govern, to guide men through life, and to fix rules for them; the duty of the other is to submit to the first, to obey, to carry out its orders and to pay it honor" (in Liebard, 1978, p. 1). The language was softened in the years that followed, but the "two orders" remained. The priest's authority was unquestioned, and he was conceived of as being "set apart" and "above" the people.

But after Vatican II, Peter Shannon (1967, p. 92), a past president of the Canon Law Society, wrote that "now we realize that the priest must be one with his people, not 'set apart' or 'above,' but united with, immersed in, a servant of his people." The role of the priest in the new church was still not clear, but the direction of change was obvious. Documents from the Second Vatican Council, such as the *Decree on the Apostolate of the Laity*, stated that lay people shared "in the priestly, prophetic and royal office of Christ," and called on secular priests to allow laity to "share actively in the life and action of His church," "in the liturgical life," and to "work in close cooperation" with the laity (in Liebard, 1978, pp. 220, 228–229).

The result was a profound loss of priestly power and authority. Ebaugh (191, p. 3) has argued that the "empowerment" of the laity caused them to cease "looking to the priest and hierarchy above them to define what it means to be Christian." She went on to note that the results of a 1974 national survey showing that only 12 percent of Catholics would acknowledge the Pope as having the right to "mandate issues of birth control" was an "indication of the fact that the hierarchical structure of control was collapsing" (p. 3).

Ebaugh sees the loss of priestly power and control as an unmixed blessing. Others have been less sanguine. Paul F. D'Arcy and Eugene C. Kennedy (1965, pp. 228–229), priests as well as psychologists, suggested:

> The aggiornamento has brought to priests not peace but a sword. Within the last year, as trumpets of new hope have been heard throughout the world, many priests have experienced deep and searing conflicts. Paradoxically, as unparalleled opportunities seem about to open for the

Church, her priests have tasted a bitter harvest of self-doubt and frustration.

The recurrent question among many serious priests concerns their own future. In a world of changed liturgy and emerged laymen, the function of the priest in relation to the Christian community is being examined. If it is true that many of the activities he now supervises . . . will gradually be assumed by an eager and better-prepared laity, what dimensions will his own work assume?

Many of these same concerns were observed by Joseph Fichter (1968) when he asked priests if they attempted to interest boys in the priestly vocations. Fichter reports "a recurring theme is that the parish priests are themselves 'unsure' of their own role" (1968, p. 80). As a result of the confusion surrounding the priesthood, the parish priest, once a primary motivator for boys to enter the vocation, was less willing to "talk up" vocations and more willing to question his own.[10]

The uncertainty of diocesan priests in the mid-sixties was warranted. In the years that followed, the relationship between the laity and the priests did change. The reestablishment of the permanent diaconate, the growing number of parish councils, and the increasing role of the laity throughout the church reduced as well as changed the role of the priest. The laity were still dependent on the priest for the Eucharistic sacrament, but in many areas of administration, liturgy, and education the laity were filling roles previously reserved for priests or sisters.

This does not mean that the priests—especially the young priests—necessarily objected to the changes being implemented. Seventy-six percent reported that the inclusion of the laity in parish planning was occurring too slowly, and 65 percent thought that the pace of liturgical adaptations was "about right"—with 30 percent responding "too slowly" (Fichter, 1968). But their support for change did not ensure that they would remain in the priesthood. To the contrary, priests scoring high on "modern values" relating to the church and its teachings were more inclined to leave (Schoenherr and Greeley, 1974).

For the priesthood, the result of Vatican II was a reduction of benefits without a reduction of costs. Indeed, it soon became clear that while many of the former rewards of the priesthood were gone, one could attain many of the rewards that remained as a member of the laity and thus avoid the major costs of the traditional religious life, such as celibacy, entirely. No wonder many resigned and few signed up.

The religious orders, as well, must have been confused about doctrine. And they too found the laity performing activities that were once reserved for the religious.[11] The *Decree on the Apostolate of the Laity* directed "religious nuns and brothers" to "respect the apostolic works of lay people, and willingly lend themselves to promote their programs" (in Liebard, 1978, p. 240).

The *Decree on the Up-to-Date Renewal of Religious Life* asked the religious orders to change their disciplines to "be in harmony with the present-day physical and psychological condition of the members" (in Flannery, 1975, p. 613). As a result, today it often is difficult to tell who is a sister; most have abandoned distinctive dress, and many live in secular housing. It seems that for many religious their "community" now consists of a roommate and friends who drop by from time to time. These changes have surely resulted in far greater personal freedom, but many of the distinctive rewards of the religious life were abandoned along the way. Once the religious constituted a community clearly separated from the laity; now religious and lay often work side by side. The religious have lost the many rewards available from belonging to a community, yet they are still asked to make sacrifices not required of their co-workers. Membership in a religious order is no longer a good bargain except for those with a remarkable *personal* ability to transmute sacrifice into powerful religious fulfillments.

## Future Prospects

Are the American Catholics going to go the way of the Congregationalists, Presbyterians, Episcopalians, and Methodists? Will they come to be just another mainline body specializing in comfortable pews, while slowly sliding downhill? Can the process somehow be reversed? We believe that in principle people can always reverse themselves and make different choices. But often they do not, and this makes it difficult to anticipate history. Nevertheless, some aspects of the future of American Catholicism seem relatively clear.

First, unless the church is able to re-establish greater tension with its environment it will not be able to restore the rewards needed to maintain high levels of sacrifice by the religious. It takes a vivid conception of active and potent supernatural forces to motivate people to make major sacrifices on behalf of faith, because only such active forces can plausibly deliver the great rewards on which a favorable exchange ratio rests. Keep in mind that the perceived rewards of the Catholic religious life must rise not only considerably but very rapidly if acute shortages are to be avoided. For example, the best current projections anticipate a

40 percent decline in the number of diocesan priests by 2005 (Schoenherr and Young, 1990).

It may be that when priests become sufficiently rare, their rewards
will rise greatly. But it seems more likely that the only way the American
Catholic Church can begin once more to recruit the people needed to
staff the institution is by *reducing the costs*. The church probably will
need to attract and hold personnel the way the mainline Protestant bodies do, by offering good salaries, fringe benefits, and job security and
by not imposing very stringent limits on their behavior.

This means, of course, that many people holding jobs once performed by the religious will be lay members. This change is already
evident in the parochial schools, where lay teachers are rapidly replacing sisters. It also means that the line between religious and lay will
become very indistinct, just as the line between Protestant pastors and
their members is slight.

If the church takes this solution to the crisis of vocations, it also
thereby becomes substantially more mainline—with all of the eventual
consequences of such a shift. Currently the high cost of vocations
screens out those with tepid commitment or a wavering faith. But
should the church accept a married clergy, the costs of entering the
priesthood will become similar to those of Protestant clergy. Moreover,
the priesthood will soon be attracting second- and third-generation
priests, a phenomenon common among Protestants. This will reduce
the average level of religious concern and dedication of the clergy—
those who pursue the family occupation will seldom be as motivated by
religious conviction as are those who enter from other backgrounds,
and this is especially true when the sacrifices asked of clergy are minor.

The second major point to be recognized is that unlike Protestant
bodies in America, Catholicism is an international faith. Decisions made
in Rome can have substantial impact on Catholicism in other nations.
Some recent decisions have been meant to make the church more otherworldly again and to restore firmer hierarchical authority. Conservatives appear to outnumber liberals among American bishops once more,
for example, and disciplinary actions have been taken against several
liberal Catholic theologians who have challenged various doctrines of
the church. Clearly, John Paul has been trying to make the church less
mainline in terms of theology.

But unlike the Southern Baptist reformers, the Pope and other opponents of liberalization in the Catholic Church cannot win through an
appeal to lay support. The majority of rank-and-file Catholics in the

United States and Europe seem to favor a much lower-tension faith. Of course, anyone seeking to restore traditional Catholicism would not appeal to the laity for authority in any event.

A third point has to do with why these changes in the church have not spawned sect movements. But they have. A large number of Catholic groups committed to a substantially higher-intensity version of their faith now exist in the United States—the large and well-known Catholic charismatic movement is but one among many. Unlike sect movements within Protestant bodies (which often depart in anger when their demands for reform are not met), however, thus far the Catholic sect groups have remained within the formal structure of the church and no liberalization by defection has taken place. For doctrinal reasons these sect movements are determined to remain within the church. The Catholics most opposed to the liberalizing trends going on in the church are also those most committed to traditional Catholic doctrines concerning the Apostolic Succession and the One True Church. How can they defect to form a church lacking legitimacy? And Catholic leaders show no interest in causing them to do so. Internal renewal movements must thus always be taken into account when trying to read the future of American Catholicism.[12]

Yet after considering all these possibilities, we think it unlikely that the American Catholic Church will be able to halt its transformation from an energetic sect into a sedate mainline body. For all the reasons we have discussed throughout this book, it would be surprising if the Catholic Church reversed its direction. But this prognosis by no means indicates that we expect it to disappear in the foreseeable future. After all, there are still 1.6 million Congregationalists (United Church of Christ) in our midst. What we do expect is that the American Catholic Church will behave like a member of the mainline. No longer in tension with the surrounding culture, the church will generate less commitment from its membership and will gradually fail to compete with a new generation of upstart sects. We believe that, as has been true for the Methodists and many other bodies, its contribution to the churching of America is drawing to an end. The recent inability of the church to hold its own within the rapidly growing Hispanic community reinforces this judgment. Although it turned out not to be true that nineteenth-century Catholic immigrants from Europe failed to keep the faith, there has been a high rate of defection to Protestant sects by Hispanics, especially recent immigrants (Christiano, 1991). Greeley (1988, p. 62) has called these losses an "ecclesiastical failure of unprecedented proportions."

But on February 28, 1990, thirty bishops from California and northwestern Mexico issued a statement charging Protestant sects with the use of "unfair and coercive" practices to steal Catholics from their proper flock. The Pope repeated these same charges during his visit to Mexico.

This book began as an effort to describe and explain the churching of America—how it went from a nation in which most people did not belong to a church to one in which most people do. In pursuit of this goal, we found ourselves driven to dispute many received truths about American religion. The first of these is the portrayal of American religious history in terms of sudden shifts during which religiousness rises or falls willy-nilly in response to various cultural crises and social concerns. We find no basis for these claims, not in recent decades or in the past several centuries. What we do find to be the master trend of American religious history is a long, slow, and consistent increase in religious participation from 1776 to 1926—with the rate inching up slightly after 1926 and then hovering near 60 percent. We recognized that sudden shifts do occur in our religious economy, but these involve the rising and falling fortunes of religious firms, not the rise and fall of religion per se. Here we have been forced to dispute a second major misperception common to the general religious histories of America. Their authors have invariably managed to depict certain mainline Protestants as the winners, while a succession of sectarian challengers either slumped off into obscurity or mended their ways and joined the mainline. This is to tell the story entirely backwards.

But whatever we have managed to accomplish in terms of amending some of these basic notions about American religious history, we place far greater importance on our attempt to place this history within a dynamic sociological model. It is the idea of religious economies and the recognition of the sect-church process as its primary dynamic that we think justifies our efforts. Thus, in closing, we should like to offer a caveat about our theory of the fate of religious firms.

We do not believe that the sect-church process has the blind inevitability of Marx's dialectic or even of the wheel of *karma*. Humans are rational beings, not puppets enslaved to the strings of "history," and always have the capacity to choose. What is history other than the record of the choices particular humans have made and the actions they have taken on the basis of their choices? The sect-church process appears so unstoppable because humans seems to have rather mixed motives when they make choices about religion. What we have in mind here is a sociological version of what John Wesley recognized as the inevitability of temptation.

Humans want their religion to be sufficiently potent, vivid, and compelling so that it can offer them rewards of great magnitude. People seek a religion that is capable of miracles and that imparts order and sanity to the human condition. The religious organizations that maximize these aspects of religion, however, also demand the highest price in terms of what the individual must do to qualify for these rewards. Moreover, because of the long-term exchange relations that religious organizations require, people are forever paying the costs in the here and now while most of the rewards are to be realized elsewhere and later. As a result, humans are prone to backslide, to get behind on their payments. As Mark put it, "The spirit truly is ready, but the flesh is weak." Thus, other things being equal, people will always be in favor of a modest reduction in their costs. In this fashion, humans begin to bargain with their churches for lower tension and fewer sacrifices. They usually succeed, both because it is those with the most influence—the clergy and the leading laity—who most desire to lower the level of sacrifice and because each reduction seems so small and engenders widespread approval. No doubt most Methodists were glad to be permitted to go to the circus, just as most Catholics probably welcomed the chance to skip mass from time to time. Thus does the sect-church process ensue.

There comes a point, however, when a religious body has become so worldly that its rewards are few and lacking in plausibility. When hell is gone, can heaven's departure be far behind? Here people begin to switch away. Some are recruited by very high tension movements. Others move into the newest and least secularized mainline firms. Still others abandon all religion. These principles hardly constitute a wheel of *karma*, but they do seem to reveal the primary feature of our religious history: the mainline bodies are always headed for the sideline.

# Appendix
# Profile Tables, 1776 and 1850

TABLE A.1
Denominational Percentages by Colony,
1776, Based on Number of Congregations

MAINE (*N* = 64)

| | |
|---|---:|
| Congregationalist | 60.9 |
| Presbyterian | 17.2 |
| Episcopal | 9.4 |
| Baptist | 7.8 |
| Quaker | 3.1 |
| Lutheran | 1.6 |

NEW HAMPSHIRE (*N* = 125)

| | |
|---|---:|
| Congregationalist | 63.2 |
| Presbyterian | 21.6 |
| Baptist | 8.8 |
| Quaker | 3.2 |
| Episcopal | 1.6 |
| Other* | 1.6 |

TABLE A.1 (*Continued*)

| | |
|---|---|
| VERMONT (N = 20) | |
| Congregationalist | 65.0 |
| Presbyterian | 10.0 |
| Baptist | 10.0 |
| Episcopal | 10.0 |
| Other* | 5.0 |
| | |
| MASSACHUSETTS (N = 433) | |
| Congregationalist | 71.6 |
| Baptist | 14.3 |
| Quaker | 4.2 |
| Episcopal | 3.7 |
| Presbyterian | 3.0 |
| Methodist | 0.2 |
| Other* | 3.0 |
| | |
| RHODE ISLAND (N = 87) | |
| Baptist | 57.5 |
| Congregationalist | 17.2 |
| Quaker | 12.6 |
| Episcopal | 6.9 |
| Presbyterian | 1.1 |
| Moravian | 1.1 |
| Other* | 3.4 |
| | |
| CONNECTICUT (N = 310) | |
| Congregationalist | 64.2 |
| Episcopal | 17.7 |
| Baptist | 9.4 |
| Quaker | 1.6 |
| Presbyterian | 1.3 |
| Other* | 5.8 |

TABLE A.1 *(Continued)*

---

NEW YORK (*N* = 220)

| | |
|---|---|
| Dutch Reformed | 26.4 |
| Presbyterian | 15.9 |
| Episcopal | 15.5 |
| Quaker | 10.9 |
| Lutheran | 8.6 |
| Baptist | 8.2 |
| German Reformed | 4.5 |
| Methodist | 3.2 |
| Moravian | 2.3 |
| Congregationalist | 1.8 |
| Roman Catholic | 0.5 |
| Other* | 2.3 |

NEW JERSEY (*N* = 252)

| | |
|---|---|
| Presbyterian | 30.5 |
| Baptist | 18.3 |
| Quaker | 15.5 |
| Episcopal | 11.5 |
| Lutheran | 9.5 |
| Methodist | 6.0 |
| Dutch Reformed | 3.2 |
| German Reformed | 2.4 |
| Roman Catholic | 2.0 |
| Moravian | 0.8 |
| Congregationalist | 0.4 |

PENNSYLVANIA (*N* = 535)

| | |
|---|---|
| Presbyterian | 27.9 |
| German Reformed | 17.6 |
| Quaker | 15.3 |
| Lutheran | 9.7 |
| Dutch Reformed | 8.6 |
| Episcopal | 6.0 |

TABLE A.1 (*Continued*)

| | |
|---|---:|
| Baptist | 4.9 |
| Moravian | 2.6 |
| Roman Catholic | 1.9 |
| Methodist | 0.2 |
| Other* | 5.4 |

DELAWARE (*N* = 67)

| | |
|---|---:|
| Presbyterian | 37.3 |
| Episcopal | 22.4 |
| Quaker | 19.4 |
| Roman Catholic | 9.0 |
| Methodist | 4.5 |
| Baptist | 4.5 |
| Lutheran | 1.5 |
| Dutch Reformed | 1.5 |

MARYLAND (*N* = 211)

| | |
|---|---:|
| Episcopal | 26.5 |
| Roman Catholic | 15.6 |
| Presbyterian | 14.2 |
| Methodist | 10.9 |
| Quaker | 10.9 |
| German Reformed | 7.6 |
| Lutheran | 7.1 |
| Baptist | 2.4 |
| Moravian | 1.0 |
| Other* | 2.8 |

VIRGINIA (*N* = 491)

| | |
|---|---:|
| Episcopal | 34.6 |
| Baptist | 29.9 |
| Presbyterian | 22.0 |
| Quaker | 7.1 |
| Methodist | 2.0 |
| Lutheran | 1.8 |

## TABLE A.1 (*Continued*)

| | |
|---|---|
| German Reformed | 1.6 |
| Roman Catholic | 0.2 |
| Other* | 0.6 |

### NORTH CAROLINA (*N* = 165)

| | |
|---|---|
| Presbyterian | 28.5 |
| Baptist | 25.5 |
| Quaker | 18.2 |
| Episcopal | 14.5 |
| German Reformed | 7.2 |
| Moravian | 3.0 |
| Lutheran | 1.8 |
| Methodist | 1.2 |

### SOUTH CAROLINA (*N* = 166)

| | |
|---|---|
| Presbyterian | 31.3 |
| Baptist | 24.7 |
| Episcopal | 22.9 |
| Lutheran | 9.0 |
| Quaker | 4.8 |
| German Reformed | 2.4 |
| Congregationalist | 1.2 |
| Other* | 3.6 |

### GEORGIA (*N* = 23)

| | |
|---|---|
| Baptist | 30.4 |
| Lutheran | 21.7 |
| Presbyterian | 13.0 |
| Quaker | 13.0 |
| Episcopal | 13.0 |
| Congregationalist | 4.3 |
| Other* | 4.3 |

SOURCE: See Table 2.2.
*Includes Separatist and Independent, Dunker, Mennonite, Huguenot, Sandemanian, and Jewish.

TABLE A.2
Denominational Adherents
per 1,000 Population, 1850

---

NEW ENGLAND
Maine (upstart ratio* = 2.80)

| | |
|---|---:|
| Congregationalists | 48 |
| Episcopalians | 2 |
| Presbyterians | 3 |
| Baptists | 89 |
| Methodists | 58 |

New Hampshire (upstart ratio = 1.33)

| | |
|---|---:|
| Congregationalists | 90 |
| Episcopalians | 3 |
| Presbyterians | 8 |
| Baptists | 82 |
| Methodists | 54 |

Vermont (upstart ratio = 1.35)

| | |
|---|---:|
| Congregationalists | 92 |
| Episcopalians | 8 |
| Presbyterians | 5 |
| Baptists | 56 |
| Methodists | 86 |

Massachusetts (upstart ratio = 1.03)

| | |
|---|---:|
| Congregationalists | 94 |
| Episcopalians | 7 |
| Presbyterians | 3 |
| Baptists | 58 |
| Methodists | 50 |

Rhode Island (upstart ratio = 3.22)

| | |
|---|---:|
| Congregationalists | 32 |
| Episcopalians | 22 |
| Presbyterians | 0 |

## TABLE A.2 (*Continued*)

| | |
|---|---|
| Baptists | 140 |
| Methodists | 34 |

Connecticut (upstart ratio = 0.80)

| | |
|---|---|
| Congregationalists | 134 |
| Episcopalians | 32 |
| Presbyterians | 8 |
| Baptists | 58 |
| Methodists | 81 |

### FORMER "MIDDLE COLONIES"

New York (upstart ratio = 1.86)

| | |
|---|---|
| Congregationalists | 13 |
| Episcopalians | 13 |
| Presbyterians | 51 |
| Baptists | 55 |
| Methodists | 88 |

New Jersey (upstart ratio = 1.95)

| | |
|---|---|
| Congregationalists | 3 |
| Episcopalians | 12 |
| Presbyterians | 77 |
| Baptists | 47 |
| Methodists | 131 |

Pennsylvania (upstart ratio = 1.58)

| | |
|---|---|
| Congregationalists | 1 |
| Episcopalians | 8 |
| Presbyterians | 67 |
| Baptists | 30 |
| Methodists | 90 |

Maryland (upstart ratio = 4.60)

| | |
|---|---|
| Congregationalists | 0 |
| Episcopalians | 25 |

## TABLE A.2 (*Continued*)

| | |
|---|---:|
| Presbyterians | 19 |
| Baptists | 15 |
| Methodists | 189 |
| **Delaware (upstart ratio = 3.03)** | |
| Congregationalists | 0 |
| Episcopalians | 21 |
| Presbyterians | 48 |
| Baptists | 18 |
| Methodists | 191 |

### FORMER SOUTHERN COLONIES

| | |
|---|---:|
| **Virginia (upstart ratio = 5.31)** | |
| Congregationalists | 0 |
| Episcopalians | 13 |
| Presbyterians | 32 |
| Baptists | 96 |
| Methodists | 143 |
| **North Carolina (upstart ratio = 8.19)** | |
| Congregationalists | 0 |
| Episcopalians | 4 |
| Presbyterians | 31 |
| Baptists | 129 |
| Methodists | 163 |
| **South Carolina (upstart ratio = 4.88)** | |
| Congregationalists | 2 |
| Episcopalians | 12 |
| Presbyterians | 46 |
| Baptists | 136 |
| Methodists | 158 |
| **Georgia (upstart ratio = 16.13)** | |
| Congregationalists | 0 |

## TABLE A.2 (*Continued*)

| | |
|---|---|
| Episcopal | 3 |
| Presbyterians | 21 |
| Baptists | 202 |
| Methodists | 173 |

FRONTIER: SOUTH

Florida (upstart ratio = 5.33)

| | |
|---|---|
| Congregationalists | 0 |
| Episcopalians | 11 |
| Presbyterians | 30 |
| Baptists | 77 |
| Methodists | 140 |

Alabama (upstart ratio = 7.85)

| | |
|---|---|
| Congregationalists | 0 |
| Episcopalians | 2 |
| Presbyterians | 34 |
| Baptists | 140 |
| Methodists | 143 |

Mississippi (upstart ratio = 6.32)

| | |
|---|---|
| Congregationalists | 0 |
| Episcopalians | 2 |
| Presbyterians | 35 |
| Baptists | 107 |
| Methodists | 129 |

Louisiana (upstart ratio = 4.74)

| | |
|---|---|
| Congregationalists | 0 |
| Episcopalians | 3 |
| Presbyterians | 8 |
| Baptists | 16 |
| Methodists | 36 |

## TABLE A.2 (*Continued*)

| | |
|---|---|
| Texas (upstart ratio = 6.67) | |
| Congregationalists | 0 |
| Episcopalians | 1 |
| Presbyterians | 17 |
| Baptists | 29 |
| Methodists | 94 |
| | |
| FRONTIER: BORDER | |
| Missouri (upstart ratio = 3.67) | |
| Congregationalists | 0 |
| Episcopalians | 2 |
| Presbyterians | 30 |
| Baptists | 62 |
| Methodists | 56 |
| | |
| Kentucky (upstart ratio = 5.93) | |
| Congregationalists | 0 |
| Episcopalians | 2 |
| Presbyterians | 45 |
| Baptists | 168 |
| Methodists | 111 |
| | |
| Tennessee (upstart ratio = 4.48) | |
| Congregationalists | 0 |
| Episcopalians | 2 |
| Presbyterians | 60 |
| Baptists | 112 |
| Methodists | 164 |
| | |
| Arkansas (upstart ratio = 5.42) | |
| Congregationalists | 0 |
| Episcopalians | 0 |
| Presbyterians | 23 |
| Baptists | 52 |
| Methodists | 74 |

TABLE A.2 (*Continued*)

---

FRONTIER: NORTH

Ohio (upstart ratio = 3.13)

| | |
|---|---|
| Congregationalists | 9 |
| Episcopalians | 4 |
| Presbyterians | 59 |
| Baptists | 52 |
| Methodists | 174 |

Indiana (upstart ratio = 5.18)

| | |
|---|---|
| Congregationalists | 1 |
| Episcopalians | 2 |
| Presbyterians | 48 |
| Baptists | 80 |
| Methodists | 180 |

Illinois (upstart ratio = 3.67)

| | |
|---|---|
| Congregationalists | 8 |
| Episcopalians | 4 |
| Presbyterians | 44 |
| Baptists | 63 |
| Methodists | 141 |

Michigan (upstart ratio = 1.88)

| | |
|---|---|
| Congregationalists | 11 |
| Episcopalians | 5 |
| Presbyterians | 24 |
| Baptists | 25 |
| Methodists | 52 |

Wisconsin (upstart ratio = 2.22)

| | |
|---|---|
| Congregationalists | 15 |
| Episcopalians | 4 |
| Presbyterians | 12 |
| Baptists | 30 |
| Methodists | 40 |

## TABLE A.2 (*Continued*)

| | |
|---|---|
| Iowa (upstart ratio = 1.99) | |
| Congregationalists | 11 |
| Episcopalians | 1 |
| Presbyterians | 18 |
| Baptists | 12 |
| Methodists | 47 |

SOURCES: The adherence rates were estimated from Bureau of the Census (1854) reports on the number of churches the seating capacity of churches and the value of church property. See Finke and Stark (1986) for a complete discussion of the statistical procedures used to generate the estimates.

*The upstart ratio represents the number of Methodists and Baptists for each Congregationalist, Episcopalian, and Presbyterian.

# Notes

## Chapter 1    A New Approach to American Religious History

1. The criticisms we direct toward historians of American religion are limited primarily to those who have written general or comprehensive works. We greatly admire the work of many historians who have specialized in specific periods and topics, especially Jon Butler, Whitney R. Cross, Jay P. Dolan, Nathan O. Hatch, William G. McLoughlin, Jr., Mark Noll, Douglas H. Sweet, Ann Taves, and James Turner.
2. A comparison of the 1926 census data for the city of Seattle with data collected in 1925 by the local church council gave strong support for the accuracy of the census data (Stark, 1992b).
3. See Christiano (1987) for a more complete discussion of the undercounting that afflicted the 1936 religious census. Despite the troubles with the 1936 data collection, Christiano claims that the religious "censuses were the grandest research projects ever undertaken in the quantitative study of religion" (p. 40). We agree.
4. We use the term "adherence rate" rather than the more familiar "church membership rate" in order to alert readers that we have standardized the membership data to eliminate different definitions of membership across religious bodies. Some groups count children, others do not. We therefore inflated the membership statistics of groups that do not count children. The inflations were based on the local age profile. Because the results do not really represent "members," we have substituted the word "adherents."

## Chapter 2    The Colonial Era Revisited

1. Granted that Stiles believed the total population to be larger than that, placing the number of dissenters at 62,420. Thus he only claimed that 88 percent

of New Englanders were Congregationalists. The actual proportion was closer to 13 percent.

2. We are aware that Patricia U. Bonomi and Peter R. Eisenstadt (1982) estimated the average membership of churches in this era as 480 adherents, or more than six times greater than our estimate. They arrived at their average by assuming the average church included 80 families and multiplying that times six—the size of the average household as reported by the census of 1790. Although we admire the fine scholarship of these authors, we must disagree with their conclusion that from 60 to 70 percent of the white colonists were churched. Our informal tours of colonial churches reveal them to be exceptionally small. It would be difficult to seat 100 people in most of those that either author has been in. Bonomi and Eisenstadt admit as much in their footnote 35 where they note, vis-à-vis Anglican churches, that "many Virginia churches and chapels were 60′ × 30′ or larger by the 1720s; with galleries added and single pews made double, they could seat several hundred people" (p. 254). As far back as good records go, American Protestants have always been optimistic builders—in 1890 Protestants averaged three seats per member nationwide (Finke and Stark, 1986). Most of Bonomi and Eisenstadt's membership data come from reports written by local Anglican pastors in response to a letter of inquiry from the Bishop of London. These reports strike us as far less careful than Bonomi and Eisenstadt's assessment would suggest. Moreover, Anglicans tended to be located in more densely populated areas, where congregations no doubt were larger than average. But our major basis for dissent is simply that too much data, from too many independent sources, suggest a lower figure.

3. In the words of Frederick Jackson Turner (1920), the "oldest west was the Atlantic Coast," and "the frontier towns of 1695 were hardly more than suburbs of Boston." Turner began his analysis of the significance of frontiers using Massachusetts of 1695 as his "early prototype."

4. Bailyn's extraordinary study is based on records made by British port officials, including 5,196 individuals leaving England and 3,872 leaving Scotland. Bailyn has managed to locate American records on many of these people, giving him the means for an immense study, only the first volume of which has appeared.

5. Muhlenberg later concluded that Pennsylvania, the colony with the most Lutherans and one of the highest rates of religious adherence, had "more necromancers . . . than Christians" (in Butler, 1990, p. 87).

6. Sometimes the liberal faction will leave, but usually those seeking higher tension lack the power to win the internal dispute, which is why the denomination had moved into lower tension in the first place.

7. For a complete explanation of why and how this occurs see Stark and Bainbridge (1985, 1987).

8. For an extended treatment of this matter, see Stark and Bainbridge (1987), chap. 9.

## Chapter 3     The Upstart Sects Win America

1. Some Congregational leaders still do not grasp the idea of market share. When discussing the process by which the Congregational and the Evangelical and Reformed Churches merged, Louis H. Gunneman (1977), a major figure in American Congregationalism, noted that the Congregationalists grew by 57, 490 members between 1956 and 1960 while the Evangelical and Reformed grew by 33,681. He then acknowledged that these rates of growth fell far short of the national average for all churchs during these years. Nevertheless, two sentences later he could write, "The obvious conclusion to be drawn is that during the time of the consummation of union both churches maintained rates of growth exhibiting high spirit and morale" (p. 59). This in 1977, after more than a decade of rapid membership declines.

2. Sweet (1976, p. 346) remarked that Beecher's account was dictated seventy years after the fact: "In his dotage, he constructed an exaggerated ash-heap of debauchery and irreligion at Yale." Beecher attributed the situation at Yale to the decay of religion in general.

3. Examination of Methodist membership statistics year by year does show a decline in six of the thirty-five years between 1776 and 1810. These could be noted as momentary ebb tides, but they cannot justify claims that religion fell on hard times for two decades or more. Moreover, we found no year during this period when Baptist membership declined.

4. For a more complete discussion of religious deregulation, see Finke (1990).

5. AHMS officials were entirely aware of the abundance of Methodists and Baptists in areas they sought funds to "church." More recently general historians, too, should have been aware of this fact, because it is a matter easily learned from denominational reports of the period, which are widely available.

6. For a complete account of the duties of the local exhorters, stewards, class-leaders, trustees, and local preachers, see Gorrie (1852).

7. Francis Asbury often referred to his circuit riders as "traveling bishops."

8. For example, Peter Cartwright helped to establish both McKendree and MacMurray Colleges and, while serving in the Illinois legislature, introduced the first bill to establish a state university (Miyakawa, 1964).

9. Cokesbury College was founded by the Methodists in 1787, but it burned to the ground in 1795. According to Sweet (1933, p. 112), Bishop Asbury took this as "an indication of Providence that it was not the duty of the Methodist Episcopal Church to found and operate colleges."

10. See the 1871 *Baptist Quarterly* for a survey of Baptist opinion on an educated clergy.

11. When a circuit rider married he soon wanted to cease traveling and to "locate." This reduced the scope of his effect and made him far more expensive to sustain—he could no longer depend on the free meals and lodging often provided by families along the way, and soon had his own extra mouths to feed. Asbury frequently complained in his journals that women would get all his best traveling preachers.
12. In his day Asbury was thought to be the most famous man in the nation. He often received mail from abroad addressed to Francis Asbury, United States of America. Because he traveled a well-known itinerary from one conference meeting to another, the postal service prided itself in being able to deliver his mail.
13. We accept that instances of what might be classified as hysteria occurred during revival services—Finney provides quite complete descriptions of some. These symptoms, however, arose as a result of participation in a highly emotional service, and therefore cannot be claimed as a cause of the revival meeting. Moreover, nothing is explained by postulating some generalized angst or other equally vague psychological state as the precipitating cause of an awakening. We might just as well embrace the Zeitgeist as a major scientific force.
14. For a formal analysis of the functions of revival within religious organizations, see Stark and Bainbridge (1987).

### Chapter 4    The Coming of the Catholics

1. Notice, however, that these lumberjacks were not tithing.
2. It must be noted that Pope Leo had been misled to think that there had been massive defections, running into millions of members, to the Protestants.
3. Dolan (1978, p. 22) described a revival as an "occasion for a religious roundup of Catholics."
4. The religious orders were not alone in their outreach efforts, however. Aaron Abell (1960) reports that by 1908 thirty bands of diocesan priests were involved in missions to interested non-Catholics. Moreover, the laity often invited non-Catholics to attend church, especially during the time of a parish mission (Hennesey, 1981).
5. In the beginning Weninger preached four times a day in German during his missions. But, when his revivals attracted French- and English-speaking audiences he added sermons in these languages as well. Soon he was preaching as many as twelve times a day in three languages. He admitted that such a pace was "very taxing on the minister," but also noted that "the effect is far greater" (in Garraghan, 1984, p. 58).
6. Each car could seat about one hundred worshipers, and each was equipped with an organ and with living quarters for a missionary couple. When a chapel car arrived in a new town or village it was unhooked from the train and placed on a siding. Services were held nightly until a sufficient number

had been gathered to found a new congregation, whereupon the chapel car was moved to another town. Despite relatively long stays in one place, each car traveled thousands of miles annually. In 1894 *Evangel,* a Baptist chapel car stationed in Minnesota, and *Emmanuel,* a Baptist car stationed in California, together logged 17,834 miles while the missionaries aboard delivered 1,313 sermons and held 207 prayer meetings (Mondello, 1987).

7. Female members of Catholic religious orders currently prefer to be called "sisters" or "women religious." We use the word "nun" in this chapter because it more accurately reflects common usage in the Catholic community during the era on which we are focusing.

## Chapter 5    Methodists Transformed, Baptists Triumphant

1. Between 1860 and 1870 both Baptists and Methodists lost members due to the dislocations of the Civil War. Following the war the Methodist rate increased again, but they never regained their prewar level and failed to keep pace with the rapid Baptist gains.

2. These trends also hold for black Baptist and Methodist bodies. Black Baptists per 1,000 blacks (in the population) rose from 299 in 1890 to 425 by 1926. In contrast, black Methodists declined from 207 to 157 during this same period.

3. According to the 1916 census of religious bodies, the seminaries of the Northern Baptist Convention enrolled 997 students while the seminaries of the Southern Baptist Convention enrolled 708 students (including 220 females "preparing for missionary and social settlement work").

4. Unfortunately only 30 percent of all Southern Baptist ministers reported their salaries to the census, and therefore the exact percentage of ministers employed outside of the church is not known. But considering that farmer-preachers were most common in the rural South, where Landmarkism and resistance to central authorities were most prominent, the percentage employed outside the church was probably much higher than the 36 percent reported.

5. The name came from a tract by James M. Pendleton, *An Old Landmark Re-Set,* which Graves published in 1854.

6. In the beginning he was called chairman of the faculty; his title was changed to president only seven months before his death in 1888.

7. In 1877 a total of eighty-one students enrolled in the seminary, and the number doubled the next year.

8. He took a position at the University of Richmond and taught there until 1909.

9. Norris was a dramatic speaker and a forceful leader, but his entire life was one of controversy. Outside of the church he was indicted for arson, tried for perjury, and acquitted on a murder charge. Within the Convention, he and his church were expelled from the Texas Southern Baptist Convention. He showed little restraint in his criticism of church or political leadership.

Indeed, in 1926 he referred to the mayor of Fort Worth and his associates as a "two by four, simian-headed, sawdust-brained, bunch of grafters" (Shurden, 1972, p. 91).

10. Ammerman's (1990) data also confirmed many of the other fears of traditionalists: modernists placed less emphasis on evangelism and were more willing to tolerate behavior traditionally regarded as "immoral," such as swearing and the drinking of alcoholic beverages.

11. The president appoints a Committee on Committees, which in turn nominates a Committee on Nominations. If approved by the messengers (voters at the convention), the Committee on Nominations then nominates agency trustees for messenger approval.

## Chapter 6    Why Unification Efforts Fail

1. If this position seems to echo the claims made on behalf of religious monopolies, keep in mind that the consequences of a fully successful ecumenical movement would be the creation of a religious monopoly.

2. An important exception is the work of Claude S. Fischer (1982). According to Fischer's subcultural theory, "urbanism bolsters ethnic and religious community, particularly if the group is small enough so that affiliation is difficult (p. 202).

3. As measured by a diversity equation wherein the more evenly people are spread across a greater number of religious denominations, the greater the pluralism.

4. Iannaccone has confirmed that the positive impact of pluralism is not confined to the United States. Using international data, Iannoccone (1991, p. 156) concludes: "Across Protestant nations, rates of church attendance and religious belief are substantially higher in highly competitive markets."

   Using U.S. county-level data, Land, Deane, and Blau (1991) support our findings for urban counties, but report that religious pluralism "retards church membership" for rural counties. We would argue, however, that their findings for rural counties are the result of an inappropriate unit of analysis. When rural counties are used, and often merged, the diversity index fails to reflect the religious options *available* to residents. Rural counties do not represent a "religious market," because residents do not have access to every church in the county and they do not choose their religious options based on county lines. Instead, they attend the most suitable local country church or one in a nearby village—regardless of the county line. For this reason some rural counties have membership rates exceeding 100 percent of their population. When data were collected on rural villages, as reported later in this chapter, religious pluralism was found to have a positive impact on religious involvement and membership—even in rural counties.

5. The American Baptist Association began in 1905, but did not officially split from the Southern Baptists until 1924. Because the ABA was included in the

1916 totals, we have included them in the 1926 totals to allow for a more accurate comparison.

6. The National Council of Churches has its headquarters in the Interchurch Center Building at 475 Riverside Drive in New York City.

7. Marked denominational differences existed in Lenski's data. When these were pointed out by Babbie (1965), Lenski (1965) continued to claim that these were merely reflections of race, ethnicity, and region of birth.

8. Although the book is co-authored with Brunner, the chapters on church unity were apparently written by Douglass. The authors report, in the Preface, that "Dr. Brunner's contribution is confined to the rural sections, while Dr. Douglass is reponsible for the rest of the volume" (1935, p. vii).

## Chapter 7    Why "Mainline" Denominations Decline

1. Here, as throughout the book, we are referring to a declining share of all church adherents.

2. We use the term "cult" in a technical rather than a pejorative sense. A sect is a new organization of a conventional faith (conventional, that is, in the society under observation); a cult is an unconventional religion. Cults can occur because someone succeeds in attracting followers to a movement based on a new religious culture. They can also occur by importation from another society. Thus a religious group can be a cult in one society while being a conventional faith in another—Hinduism is a cult in the United States and Christianity is a cult in India. For a full discussion see Stark and Bainbridge (1985, 1987).

3. We removed atheist and adventist groups on the grounds that they were not cults, and we removed purely mail-order organizations on the grounds that they were neither cults nor sects. As it turned out, the results were unchanged by these omissions.

4. We note that Melton interprets these same data as a gradually accelerating curve—that cult formation is slowly increasing. While we disagree, Melton's interpretation is as incompatible as ours with the sixties eruption thesis.

5. Under the name of Summit Lighthouse.

6. The popular mail-order guru Yogi Ramacharaka was actually an American named William Walker Atkinson (Melton, 1987).

7. In 1965 there were 467 immigrants from India, in 1966 there were 2,293, and Indian immigration now runs at about 25,000 a year.

8. We are indebted to Laurence R. Iannaccone for his pioneering work in this area. Not only have we drawn from his published work, we have benefited from many stimulating conversations.

9. For a window into the extraordinary bonds between priests and their parishioners (and, indeed of the social rewards of the priesthood) in pre–Vatican II times, we recommend seeing the 1944 Academy Award–winning movie *Going My Way* starring Bing Crosby and Barry Fitzgerald. Before the film was

released, Paramount held a special showing for the priests of Los Angeles. At the end of the movie Paramount press agents were upset by the utter silence of the audience, until they realized that the priests were too moved to speak and that there wasn't a dry eye in the house.

10. Hoge (1987) reports that the level of encouragement priests provide for potential recruits to religious vocations declined sharply after the Second Vatican Council (as reported in a 1970 survey) and increased slightly in the 1980s (based on a 1985 survey).

11. Strictly speaking, sisters and brothers are considered members of the laity, except in canon law. Here we are using the term to refer to Catholics who are not ordained and have not taken religious vows.

12. The traditional source for renewal in the church has been from religious orders. Like sect movements, their message of renewal or revival has often aroused mass religious movements and challenged traditional church teachings (Gannon, 1980; Stark and Bainbridge, 1985). Unlike sectarian movements, however, the movements led by religious orders are usually channeled into the church. It is ironic that the Second Vatican Council's attempt for renewal has inadvertently reduced the activity of a source of past renewal—religious orders.

# Reference List

Abell, Aaron. 1960. *American Catholicism and Social Action: A Search for Social Justice, 1865–1950.* Garden City, N.Y.: Hanover House.

Adams, Robert Hickman. 1970. *White Churches of the Plains.* Boulder, Colo.: Colorado Associated Press.

Ahlstrom, Sydney E. 1975. *A Religious History of the American People.* Garden City, N.Y.: Image Books

Alba, Richard D. 1990. *Ethnic Identity: The Transformation of White America.* New Haven: Yale University Press.

Alexander, June Granatir. 1987. *The Immigrant Church and Community: Pittsburgh's Slovak Catholics and Lutherans, 1880–1915.* Pittsburgh: University of Pittsburgh Press.

Alston, Jon P. 1969. "Occupational Placement and Mobility of Protestants and Catholics, 1953–1964." *Review of Religious Research* 10: 135–140.

Ammerman, Nancy Tatom. 1990. *Baptist Battles: Social Change and Religious Conflict in the Southern Baptist Convention.* New Brunswick, N.J.: Rutgers University Press.

Annarelli, James John. 1987. *Academic Freedom and Catholic Higher Education.* Westport, Conn.: Greenwood Press.

Appel, John, and Selma Appel. 1990. *Pat-riots to Patriots.* East Lansing, Mich.: Michigan State University.

Armstrong, O. K., and Marjorie M. Armstrong. 1967. *The Indomitable Baptists: A Narrative of Their Role in Shaping American History.* Garden City, N.Y.: Doubleday and Co.

Asbury, Francis. [1852] 1958. *Journal and Letters of Francis Asbury.* 3 vols. Nashville: Abingdon Press.

Asplund, John. 1790. *The Annual Register of the Baptist Denomination.*

Atkins, Gaius Glenn, and Frederick L. Fagley. 1942. *History of American Congregationalism.* Boston: Pilgrim Press.

Babbie, Earl. 1965. "The Religious Factor—Looking Forward." *Review of Religious Research* 7:42–51.

———. 1990. "Channels to Elsewhere." In Thomas Robbins and Dick Anthony, eds., *In Gods We Trust.* 2d ed. New Brunswick, N.J.: Transaction Publishers.

Babcock, Rufus. 1841. "General Summary View of the Baptist Denominations in Each of the United States." *American Quarterly Register* (November): 184–186.

Bacon, Leonard Woolsey. 1897. *A History of American Christianity.* New York: Christian Literature Co.

Bailyn, Bernard. 1986. *Voyagers to the West: A Passage in the Peopling of America on the Eve of the Revolution.* New York: Knopf.

Bainbridge, William Sims. 1985. "Collective Behavior and Social Movements." In Rodney Stark, *Sociology.* Belmost Calif.: Wadsworth Publishing Co.

Baird, Robert. 1844. *Religion in American; or, An Account of the Origin, Progress, Relation to the State, and Present Condition of the Evangelical Churches in the United States.* New York: Harper & Bros.

Baker, Robert A. 1974. *The Southern Baptist Convention and Its People, 1607–1972.* Nashville: Broadman Press.

Bangs, Carl. 1972. "Deceptive Statistics." *Christian Century* 89: 852–853.

Barkun, Michael. 1986. *Crucible of the Millennium.* Syracuse: Syracuse University Press.

Barnes, Roswell P. 1960. "The Ecumenical Movement." *The Annals: Religion in American Society* 332: 135–145.

Barnhart, Joe Edward. 1986. *The Southern Baptist Holy War.* Austin: Texas Monthly Press.

Beard, Charles A., and Mary R. Beard. 1930. *The Rise of American Civilization.* New York: Macmillan Co.

Beecher, Lyman. [1835] 1977. *Plea for the West.* New York: Arno Press.

Beecher, Lyman, and Asahel Nettleton. 1828. *Letters of the Rev. Dr. Beecher and Rev. Mr. Nettleton on the "New Measures" in Conducting Revivals of Religion.* New York: G. & C. Carvill.

Berger, Peter. 1963. "A Market Model for the Analysis of Ecumenicity." *Social Research* 30:77-93.

———. 1967. *The Sacred Canopy.* Garden City, N.Y.: Doubleday and Co.

———. 1979. *The Heretical Imperative: Contemporary Possibilities of Religious Affirmation.* New York: Doubleday and Co.

———. 1982. "From the Crisis of Religion to the Crisis of Secularity." In Mary Douglas and Steven M. Tipton, eds., *Religion and America: Spirituality in as Secular Age.* Boston: Beacon Press.

Bergin, Allen E. 1983. "Religiosity and Mental Health: A Critical Reevaluation and Meta-analysis." *Professional Psychology* 14: 170–184.

Berry, B., and J. Kasarda. 1978. *Contemporary Urban Ecology.* New York: Academic Press.

Bibby, Reginald W. 1978. "Why Conservative Churches Really Are Growing." *Journal for the Scientific Study of Religion* 2: 129–137.

Bibby, Reginald W., and Merlin B. Brinkerhoff. 1973. "The Circulation of the Saints." *Journal for the Scientific Study of Religion* 12: 273–283.

———. 1983. "Circulation of the Saints Revisited." *Journal for the Scientific Study of Religion* 22: 253–262.

Billingsley, K. L. 1990. *From Mainline to Sideline.* Washington, D.C.: Ethics and Public Policy Center.

Bird, Steven. 1990. "The Blending of Catholic Political Behavior: Presidential Voting and Political Party Affiliation." Master's thesis, University of Washington.

Blake, Eugene Carson. 1959. "The American Churches and Ecumenical Mission." In Edward J. Jurji, ed., *The Ecumenical Era in Church and Society.* New York: Macmillan Co.

Bonhoeffer, Dietrich. 1965. *No Rusty Swords: Letters, Lectures, and Notes, 1928–1936.* New York: Harper & Row.

Bonomi, Patricia U., and Peter R. Eisenstadt. 1982. "Church Adherence in the Eighteenth-Century British American Colonies." *William and Mary Quarterly* 39: 245–286.

Brackney, William Henry. 1988. *The Baptists.* New York: Greenwood Press.

Bruce, Dickson, Jr. 1974. *And They All Sang Hallelujah: Plain-Folk Camp-Meeting Religion, 1800–1845.*

Brunner, Edmund deS. 1927. *Village Communities.* New York: George H. Doran Co.

Brunner, Edmund deS., Gwendolyn S. Hughes, and Marjorie Patten. 1927. *American Agricultural Villages.* New York: George H. Doran Co.

Bryce, Mary Charles. 1986. "The Confraternity of Christian Doctrines in the United States." In D. Campbell Wyckoff, ed., *Renewing the Sunday School and CCD.* Birmingham, Ala.: Religious Education Press.

Bureau of the Census. 1854. *Compendium of the Seventh Census.* Washington, D.C.: Government Printing Office.

———. 1894. *Eleventh Census of the United States: 1890.* Vol. 9. Washington, D.C.: Government Printing Office.

———. 1910. *Religious Bodies: 1906.* Vols. 1–2. Washington, D.C.: Government Printing Office.

———. 1919. *Religious Bodies: 1916.* Vols. 1–2. Washington, D.C.: Government Printing Office.

———. 1930. *Religious Bodies: 1926.* Vols 1–2. Washington, D.C.: Government Printing Office.

———. 1941. *Religious Bodies: 1936.* Vol. 1. Washington, D.C.: Government Printing Office.

———. 1975. *Historical Statistics of the United States: Colonial Times to 1970.* Washington, D.C.: Government Printing Office.

Burns, James A. [1912] 1969. *The Growth and Development of the Catholic School System in the United States.* New York: Arno Press.

Burns, Jeffrey M. "The Parish History Project: A Descriptive Analysis of the Data." Cushwa Center for the Study of American Catholicism, University of Notre Dame.

Burr, Walter. 1924. "What's the Matter with the Rural Church?" In *Religion in Country Life: Proceedings of the Seventh National Country Life Conference.* New York.

Burrows, Robert. 1987. "A Christian Critiques the New Age." *Christianity Today* 16.

Butler, Jon. 1982. "Enthusiasm Described and Decried: The Great Awakening as Interpretive Fiction." *Journal of American History* 69: 305–325.

———. 1990. *Awash in a Sea of Faith: Christianizing the American People.* Cambridge, Mass.: Harvard University Press.

Cameron, Richard M. 1961. *Methodism and Society in Historical Perspective.* Nashville: Abingdon Press.

Cantril, Hadley. 1943. "Educational and Economic Composition of Religious Groups: An Analysis of Poll Data." *American Journal of Sociology* 48: 574–579.

Carroll, H. K. 1898. "Is Methodism Catholic?" *Methodist Review* 14: 177–186.

Cartwright, Peter, 1856. *Autobiography of Peter Cartwright, the Backwards Preacher.* Edited by W. P. Strickland. New York: Carlton and Porter.

Casino, Joseph J. 1987. "From Sanctuary to Involvement: A History of the Catholic Parish in the Northeast." In Jay P. Dolan, ed., *The American Catholic Parish.* Vol. 1. New York: Paulist Press.

Chandler, Tertius, and Gerald Fox. 1974. *3000 Years of Urban Growth.* New York: Academic Press.

*Christianity Today.* 1983. "The Historic Shift in America." 27 (August): 38–41.

Christiano, Kevin. 1987. *Religious Diversity and Social Change: American Cities, 1890–1906.* New York: Cambridge University Press.

———. 1991. "The Catholic Church and Recent Immigrants to the United States: A Review of Research." In Helen Rose Ebaugh, ed., *Vatican II and American Catholicism: Twenty-Five Years Later.* Greenwich, Conn.: JAI Press.

Clark, Elmer T. 1952. *An Album of Methodist History.* New York: Abingdon-Cokesbury Press.

Cobbett, William. 1818. *Journal of a Year's Residence in the United States of America* (as excerpted in Powell, 1967).

Coke, Thomas. 1793. *The Life of the Rev. John Wesley.* Philadelphia: John Dickens.

Cott, Nancy F. 1977. *The Bonds of Womanhood.* New Haven: Yale University Press.

Cox, Harvey. 1965. *The Secular City.* New York: Macmillan Co.

———. 1977. *Turning East: The Promise and Peril of the New Orientalism.* New York: Simon and Schuster.

————. 1983. "Interview." In Steven J. Gelberg, ed., *Hare Krishna, Hare Krishna.* New York: Grove Press.

Cross, Barbara M., ed. 1961. *The Autobiography of Lyman Beecher.* Cambridge, Mass.: The Belknap Press of Harvard University Press.

Cross, Whitney R. [1950] 1982. *The Burned-Over District.* Ithaca: Cornell University Press.

Crowe, Charles M. 1944. "Religion on the Air." *Christian Century* 61: 973–975.

Curry, Catherine Ann. 1988. "Statistical Study of Religious Women in the United States." Available from George C. Stewart, Jr., P. O. Box 7, Fayetteville, N.C. 29302.

D'Antonio, William, James Davidson, Dean Hoge, and Ruth Wallace. 1989. *American Catholic Laity in a Changing Church.* Kansas City: Sheed and Ward.

D'Arcy, Paul F., and Eugene C. Kennedy. 1965. *The Genius of the Apostolate.* New York: Sheed and Ward.

Deck, Allan Figueroa, S.J. 1989. *The Second Wave: Hispanic Ministry and the Evangelization of Cultures.* New York: Paulist Press.

Doherty, Robert W. 1967. *The Hicksite Separation.* New Brunswick, N.J.: Rutgers University Press.

Dolan, Jay P. 1975. *The Immigrant Church: New York's Irish and German Catholics, 1815–1865.* Baltimore: Johns Hopkins University Press.

————. 1978. *Catholic Revivalism: The American Experience, 1830–1900.* Notre Dame: University of Notre Dame Press.

————. 1985. *The American Catholic Experience: A History from Colonial Times to the Present.* Garden City, N.Y.: Image Books.

————., ed. 1987. *The American Catholic Parish.* Vols. 1–2. New York: Paulist Press.

Douglass, H. Paul, and Edmund deS. Brunner. 1935. *The Protestant Church as a Social Institution.* New York: Russell and Russell.

Dunn, Mary Maples. 1978. "Saints and Sisters: Congregational and Quaker Women in the Early Colonial Period." *American Quarterly* 30: 582–601.

Durkheim, Emile. [1897] 1951. *Suicide.* Glencoe, ILL.: Free Press.

Ebaugh, Helen Rose Fuchs. 1977. *Out of the Cloister: A Study of Organizational Dilemmas.* Austin: University of Texas Press.

————. 1991. "The Revitalization Movement in the Catholic Church." *Sociological Analysis* 52: 1–12.

Eighmy, John Lee. 1972. *Churches in Cultural Captivity: A History of the Social Attitudes of Southern Baptists.* Knoxville: University of Tennessee Press.

Ellis, John Tracy. 1956. *Documents of American Catholic History.* Milwaukee: Bruce Publishing Co.

————., ed. 1962. *Documents of American Catholic History.* 2d ed. Milwaukee: Bruce Publishing Co.

———. 1969. *American Catholicism.* 2d ed. Chicago: University of Chicago Press.

Ewens, Mary. 1978. *The Role of the Nun in Nineteenth-Century America: Variations on the International Theme.* New York: Arno Press.

Fichter, Joseph H. 1961. *Religion as an Occupation: A Study in the Sociology of Professions.* Notre Dame: University of Notre Dame Press.

———. 1968. *America's Forgotten Priests: What They Are Saying.* New York: Harper & Row.

Finke, Roger. 1989. "Demographics of Religious Participation: An Ecological Approach, 1850–1980." *Journal for the Scientific Study of Religion* 28: 45–58.

———. 1990. "Religious Deregulation: Origins and Consequences." *Journal of Church and State* 32: 609–626.

Finke, Roger, and Rodney Stark. 1986. "Turning Pews into People: Estimating Nineteenth-Century Church Membership." *Journal for the Scientific Study of Religion* 25: 180–192.

———. 1988. "Religious Economies and Sacred Canopies: Religious Mobilization in American Cities, 1906." *American Sociological Review* 53: 41–49.

Finney, Charles Grandison. [1835] 1960. *Lectures on Revivals of Religion.* Cambridge, Mass.: Harvard University Press.

Fischer, Claude S. 1982. *To Dwell among Friends: Personal Networks in Town and City.* Chicago: University of Chicago Press.

Flannery, Austin P., ed. 1975. *Documents of Vatican II.* Grand Rapids, Mich.: Eerdmans Publishing.

Flynt, J. Wayne. 1981. "Southern Baptists: Rural to Urban Transition." *Baptist History and Heritage* 16: 24–34.

———. 1982. "The Impact of Social Factors on Southern Baptist Expansion, 1800–1914." *Baptist History and Heritage* 17: 20–31.

Foy, Felician A., ed. 1965. *National Catholic Almanac.* Paterson, N.J.: St. Anthony's Guild.

Franklin, Benjamin. [1868] 1916. *The Autobiography of Benjamin Franklin.* Garden City, N.Y.: Garden City Publishing Co.

Freud, Sigmund. 1927. *The Future of an Illusion.* Garden City, N.Y.: Doubleday.

Galpin, Charles Josiah. 1923. *Rural Life.* New York: Century Co.

———. 1925. *Empty Churches: The Rural-Urban Dilemma.* New York: Century Co.

Gannon, Thomas M. 1980. "Catholic Religious Orders in Sociological Perspective." In Ross P. Scherer, ed., *American Denominational Organization: A Sociological View.* Pasadena, Calif.: William Carey Library.

Garraghan, Gilbert J. 1984. *The Jesuits of the Middle United States.* Vol. 2. Chicago: Loyola University Press.

Gaustad, Edwin S., ed. 1982. *A Documentary History of Religion in America to the Civil War.* Grand Rapids, Mich.: Eerdmans Publishing.

———. 1987. *Faith of Our Fathers: Religion and the New Nation.* San Francisco: Harper & Row.

Gleason, Philip. 1967. "American Catholic Higher Education: A Historical Perspective." In Robert Hassenger, ed., *The Shape of Catholic Higher Education*. Chicago: University of Chicago Press.

———. 1973. "Coming to Terms with American Catholic History." *Societas* 3: 305.

———. 1987. *Keeping the Faith: American Catholicism Past and Present*. Notre Dame: University of Notre Dame Press.

Glenn, Norval, and Ruth Hyland. 1967. "Religious Preference and Worldly Success: Some Evidence from National Surveys." *American Sociological Review* 32: 73–85.

Glock, Charles Y., and Robert N. Bellah, eds. 1976. *The New Religious Consciousness*. Berkeley: University of California Press.

Goode, Stephen, 1991. "A Struggle for Earthly Power Bruises the Baptists." *Insight* 7(22): 20–23.

Gordon-McCutchan, R. C. 1981. "The Irony of Evangelical History." *Journal for the Scientific Study of Religion* 20: 309–326.

———. 1983. "Great Awakenings." *Sociological Analysis* 44: 83–95.

Gorham, B. W. 1854. *Camp Meeting Manual: A Practical Book for the Camp Ground*. Boston: H. V. Degen.

Gorrie, P. Douglass. 1852. *Episcopal Methodism. As It Was and Is*. Auburn: Derby and Miller.

———. 1890. *History of the Methodist Episcopal Church in the United States*. Keystone Publishing Co.

Goss, C. C. 1866. *Statistical History of the First Century of American Methodism*. New York: Carlton and Porter.

Greeley, Andrew M. 1963. "Influence of the 'Religious Factor' on Career Plans and Occupational Values of College Graduates." *American Journal of Sociology* 68: 658–671.

———. 1964. "The Protestant Ethic: Time for a Moratorium." *Sociological Analysis* 25: 20–33.

———. 1969. *From Backwater to Mainstream*. New York: McGraw-Hill.

———. 1972. *The Catholic Priest in the United States: Sociological Investigations*. Washington, D.C.: United States Catholic Conference.

———. 1974. *Ethnicity in the United States: A Preliminary Reconnaissance*. New York: John Wiley and Sons.

———. 1979. "Ethnic Variations in Religious Commitment." *In* Robert Wuthnow, ed., *The Religious Dimension: New Directions in Quantitative Research*. New York: Academic Press.

———. 1982. "The Failures of Vatican II after Twenty Years." *America*, February 6, pp. 86–89.

———. 1988. "Defection among Hispanics." *America*, July 30, pp. 61–62.

———. 1989. *Religious Change in America*. Cambridge, Mass.: Harvard University Press.

Greeley, Andrew M., William C. McCready, and Kathleen McCourt. 1976. *Catholic Schools in a Declining Church*. Kansas City: Sheed and Ward.

Greeley, Andrew M., and William McManus. 1987. *Catholic Contributions: Sociology and Policy.* Chicago: Thomas More Press.

Greeley, Andrew M., and Peter H. Rossi. 1966. *The Education of Catholic Americans.* Chicago: Aldine.

Grund, Francis. 1837. *The Americans in Their Moral, Social, and Political Relations* (as excerpted in Powell, 1967).

Gunneman, Louis H. 1977. *The Shaping of the United Church of Christ.* New York: United Church Press.

Guttentag, Marica, and Paul F. Secord. 1983. *Too Many Women?* Beverly Hills, Calif.: Sage Publications.

Hadden, Jeffrey K. 1969. *The Gathering Storm in the Churches.* Garden City. N.Y.: Doubleday and Co.

Hadden, Jeffrey K., and Anson Shupe. 1988. *Televangelism Power and Politics on God's Frontier.* New York: Henry Holt and Co.

Handy, Robert T. 1969. "The City and the Church: Historical Interlockings." In Kendig Brubaker Cully and F. Nile Harper, eds., *Will the Church Lose the City?* New York: World Publishing Co.

Hargreaves, Robert. 1914. "The Rural Community and Church Federation." *American Journal of Sociology* 20: 249–260.

Harrell, David Edwin, Jr. 1985. "Pluralism: Catholics, Jews, and Sectarians." In Charles Reagan Wilson, ed., *Religion in the South.* Jackson: University of Mississippi Press.

Harrison, Paul M. 1959. *Authority and Power in the Free Church Tradition.* Princeton: Princeton University Press.

Hatch, Nathan O. 1989. *The Democratization of American Christianity.* New Haven: Yale University Press.

Hayward, John. 1836. *Religious Creeds and Statistics of Every Christian Denomination in the U.S.* Boston: John Hayward.

Hechter, Michael. 1987. *Principles of Group Solidarity.* Berkeley: University of California Press.

Hefley, James C. 1983. "The Historic Shift in America." *Christianity Today* 27: 38–41.

Hennesey, James, S.J. 1981. *American Catholics.* New York: Oxford University Press.

Herberg, Will. 1960. *Protestant-Catholic-Jew.* Garden City, N.Y.: Doubleday and Co.

Hexham, Irving, Raymond F. Currie, and Joan B. Townsend, 1985. "New Religious Movements." In *The Canadian Encyclopedia.* Edmonton: Hurtig.

Hoge, Dean R. 1987. *Future of Catholic Leadership: Responses to the Priest Shortage.* Kansas City: Sheed and Ward.

Hoge, Dear R., and David A. Roozen, eds. 1979. *Understanding Church Growth and Decline, 1950–1978.* New York: Pilgrim Press.

Hooker, Elizabeth R. 1931. *Hinterlands of the Church.* New York: Institute of Social and Religious Research.

Horgan, Paul. 1975. *Lamy of Santa Fe.* Toronto: McGraw-Hill.

Hout, Michael, and Andrew M. Greeley. 1987. "The Center Doesn't Hold: Church Attendance in the United States, 1940–1984." *American Sociological Review* 52: 325–345.

Hudson, Winthrop S. 1965. *Religion in America.* 1st ed. New York: Charles Scribner's Sons.

———. 1981. *Religion in America.* 3d ed. New York: Charles Scribner's Sons.

Iannaccone, Laurence R. 1989. "Why Strict Churches Are Strong." Paper presented at the annual meeting of the Society for the Scientific Study of Religion, Salt Lake City, Utah.

———. 1990. "Religious Practice: A Human Capital Approach." *Journal for the Scientific Study of Religion* 29: 297–314.

———. 1991. "The Consequences of Religious Market Regulation: Adam Smith and the Economics of Religion." *Rationality and Society* 3: 156–177.

———. 1992. "Sacrifice and Stigma: Reducing Free Riding in Cults, Communes, and Other Collectives." *Journal of Political Economy* (April).

Interchurch World Movement. 1920. *Standards for City Church Plants.* New York: Interchurch Press.

Jent, John W. 1924. *The Challenge of the Country Church.* Nashville: Sunday School Board of the Southern Baptist Convention.

Jernegan, M. W. 1916. "Slavery and Conversion in the Colonies." *American Historical Review* 21: 504–527.

Johnson, Benton. 1963. "On Church and Sect." *American Sociological Review* 28: 539–549.

Johnson, Charles A. 1955. *The Frontier Camp Meeting: Religion's Harvest Time.* Dallas: Southern Methodist University Press.

Johnson, Douglas W., Paul R. Picard, and Bernard Quinn. 1974. *Churches and Church Membership in the United States: An Enumeration by Region, State, and County.* Washington, D.C.: Glenmary Research Center.

Jonas, Thomas J. 1988. *The Divided Mind: American Catholic Evangelists in the 1890s.* New York: Garland Press.

Kalmijn, Matthijs. 1991. "Shifting Boundaries: Trends in Religious and Educational Homogamy." *American Sociological Review* 56: 786–800.

Kelley, Dean. 1972. *Why Conservative Churches Are Growing.* New York: Harper and Row.

———. 1984. "Why Conservative Churches Are Still Growing." In Patrick H. McNamara, ed., *Religion: North American Style.* Belmont, Calif.: Wadsworth Publishing Co.

Kirk, Dudley. 1955. "Recent Trends of Catholic Fertility in the United States." In Milbank Memorial Fund, *Current Research in Human Fertility,* pp. 93–105.

Kosmin, Barry A. 1991. *Research Report: The National Survey of Religious Identification.* New York: CUNY Graduate Center.

Lambert, Frank. 1990. "'Pedlar in Divinity': George Whitefield and the Great Awakening, 1737–1745." *Journal of American History* (December) 77: 812–837.

Lambert, Richard D. 1960. "Current Trends in Religion: A Summary." In *The Annals: Religion in American Society* 332: 146–155.

Land, Kenneth C., Glenn Deane, and Judith R. Blau. 1991. "Religious Pluralism and Church Membership: A Spatial Diffusion Model." *American Sociological Review* 56: 237–249.

Landis, Benson Y. 1922. *Rural Church Life in the Middle West.* New York: Institute of Social and Religious Research.

Larkin, Emmet. 1972. "The Devotional Revolution in Ireland, 1850–1875." *American Historical Review* 77: 625–652.

Lee, Robert. 1960. *The Social Sources of Church Unity.* New York: Abingdon Press.

Lenski, Gerhard. 1961. *The Religious Factor.* Garden City, N.Y.: Doubleday and Co.

———. 1965. "Comment." *Review of Religious Research* 7:51–53.

Leonard, Bill J. 1990. *God's Last and Only Hope: The Fragmentation of the Southern Baptist Convention.* Grand Rapids, Mich.: Eerdman's Publishing.

Liebard, Odile M. 1978. *Official Catholic Teachings: Clergy and Laity.* Wilmington, N.C.: Consortium.

Lipset, Seymour Martin, and Reinhard Bendix. 1959. *Social Mobility in Industrial Society.* Berkeley: University of California Press.

Lowry, James A. 1989. "Selected SBC Trends." *The Quarterly Review* 49: 51–61.

McBeth, Leon. 1982. "Expansion of the Southern Baptist Convention to 1951." *Baptist History and Heritage* 17: 32–43.

———. 1990. *A Sourcebook for Baptist Heritage.* Nashville: Broadman Press.

McCarthy, James. 1979. "Religious Commitment, Affiliation, and Marriage Dissolution." In Robert Wuthnow, ed., *The Religious Dimension: New Directions in Quantitative Research.* New York: Academic Press.

McClellan, Albert. 1985. "The Southern Baptist Convention, 1965–1985." *Baptist History and Heritage* 20: 7-24.

McCulloh, Gerald O. 1964. "The Theology and Practices of Methodism, 1876–1919." In E. S. Bucke, ed., *The History of American Methodism.* Vol. 2. Nashville: Abingdon Press.

McCutcheon, Alan L. 1988. "Denominations and Religious Intermarriage." *Review of Religious Research* 29: 213–227.

McLoughlin, William G. 1971. *New England Dissent, 1630–1833: The Baptists and the Separation of Church and State.* Vols. 1–2. Cambridge, Mass.: Harvard University Press.

———. 1978. *Revivals, Awakenings, and Reform.* Chicago: University of Chicago Press.

———. 1983. "Timepieces and Butterflies: A Note on the Great-Awakening–Construct and Its Critics." *Sociological Analysis* 44: 103–10.

Madison, James H. 1986. "Reformers and the Rural Church, 1900–1950." *Journal of American History* 73: 645–668.

Marsden, George M. 1982. "Preachers of Paradox: The Religious New Right in Historical Perspective." In Mary Douglas and Steven M. Tipton, eds., *Religion and America: Spirituality in a Secular Age.* Boston: Beacon Press.

Martin, David. 1990. *Tongues of Fire: The Explosion of Protestantism in Latin America.* Oxford: BAsil Blackwell.

Marty, Martin E. 1959. *The New Shape of Religion.* New York: Harper & Brothers.

———. 1964. *Church Unity and Church Mission.* Grand Rapids, Mich.: Eerdmans Publishing.

———. 1975. "Vice and Virtue: Our Moral Condition." *Time,* October 27.

———. 1976. *A Nation of Behavers.* Chicago: University of Chicago Press.

———. 1979. "Foreword." In Dean R. Hoge and David A. Roozen, eds., *Understanding Church Growth and Decline, 1950–1978.* New York: Pilgrim Press.

———. 1984. *Pilgrims in Their Own Land: 500 Years of Religion in America.* New York: Penguin Books.

———. 1991. "Never the Same Again: Post-Vatican II Catholic–Protestant Interactions." *Sociological Analysis* 52: 13–26.

Masters, Victor. 1916. *Country Church in the South.* Atlanta: Home Mission Board of the Southern Baptist Convention.

Mead, Sidney E. 1956. "From Coercion to Persuasion: Another Look at the Rise of Religious Liberty and the Emergence of Denominationalism." *Church History* 25: 317–337.

Melton, J. Gordon. 1978. *The Encyclopedia of American Religions.* Wilmington, N.C.: McGrath.

———. 1987. "How New Is New? The Flowering of the 'New' Religious Consciousness since 1965." In David G. Bromley and Phillip E. Hammond, eds., *The Future of New Religious Movements.* Macon, Ga.: Mercer University Press.

———. 1988. "Testing the Truisms about the 'Cults': Toward a New Perspective on Nonconventional Religion." Paper presented at the annual meetings of American Academy of Religion, Chicago.

———. 1989. *The Encyclopedia of American Religions.* 3d ed. Detroit: Gale Research.

———. 1990. *New Age Encyclopedia.* Detroit: Gale Research.

Miller, Paul M. 1978. "Yes, Dean Kelly [*sic*], there has been growth." *Gospel Herald,* March 28.

Miller, Perry. 1935. "The Contribution of the Protestant Churches to Religious Liberty in America." *Church History* 4: 57–66.

Miyakawa, T. Scott. 1964. *Protestants and Pioneers.* Chicago: University of Chicago Press.

Modde, Margaret Mary, O.S.F. 1974. "A Study of Entrances and Departures in Religious Communities of Women in the United States, 1965–1972." As reported in the 1975 *Catholic Almanac.*

Mondello, Salvatore. 1987. "Baptist Railroad Churches in the American West, 1890–1946." In Carl Guarneri and David Alvarez eds., *Religion and Society in the American West.* New York: University Press of America.

Moore, R. Laurence. 1986. *Religious Outsiders and the Making of Americans.* New York: Oxford University Press.

Morgan, Edmund. 1961. "New England Puritanism: Another Approach." *William and Mary Quarterly* 18: 236–242.

Morrill, Miron A. 1945. "Will Churches Surrender Sovereignty?" *Christian Century* 62: 460–461.

Morris, Loretta M. 1989. "Secular Transcendence: From ACSS to ASR." *Sociological Analysis* 50: 329–349.

Morse, Hermann N., and Edmund deS. Brunner. 1923. *Town and Country Churches in the United States.* New York: Institute of Social and Religious Research.

Muhlenberg, Henry. 1959. *The Notebook of a Colonial Clergyman.* Philadelphia: Fortress Press.

Murray, John Courtney. 1960. *We Hold These Truths: Catholic Reflections on the American Proposition.* New York: Sheed and Ward.

Nelson, Lynn D., and David G. Bromley. 1988. "Another Look at Conversion and Defection in Conservative Churches." In David G. Bromley, ed. *Falling from the Faith.* Newbury Park, Calif.: Sage Publications.

Nettles, Tom J. 1981. "Southern Baptists: Regional to National Transition." *Baptist History and Heritage* 16: 13–23.

Neuhaus, Richard John. 1987. *The Catholic Moment.* San Francisco: Harper & Row.

Newman, Albert Henry. 1915. *A History of the Baptist Churches in the United States.* 6th ed. New York: Charles Scribner's Sons.

Nickerson, Michael G. 1983. "Historical Relationships of Itineracy and Salary." *Methodist History* 21: 43–59.

Niebuhr, Richard H. 1929. *The Sources of Denominationalism.* New York: Henry Holt.

Norwood, Frederick A., 1982. *Sourcebook of American Methodism.* Nashville: Abingdon Press.

Oates, Mary J. 1980. "Organized Voluntarism: The Catholic Sisters in Massachusetts, 1870–1940." In Janet Wilson James, ed., *Women in American Religion.* Philadelphia: University of Pennsylvania Press.

Oblinger, Carl. 1973. *Religious Mimesis: Social Basis for the Holiness Schism in Late Nineteenth-Century Methodism—the Illinois Case, 1869–1885.* Evanston, Ill.: Institute for the Study of American Religion.

O'Callaghan, E. B., ed. 1855. *Documents Relative to the Colonial History of the State of New York.* Vol. 5. Albany, N.Y.: Weed, Parsons, and Co.

O'Connell, Eugene [1853] 1956. "Letter to Father Moriarty." In John Tracy Ellis, ed., *Documents of American Catholic History*. Milwaukee: Bruce Publishing Co.

*The Official Catholic Directory*. 1950–1990. P. J. Kenedy and Sons.

Olmstead, Clifton E. 1961. *Religion in America: Past and Present*. Englewood Cliffs, N.J.: Prentice-Hall.

Orsi, Robert A. 1985. *The Madonna of 115th Street: Faith and Community in Italian Harlem*. New Haven: Yale University Press.

Patterson, L. Dale. 1985. "Improvement in Methodist Ministerial Education at the End of the Nineteenth Century." *Methodist History* 23: 68–78.

Patterson, W. Morgan. 1979. "Baptist Growth in America: Evaluation of Trends." *Baptist History and Heritage* 14: 16–26.

Paullin, Charles O. 1932. *Atlas of the Historical Geography of the United States*. Washington, D.C.: Carnegie Institution, and New York: American Geographical Society.

Perko, F. Michael, S.J. ed. 1988. *Enlightening the Next Generation: Catholics and Their Schools, 1830–1980*. New York: Garland Press.

Peters, John Leland. [1956] 1985. *Christian Perfection and American Methodism*. Grand Rapids, Mich.: Francis Asbury Press.

Petersen, William. 1962. "Religious Statistics in the United States." *Journal for the Scientific Study of Religion* 1: 165–178.

Phares, Ross. 1964. *Bible in Pocket, Gun in Hand*. Lincoln: University of Nebraska Press.

Pollock, John. 1972. *George Whitefield and the Great Awakening*. Belleville, Mich.: Lion Publishing.

Powell, Milton B., ed. 1967. *The Voluntary Church: Religious Life, 1740–1860, Seen through the Eyes of European Visitors*. New York: Macmillan Co.

Power, Edward J. 1972. *Catholic Higher Education in America*. New York: Appleton-Century-Crofts.

*The Quarterly Review*. 1990. Vol. 50 (4): 62.

Raboteau, Albert. 1978. *Slave Religion: The "Invisible Institution" in the Antebellum South*. New York: Oxford University Press.

Reichley, A. James. 1986. *Religion in American Public Life*. Washington, D.C.: Brookings Institution.

Ritchie, Carson I.A. 1976. *Frontier Parish*. London: Associated University Presses.

Robbins, Thomas, and Dick Anthony, eds. 1990. "Introduction." In *In Gods We Trust*. 2d ed. New Brunswick, N.J.: Transaction Publishers.

Rogers, James R. 1910. *The Cane Ridge Meeting-house*. 2d ed. Cincinnati: Standard Publishing Co.

Roof, Wade Clark, and William McKinney. 1987. *American Mainline Religion: Its Changing Shape and Future*. New Brunswick, N.J.: Rutgers University Press.

Rose, Royce A. 1983. "The Rural Church: Not Gone, But Forgotten." *Baptist History and Heritage* 18: 44–46.

Rowe, Kenneth E. 1971. "New Light on Early Methodist Theological Education." *Methodist History* 10: 58–62.

Ryder, Norman B., and Charles F. Westoff. 1971. *Reproduction in the United States, 1965.* Princeton: Princeton University Press.

Sanders, James W. 1977. *The Education of an Urban Minority: Catholics in Chicago, 1833–1965.* New York: Oxford University Press.

Sanderson, Dwight. 1942. *Rural Sociology and Rural Social Organization.* New York: John Wiley and Sons.

Scherer, F. M. 1970. *Industrial Market Structure and Economic Performance.* Chicago: Rand McNally and Co.

Schneider, Herbert W. 1952. *Religion in Twentieth-Century America.* Cambridge: Harvard University Press.

Schoenherr, Richard A., and Andrew M. Greeley. 1974. "Role Commitment Processes and the American Catholic Priesthood." *American Sociological Review* 39: 407–426.

Schoenherr, Richard A., and Lawrence A. Young. 1990. *The Catholic Priest in the U.S.: Demographic Investigations.* Final report for the United States Catholic Conference, Washington, D.C.

Schofield, Charles Edwin. 1939. *We Methodists.* New York: Methodist Publishing House.

Seidler, John. 1979. "Priest Resignations in a Lazy Monopoly." *American Sociological Review* 44: 763–783.

Seidler, John, and Katherine Meyer. 1989. *Conflict and Change in the Catholic Church.* New Brunswick, N.J.: Rutgers University Press.

Shannon, James P. 1957. *Catholic Colonization on the Western Frontier.* New Haven: Yale University Press.

Shannon, Peter M. 1967. "Future Laws for the Secular Priest." In Gerard S. Sloyan, ed., *Secular Priest in the New Church.* New York: Herder and Herder.

Shaughnessy, Gerald. 1925. *Has the Immigrant Kept the Faith.* New York: Macmillan Co.

Shaw, Stephen J. 1987. "The Cities and the Plains, a Home for God's People." In Jay P. Dolan, ed., *The American Catholic Parish.* Vol. 2. New York: Paulist Press.

Shiels, Richard D. 1981. "The Feminization of American Congregationalism, 1730–1835." *American Quarterly* 33: 45–62.

Shinn, Larry D. 1985. "Conflicting Networks: Guru and Friend in ISKCON." In Rodney Stark, ed., *Religious Movements: Genesis, Exodus, and Numbers.* New York: Paragon.

Shurden, Walter B. 1972. *Not a Silent People: Controversies That Have Shaped Southern Baptists.* Nashville: Broadman Press.

———. 1980. "Documents on the Ministry in Southern Baptist History." *Baptist History and Heritage* 15: 45–54.

Sjoberg, Gideon. 1960. *The Preindustrial City.* New York: Free Press.

Smith, Adam. [1776] 1937. *The Wealth of Nations.* New York: Modern Library.

Smith, Daniel Scott. 1985. "The Dating of the American Sexual Revolution: Evidence and Interpretation." In John F. Crosby, ed., *Reply to Myth: Perspectives on Intimacy.* New York: John Wiley.

Smith, Timothy L. 1978a. "Religion and Ethnicity in America." *American Historical Review* 83(5): 1155–1185.

———. 1978b. "Lay Initiative in the Religious Life of American Immigrants, 1880–1950." In John M. Mulder and John F. Wilson, eds., *Religion in American History.* Englewood Cliffs, N.J.: Prentice-Hall.

———. 1983. "My Rejection of a Cyclical View of 'Great Awakenings' in American Religious History." *Sociological Analysis* 44: 97–101.

Spalding, John Lancaster. [1880] 1967. "The Country and the City, 1880." In Robert D. Cross, ed., *The Church and the City, 1865–1910.* New York: Bobbs-Merrill Co.

Stark, Rodney. 1971. "The Economics of Piety: Religion and Social Class." In Gerald W. Thielbar and Saul D. Feldman, eds., *Issues in Social Inequality.* Boston: Little, Brown and Co.

———. 1985. "Church and Sect." In Phillip E. Hammond, ed., *The Sacred in a Secular Age.* Berkeley: University of California Press.

———. 1990. "Do Catholic Societies Exist?" Paper presented at the annual meeting of the Society for the Scientific Study of Religion, Virginia Beach, Virginia.

———. 1991. "Antioch as the Social Situation for Matthew's Gospel." In David L. Balch, ed., *Social History of the Matthean Community: Cross-Disciplinary Approaches to an Open Question.* Minneapolis: Augsburg-Fortress.

———. 1992a. "Epidemics, Networks, and the Rise of Christianity." *Semeia* (issue edited by L. Michael White).

———. 1992b. "A Note on the Reliability of Historical U.S. Census Data on Religion." *Sociological Analysis.*

Stark, Rodney, and William Sims Bainbridge. 1980. "Networks of Faith: Interpersonal Bonds and Recruitment to Cults and Sects." *American Journal of Sociology* 85: 1376–1395.

———. 1985. *The Future of Religion: Secularization, Revival, and Cult Formation.* Berkeley: University of California Press.

———. 1987. *A Theory of Religion.* New York and Bern: Peter Lang.

Stark, Rodney, William Sims Bainbridge, Robert D. Crutchfield, Daniel Doyle, and Roger Finke. 1983. "Crime and Delinquency in the Roaring Twenties." *Journal of Research in Crime and Delinquency* 20: 4–23.

Stark, Rodney, and Roger Finke. 1988. "American Religion in 1776: A Statistical Portrait." *Sociological Analysis* 49: 39–51.

Stark, Rodney, and Charles Y. Glock. 1965. "The New Denominationalism." *Review of Religious Research* 7: 8–17.

———. 1968. *American Piety.* Berkeley: University of California Press.

Stark, Rodney, and Laurence R. Iannaccone. 1991. "Sociology of Religion." In Edgar F. Borgotta, ed., *Encyclopedia of Sociology.* New York: Macmillan Co.

————. 1992. "Cult and Sect Movements within Religious Economies." In David G. Bromley and Jeffrey K. Hadden, eds., *Handbook of Cults and Sects in America*. Greenwich, Conn.: JAI Press.

————. Forthcoming. "The Secularization of Europe Reconsidered."

Stark, Rodney, and James McCann. 1989. "The Weakness of Monopoly Faiths: Market Forces and Catholic Commitment." Paper presented at the annual meetings of the Association for the Sociology of Religion.

Steinberg, Stephen. 1974. *The Academic Melting Pot*. New York: McGraw-Hill.

Stone, Barton W. 1910. *Autobiography*. Boston: Beacon Press. Incorporated in Rogers, 1910, pp. 113–204.

Stout, Harry S. 1986. *The New England Soul: Preaching and Religious Culture in Colonial New England*. New York: Oxford University Press.

Swanson, Merwin. 1977. "The 'Country Life Movement' and the American Churches." *Church History* 46: 368–369.

Sweet, Douglas H. 1976. "Church Vitality and the American Revolution: Historiographical Consensus and Thoughts toward a New Perspective." *Church History* 45: 341–357.

Sweet, William Warren, ed. 1920. *The Rise of Methodism in the West: Being the Journal of the Western Conference, 1800–1811*. New York: Methodist Book Concern.

————. [1930] 1950. *The Story of Religion in America*. New York: Harper & Row.

————. 1933. *Methodism in American History*. New York: Methodist Book Concern.

————. 1939. *Religion on the American Frontier, 1783–1850: The Congregationalists*. Chicago: University of Chicago Press.

————. 1944. *Revivalism in America*. New York: Charles Scribner's Sons.

————. 1946. *Religion on the American Frontier, 1783–1840: The Methodists*. Chicago: University of Chicago Press.

————. 1947. *Religion in Colonial America*. New York: Charles Scribner's Sons.

————. 1948. "The Protestant Churches." *The Annals* 256: 43–52.

————. 1952. *Religion in the Development of American Culture, 1765–1840*. New York: Charles Scribner's Sons.

————. 1964a. *Religion on the American Frontier, 1783–1840: The Baptists*. New York: Cooper Square Publishers.

————. 1964b. *Religion on the American Frontier, 1783–1840: The Presbyterians*. New York: Cooper Square Publishers.

Szafran, Robert F. 1976. "The Distribution of Influence in Religious Organizations." *Journal for the Scientific Study of Religion* 15: 339–350.

Taves, Ann. 1986. *The Household of Faith: Roman Catholic Devotions in Mid-Nineteenth-Century America*. Notre Dame: University of Notre Dame Press.

Taylor, John. 1843. *History of Ten Baptist Churches*. Frankfort, Ky.: J. H. Holeman.

*The Testimony of an Association of Ministers Convened at Marlborough, January 22,*

*1744, against the Reverend George Whitefield and His Conduct.* 1745. Boston, N.E.: T. Fleet.

*The Testimony of the President, Professors, Tutors and Hebrew Instructor of Harvard College in Cambridge, against the Reverend Mr. George Whitefield and His Conduct.* 1744. Boston, N.E.: T. Fleet.

Tharp, Clifford J. 1985. "A Study of the Forced Termination of Southern Baptist Ministers." *The Quarterly Review* 46: 50–56.

Thernstrom, Stephan. 1980. *The Harvard Encyclopedia of American Ethnic Groups.* Cambridge, Mass.: The Belknap Press of Harvard University Press.

Thompson, James J. 1982. *Tried as by Fire: Southern Baptists and the Religious Controversies of the 1920s.* Macon, Ga.: Mercer University Press.

Thompson, Robert C. 1974. "A Research Note on the Diversity among American Protestants: A Southern Baptist Example." *Review of Religious Research* 15: 87–92.

Tipton, Steven M. 1982. "The Moral Logic of Alternative Religions." In Mary Douglas and Steven M. Tipton, eds., *Religion and America: Spirituality in a Secular Age.* Boston: Beacon Press.

Tolles, Frederick B. 1948. *Meeting House and Counting House: The Quaker Merchants of Colonial Philadelphia, 1682–1763.* Chapel Hill: University of North Carolina Publishing.

Torbet, Robert G. 1963. *A History of the Baptists.* Valley Forge, Pa.: Judson Press.

———. 1976. "Baptists of the North." In James E. Wood, Jr., ed. *Baptists of the American Experience. Valley Forge, Pa.: Judson Press.*

Turner, Frederick Jackson. 1920. *The Frontier in American History.* New York: Henry Holt and Co.

Turner, James. 1985. *Without God, Without Creed: The Origins of Unbelief in America.* Baltimore: Johns Hopkins University Press.

Verdieck, Mary Jeanne, Joseph J. Shields, and Dean R. Hoge. 1988. "Role Commitment Processes Revisited." *Journal for the Scientific Study of Religion* 27: 524–535.

Villeneuve, Alphonse. 1891. "Les Etats-Unis d'Amérique et l'émigration." *Siècle*, tome 2, année.

Visser t' Hooft, W.A. 1959. "The Gathering of the Scattered Children of God." In Edward J. Jurji, ed., *The Ecumenical Era in Church and Society.* New York: Macmillan Co.

Vogt, Paul L. 1917. *Introduction to Rural Sociology.* New York: D. Appleton and Co.

Walker, Williston. 1894. *A History of the Congregational Churches in the United States.* New York: Christian Literature Co.

Wamble, G. Hugh. 1976. "Baptists of the South." In James E. Wood, Jr., ed., *Baptists and the American Experience,* Valley Forge, Pa: Judson Press.

Warner, R. Stephen. 1988. *New Wine in Old Wineskins: Evangelicals and Liberals in a Small-Town Church.* Berkeley: University of California Press.

Weaver, R. M. 1943. "The Older Religiousness in the South." *Sewanee Review* 51: 248.

Weber, Herman C. 1927. *Presbyterian Statistics through One Hundred Years: 1826–1926*. Presbyterian Board of Christian Education.

Weber, Max. 1946. *From Max Weber: Essays in Sociology*. Edited by H. H. Gerth and C. Wright Mills. New York: Galaxy.

Weis, Federick Lewis. 1936. *The Colonial Clergy and the Colonial Churches of New England*. Society of the Descendants of the Colonial Clergy. Massachusetts.

———. 1938. *The Colonial Churches and the Colonial Clergy of the Middle and Southern Colonies, 1607–1776*. Society for the Descendants of the Colonial Clergy. Massachusetts.

———. 1950. *The Colonial Clergy of Maryland, Delaware, and Georgia*. Society for the Descendants of the Colonial Clergy. Massachusetts.

———. 1955. *The Colonial Clergy of Virginia, North Carolina, and South Carolina*. Society for the Descendants of the Colonial Clergy. Massachusetts.

Welch, Kevin. 1983. "Community Development and Metropolitan Religious Commitment: A Test of Two Competing Models." *Journal for the Scientific Study of Religion* 22: 167–181.

Welch, Michael R., and John Baltzell. 1984. "Geographic Mobility, Social Integration, and Church Attendance." *Journal for the Scientific Study of Religion* 23: 75–91.

Westoff, Charles F. 1979. "The Blending of Catholic Reproductive Behavior." In Robert Wuthnow, ed., *The Religious Dimension*. New York: Academic Press.

Whitefield, George. [1756] 1969. *George Whitefield's Journals*. Gainesville, Fl.: Scholars' Facsimiles and Reprints.

Whitehead, John. 1982. *The Second American Revolution*. Westchester, Ill.: Crossway Books.

Whitehead, John, and John Conlan. 1978. "The Establishment of the Religion of Secular Humanism and Its First Amendment Implications." *Texas Tech Law Review* (Winter): 1–66.

Wilke, Richard B. 1986. *And Are We Yet Alive?* Nashville: Abingdon Press.

Wilson, Bryan. 1966. *Religion in Secular Society*. London: C. A. Watts.

Wilson, George W. 1904. *Methodist Theology vs. Methodist Theologians*. Cincinnati: Press of Jennings and Pye.

Wilson, John F. 1983. "Perspectives on the Historiography of Religious Awakenings." *Sociological Analysis* 44: 117–120.

Wilson, Warren H. 1911a. *The Church of the Open Country: A Study of the Church of the Working Farmer*. New York.

———. 1911b. "The Church and the Rural Community." *American Journal of Sociology* 16: 668–693.

———. 1913. *A Rural Survey in Indiana*. New York: Department of Church and Country Life of the Board of Home Missions of the Presbyterian Church in the U.S.A.

———. 1923. "The Church and the Country Life Movement." *Journal of Social Forces* 2: 23–28.

———. 1925. *The Farmer's Church.* New York: Century Co.

Wind, James P. 1990. *Places of Worship.* Nashville: American Association for State and Local History.

Wingo, Lewis. 1984. "Little-Known Facts about the Southern Baptist Convention." *The Quarterly Review* 44: 40–51.

Wissel, Joseph. 1886. *The Redemptorist on the American Missions.* New York: John Ross and Son.

Wood, James R., and Mayer N. Zald. 1966. "Aspects of Racial Integration in the Methodist Church: Sources of Resistance to Organizational Policy." *Social Forces* 45: 255–265.

Wuthnow, Robert. 1973. "Religious Commitment and Conservatism: In Search of an Elusive Relationship." In Charles Y. Glock, ed., *Religion in Sociological Perspective.* Belmont, Calif.: Wadsworth Publishing Co.

———. 1976. *The Consciousness Reformation.* Berkeley: University of California Press.

———. 1978. *Experimentation in American Religion.* Berkeley: University of California Press.

Wuthnow, Robert, and Kevin Christiano. 1979. "The Effects of Residential Mobility on Church Attendance." In Robert Wuthnow, ed., *The Religious Dimension: New Directions in Quantitative Research.* New York: Academic Press.

*Yearbook of American and Canadian Churches.* 1988. Edited by Constant H. Jacquet. Nashville: Abingdon Press.

Young, Jacob. 1857. *Autobiography of a Pioneer.* Cincinnati: Cranston and Curt's.

Zelinsky, W. 1961. "An Approach to the Religious Geography of the United States: Patterns in 1952." *Annals of the American Association of Geographers* 51: 139–193.

# Index

Currie, Raymond, 241
Curry, Catherine Ann, 135–136
Cutler, Timothy, 201

Damen, Arnold, 118
D'Antonio, William, 264
D'Arcy, Paul, 269–270
data on American religion, 6–16
Daughters of the American Revolution, 139
Davies, G. Henton, 189
decline of religious denominations: Congregationalists, 4, 46, 54–56, 57, 70–71, 208, 249; and ecumenical movement, 231–234; Episcopalians, 54–55, 56, 57, 74–75, 237; and mainline denominations, 208, 231–234, 236–275; Methodists, 2, 144–150, 166–168, 208; Roman Catholics, 259–271. *See also* church membership
*Decree on the Apostolate of the Laity,* 269, 271
*Decree on the Up-to-Date Renewal of Religious Life,* 271
Delaware, Quakers in, 30
De Paul University, 140
De Pauw, Washington C., 160
De Pauw University, 160
Disciples of Christ, 231; decline, 208
doctrine, 83–86, 107, 108, 266–271; and biases of historians of religion, 4–6; and church membership, 1, 18; and ecumenical movement, 213–214, 226–229, 233–236; liberalism and decline of churches, 4–5, 18
Doherty, Robert W., 44–45
Dolan, Jay P., 112, 117, 118–119, 122, 126, 132, 134, 140, 289n1, 292n3
Douglass, H. Paul, 210, 225–226, 230–231, 233–234, 238
Draper, Jimmy, 195
Druggist Guild of St. James, 139
Dubuque, Iowa, 142
Durkheim, Emile, 203
Dutch Reformed Church, 28; clergy, 36

Eastern faiths and cults, 239, 240, 242–244
Eastman, Fred, 221
Ebaugh, Helen Rose, 267, 269
economics of religion, *see* religious economies

*Ecumenical Era in Church and Society, The* (Blake), 200
ecumenical movement, 199–236; and Baptists, 217–218, 231; and Congregationalists, 227, 231, 233; and country churches, 207–216; doctrinal divisions, 213–214, 226–229, 233–236; and Episcopalians, 227; and growth or decline, 231–234; and mainline denominations, 216–225, 227–229; and media, 218–223; and Methodists, 227, 231; and Presbyterians, 227; and Roman Catholics, 258–259, 263–271; and salaries of clergy, 211, 216; and secularization, 230–236; and suburban life, 225–236
education: and Baptists, 77–78; circuit riders, 76, 155; and clergy, 36, 45–46, 76–79, 154–159; and Congregationalists, 36, 45–46, 73; and Methodists, 76–78, 154–159, 160–161, 166; and Roman Catholics, 132, 133–134, 139–140, 264, 272; and secularization, 45–46, 84, 154–159. *See also* colleges; seminaries
Edwards, Jonathan, 49
Eisenstadt, Peter R., 290n2
Elliott, Ralph H., 187–189
Emerson, Ralph Waldo, 243
England, John, 110–111
England, immigrants from, 28, 33, 35
Episcopalians, 4; church membership, 24; church property, 160; clergy, 36–37, 76; colleges, 76; and colonial era, 24, 36–37; decline, 54–55, 56, 57, 74–75, 237; disestablishment, 59; and ecumenical movement, 227; as established church, 39–40, 52, 57, 59; missions, 65; in New England, 28; organizational structure, 72; and Revolutionary War, effects of, 74–75; and urban areas, 206
established church, 39–40; Congregationalists, 40, 57, 59–60, 73–74; Episcopalians, 39–40, 52, 57, 59; Adam Smith on, 51–52, 223
ethnic issues, 28, 126–135
Eugene, Oregon, 241
Evangelical and Reformed Church, 227
Evangelical Lutheran Church in America, 237
Evangelical Synod, 231